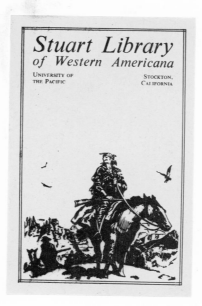

SCOTTY PHILIP,
THE MAN WHO SAVED THE BUFFALO

JAMES (SCOTTY) PHILIP

SCOTTY PHILIP,
THE MAN WHO SAVED THE BUFFALO

by
WAYNE C. LEE

The CAXTON PRINTERS, Ltd.
Caldwell, Idaho
1975

© 1975 by
Wayne C. Lee

International Standard Book Number 0-87004-242-4

Library of Congress Catalog Number 73-83113

Lee, Wayne C
Scotty Philip, the man who saved the buffalo.

Bibliography: p.
1. Philip, Scotty, 1858-1911.   I. Title.
F655.P55L43   639'.97'973580924   [B]   73-83113
ISBN 0-87004-241-6

Printed, lithographed and bound in the United States of America by
The CAXTON PRINTERS, Ltd.
Caldwell, Idaho 83605
122085

To

the Philip family, generations past, present, and
to come; particularly to Billie Ann Rheborg,
Jean Mitchell, and Douglas Philip, Scotty's
grand-daughter, grand-niece, and grand-
nephew, respectively, and to Flora Ziemann,
the "Scotty Philip historian." Without their
help, this book would not have been possible.

TABLE OF CONTENTS

LIST OF ILLUSTRATIONS

ACKNOWLEDGMENTS

SO MANY PEOPLE gave me help in running down the story of Scotty Philip's life that it is impossible to name them all. But even if I can't record them all here, I will never forget the wonderful help they gave me.

Although many people figured prominently in my research, two were outstanding. Senator Arthur Carmody of Trenton, Nebraska, very accurately described as the best historian in the state of Nebraska, went with me on most of my ventures into the land of Scotty Philip. Often our wives, Grace Carmody and Pearl Lee, went along to help probe into history and then remember things that we failed to get in our notes or on our tape recorder.

Flora Ziemann, of Fort Pierre, South Dakota, is a real "Scotty Philip historian." She grew up in Scotty's land. She visited almost daily with Scotty's wife, Sally, in Sally's latter days and listened repeatedly to stories of life with Scotty on the Nebraska and Dakota plains. Flora has gathered pictures, letters, and Scotty Philip mementos of every kind and we were given access to all these for use in this biography.

Billy Ann Rheborg, Scotty's granddaughter, now living in Pierre, South Dakota, showed us old letters of Scotty's, pictures and documents, including his marriage certificate, which we particularly needed to settle some controversial questions.

Doug and Mary Allyn Philip of Hays, Kansas, who

live on the old original Philip ranch on Big Creek, are great historians themselves. For years they have been collecting everything possible about Scotty. I thank them especially for the geneaology of the Philip family, tracing it from the days in Scotland to the present.

Lavern and Jean Mitchell of Sturgis, South Dakota, are also great collectors of Scotty Philip history. Jean is the daughter of George Philip, Scotty's orphan nephew, who lived with Scotty's family in his teens and early twenties and wrote more about Scotty than Scotty himself or any of his children. From Mrs. Mitchell's collections came many first hand accounts of Scotty's escapades written as eye witness accounts by her father.

"Scotty" Philip, grandson of George Philip, Scotty's older brother, showed us pictures and mementos of Scotty that he has on display in his hardware store in Hays, Kansas.

Ralph Jones of Midland, South Dakota, is the son of Tom Jones, one of Scotty's partners in the cattle business just after the turn of the century. His wife is the daughter of the late Tom Berry, cowboy governor of South Dakota. They are prominent ranchers on Bad River and real historians, with great collections of books, pictures and stories which they made available to us.

I also want to thank the Nebraska State Historical Society for its help and especially Leigh DeLay, Historian of the Society, and Paul Riley, Research Assistant of the Society.

The same appreciation goes to the South Dakota State Historical Society with special thanks to Dayton W. Canady, Director of the Society, and Bonnie Gardner, Research Assistant. They not only furnished microfilm and back issues of old papers published along Bad River and at Pierre and Fort Pierre but displayed great numbers of pictures, some of which I had reproduced for this book.

My thanks go also to Vance Nelson, curator of the Ft. Robinson Museum near Crawford, Nebraska, where Scotty spent many exciting years. He pinpointed both geographical sites and sources of research in the beginning of our work on Scotty's life story.

Fr. Joseph Karol of the St. Francis Mission on the Rosebud Indian Reservation, furnished names and dates on the Indian side of the Scotty story.

Elnor Brown, librarian at the Imperial Public Library at Imperial, Nebraska, willingly searched through files, tracing down research books that were needed.

I also want to acknowledge the help received from the many historical societies, both state and local, and the museums, especially the Verendrye Museum at Fort Pierre, South Dakota, as well as the newspapers who let me go through their old files. In this respect, I want to give particular thanks to the Rapid City Daily Journal of Rapid City, South Dakota.

PREFACE

THE STORY OF Scotty Philip's life could be made into a thrilling Western novel with only a little fiction added here and there to tie his adventures together. But his life was much more significant than a novel. A Scottish lad of sixteen with only enough money to get to America where he dreamed he would make a fortune, he proceeded not only to make that fortune but to prove himself a giant in a land of big men.

From a wandering cowboy to a prospector in the Black Hills before they were legally opened to the white men, to freighter, to army scout during one of the most thrilling periods in the development of our frontier, to rancher, and finally to the spot in history for which he will always be remembered, the preserver of the buffalo, he followed his dream and made it come true.

He saw and understood the rich heritage that belonged to the people of this new land much better than those who were born into it. He used all his foresight, energy and accumulated resources to preserve a part of that heritage when he gathered the last of the vanishing buffalo on the northern plains and put them in a tightly fenced pasture. When Scotty died, his herd numbered nearly a thousand head. Most of the buffalo we are privileged to see today in parks and reserves are descendants of Scotty's herd.

For this and other accomplishments, he is today

enshrined in the National Cowboy Hall of Fame at Oklahoma City. A country without a knowledge and pride in its history does not have a solid foundation on which to build a successful future. Without men like Scotty Philip, who not only helped develop the raw frontier of this nation but also preserved the heritage from which it sprang, this country would be poor indeed.

SCOTTY PHILIP,
THE MAN WHO SAVED THE BUFFALO

SCOTTY PHILIP, DAKOTA GIANT

I

THE SOLDIERS came when the sun was only half way to its zenith. It was the most frustrating moment of Scotty Philip's seventeen years of life.

James Philip, Jimmie or Jamie to his family back home but Scotty to the strangers who detected the rich Scottish burr on his words when he spoke, was only a little more than a year out of the highlands of Scotland and just a few months away from his brothers and friends back in Victoria, Kansas.

Although Scotty had already endured several disappointments, this had to be the worst. He hadn't been in the Black Hills long enough even to stake a claim. Now the soldiers were here, and that meant that he and all the other prospectors in this camp who had sneaked into the Hills illegally would be herded out like stray cattle.

Captain Edwin Pollack, in command of the soldiers, gave the prospectors an hour to gather up their possessions. Anything they left behind would probably be picked up or burned by the Indians.

This was Indian land, allotted to them by the Treaty of 1868.[1] It was September, 1875, now, and no white man supposed to be in these hills except for soldiers passing through. But after the announcement last year that gold had been found in the Hills, no treaty was strong enough to keep white men out. They had sneaked into the Hills, and Scotty had come with them.

It was the soldiers' task to drive out the prospectors and keep them out. An impossible assignment, they all knew. But for the men that the soldiers discovered, it meant giving up everything they had found here and going back where they came from.

The column started out at noon. Scotty had paid a member of the company who had a wagon to haul his supplies in from Cheyenne. Now he'd have to pay him to haul his stuff out. Some of the miners had pack horses to carry their equipment. Only a few had teams and wagons. A dozen shacks had been thrown up hastily in preparation for the winter that was only a short season away. Those shacks would likely be ashes before the sun set tonight.

Scotty looked around at the hills. Indians might be there, just waiting until the soldiers had pushed the prospectors out of the valley before coming down to put the torch to anything left in camp.

The captain rode at the head of the column and there were a dozen soldiers close behind him. More were in the rear of the column to make sure nobody stayed behind. A few soldiers rode along the sides. It reminded Scotty of a cattle drive. He had seen several weary trail herds come into Cheyenne this past summer on their way to the wide open grasslands of Wyoming. There were point riders and flankers and men who rode drag, back in the dust. They virtually surrounded the herd and kept it moving, preventing any strays from getting away or staying behind. The soldiers were doing the same with the prospectors they were herding out of the Hills. The miners weren't in chains, but Scotty wasn't fooling himself. They were prisoners.

Scotty didn't want to go back to Cheyenne, but he had no choice. If these prospectors in the camp, hardened by years on the plains and in the hills, couldn't rebel successfully against the soldiers, then a seventeen-year-old lad had no business trying it. But he'd come back the first chance he got. He'd been primed to try his hand at finding gold, and he hadn't had the chance to prove whether or not he could. He wasn't going to let a few soldiers prevent him from becoming a rich man.

The column headed south toward Camp Robinson. Scotty wondered if they'd be put in a stockade or the guard house. Captain Pollack seemed angry enough to have them put in irons. But maybe he was just angry at the assignment he had drawn. Running prospectors out of the Black Hills was not exactly the kind of duty most officers dreamed of.

It was a crisp early September day with the leaves of some trees already promising fall. Not even the warm sun could take away the feeling of autumn.

Although he was less than five months past his seventeenth birthday, Scotty was a husky lad, already standing over six feet tall. He had black hair and dark eyes with broad shoulders that foreshadowed a strength not yet fully developed. The fuzz on his face had not been shaved off for several days, and it gave promise of the black beard that would someday be shaved regularly except for a mustache.

Scotty had already come to love this great open country. It presented a sharp contrast to his native highlands of Scotland with their fog-shrouded coasts, high mountains and deep valleys. It was on the farm of Auchness, back a short distance from the sea near the village of Dallas in Morayshire, that he had been born and christened James Philip. Here he had grown up and gone to school.

Jimmie had always been big for his age and he found this to his advantage in the games played at school. He received the rudiments of education in a school house built of the native rock of the highlands. But the sturdiness of the building didn't necessarily lend to the quality of the education garnered within its walls.

He didn't take a particular liking to the education portioned out by the teacher, especially when it was driven home with a stout stick or a stinging leather strap. He did enjoy the games played at school. He quickly learned that he could win more with his brain than he could with his muscles, even though he took a back seat to no boy his age when it came to strength.

On one occasion he was included in a blindfold race in which each lad had his eyes carefully covered before the race began. Jimmie was sure he could out-run his opponents in an ordinary race. But a big blind-folded boy could fall just as easily and just as hard as a small one.

The race was started, and he skimmed down the course like a deer, never varying from the smooth path. Some lads ran off at odd angles or fell. Others stumbled around trying to locate the smooth race course. Jimmie, of course, was questioned the minute he completed the race.

"Could you see under your blindfold?"

Jimmie shook his head. "No, sir. But I got the wind spotted."[2]

The race had been run directly into the wind and he had simply kept the wind in his face. It had easily won him a race that day, and he never forgot the lesson. Whenever the winds of opposition blew strong, he only worked harder and kept the wind in his face.

Jimmie spent long hours hunting the hills around the farm and fishing in the Lossie close by. There were some laws governing hunting and fishing, but he paid little heed to them. Bringing home the game was the important thing, and he let that be his guide.

He worked long hours on the farm, but the tasks assigned to him were meant for boys his age with average strength and energy. Jimmie handled his chores easily and had plenty of vitality left for other things.

Although he liked the country and everything

Long range view of Auchness, Scotty's birthplace. The three nurses are Clara Philip and Scotty's two nieces, Ann and Margaret Garrow.

about it, except the dull hours of drudgery in the stone school house, his mind and imagination reached far out beyond the hills surrounding him. America was a magic word on the lips of many of his neighbors. More than a few intrepid souls had left their shops in town or their hillside farms and embarked for the land of golden promise so far across the ocean. At a young age, Jimmie began dreaming the impossible dream.

He had four brothers, all older than he was, and they were talking of America, too. It helped fire the furnace of the lad's imagination, and he resolved that someday he'd go to the United States. His decision had been reached even before any of his brothers decided to make the long one-way journey. He also had four sisters, two older and two younger than he was. Before the migration was complete, most of them would yield to the strong pull of the foreign land.

After four years in the stone school house, Jimmie

Scotty Philip as a Scottish lad.

Scotty's father and sisters, Maggie and Tina. Taken in Scotland in 1884.

was convinced that he had all the education he would
ever need, and he stopped knuckling under to the
school master and put all his energy into the farm.
Although his formal education ended here, he never
stopped learning and became a well educated man
through a never-ending drive to better himself and
satisfy a thirst for knowledge of things around him. He
was a great reader, and when elected to represent his
district in the South Dakota senate many years later, he
proved that he could hold his own with the best educated men of his day.

When the talk at home turned to America, Jimmie
was at the fringe of every conversation listening eagerly, or at times, forcing his way right into the conversation. He watched his father add years to his life on
the farm in the Highlands close to the Lossie, where he
had always lived and would likely spend the remainder of his life. That was what his father wanted, but it
wasn't what he wanted.

When Jimmie was fifteen, his older brother,
George, left for America. Jimmie pined away the hours
vainly wishing he could have gone with his brother
and making his plans to go as soon as possible. George
had gone with a group of men, some with their families,
to establish a colony in the new world. George Grant
was the leader of this colony, made up of men from
England and Scotland.[3]

Jimmie could hardly wait for word from his brother
on how things really were in America. He had learned
that not all things proved to be exactly the way people
claimed they were, but he could believe whatever his
brother George said about the new land.

A letter came from George. Jimmie read it over and
over. The new land was just as wonderful as they had
heard it was. Great oceans of space, room for everyone.
The colony had settled in some state called Kansas out
in the middle of the United States. Miles and miles of

flat land for farming and the richest grass in the world for grazing cattle.

It was the end of George's letter that intrigued him the most, however. George Grant's colony needed more workers. Jimmie decided immediately that he would be one of those workers. He'd go to America the next spring.

Jimmie wasn't the only member of the Philip family impressed with George's report. Two of his brothers, Alexander and David, were just as enthusiastic about making the pilgrimage. Their father was not so impressed with George's report on America, but he did not stand in the way of his three sons. He still had one son, Robert, who would stay with him and work the Auchness farm.

Jimmie's excitement grew through the winter months of 1873 and '74 as he prepared for the great voyage to the new land. When it came time to say good-bye to those who would stay behind, he was the least reluctant to leave. Perhaps it was because his brothers were older, and they thought more about what they were leaving. He realized that it wasn't likely he would ever see either of his parents again and that depressed him. But the magic of the new world had him completely in its grip, and he could see little else than the fortune he was sure was waiting for him in America.

The trip across the ocean seemed very long to Jimmie. His mind was already ahead of him, trying to imagine what life would be like on the plains of Kansas.

After the three brothers landed in New York, long train rides followed, but he was so engrossed in the country they were passing through that he didn't mind the long hours.

Then they were in Kansas City and finally out on the plains. The trees that lined the river grew fewer, and there were places where there were no trees at all.

This was hard for Jimmie to understand; it wasn't what he thought Kansas would be like.

They went through towns he had read about: Topeka, Abilene, Ellsworth, Russell. Hays would be next. But at the station just before they reached Hays, they got off. Victoria, named by George Grant, wasn't much of a town compared to Lossiemouth on the sea back home.

George Philip was at Victoria to meet his three brothers, and he took them out to the place where he lived. Jimmie stared around in every direction at the endless rolling prairies. It was hard for him to realize that this was his home now.

Jimmie had expected life to be different in Kansas than it had been in the Highlands of Scotland, but not even in his dreams had he expected such a big change. He and his brothers worked the soil as they had back home, but here the work was on a much grander scale. The soil wasn't rocky and it was level. Once the ground was turned by a plow, it was ready to plant.

Cattle were just turned loose to roam over the prairie on either side of Big Creek. Instead of fencing the cattle into pastures, here they fenced them out of the fields. There was very little rain compared to the moisture back in his native Scotland, but the grass grew well and the cattle thrived on it.

Jimmie worked hard through the summer, for it was his nature to work hard. But he was restless. He had thought that just getting over here in this new country would fulfill all his dreams. But now that he was here, he knew it wasn't enough. He had read of excitement, adventure, of fortunes to be made overnight in this new country. There was no evidence of any of that here at Victoria.

He talked to his brothers about the things he had read concerning the American frontier. George and Alex were satisfied where they were. Both were sure they could see a fortune to be made by hard work right

Doug Philip Collection

Victoria Manor, the depot at Victoria, Kansas. It was here that Scotty landed when he came to America.

here in this rich soil. David already was thinking of moving on, perhaps to Canada.

Canada held no special allure for Jimmie. He yearned to be a part of the adventure that the frontier just beyond the western horizon promised. Maybe his fortune was there, just waiting for him to pick it up. His restless soul couldn't be content farming and running cattle on Big Creek when the material from which his dreams had been made was almost within his grasp.

The crops were finally harvested and winter came. When the snows started to melt and winter began to wear away, Jimmie packed his few belongings in a saddle roll and bid his brothers good-bye. Then he rode west.

II

HE WENT FIRST to Hays City to the northwest of Grant's colony on Big Creek. Here he bought the supplies he thought he would need on the trail. He had been to Hays a few times since coming to Grant's colony, but the town had been a disappointment. He realized he had expected too much after hearing all the stories about it when Hays was the main shipping point for Texas cattle and Wild Bill Hickok was marshal in '69 and '70.

Ninety miles to the southwest was Dodge City from which hundreds of thousands of buffalo hides had been shipped in the last couple of years. It was as rough and tough as Hays ever was, Jimmie had heard, and it seemed to this sixteen-year-old lad that it ought to be investigated. So he pointed his horse toward the town on the Arkansas River.

He crossed the Smoky Hill, and for long weary miles he rode over the prairie, broken only now and then by small streams, all of them running east to empty into the Arkansas where it looped to the northeast after passing Dodge City.

Then he reached the Arkansas, and the town that still had most of its reputation to make because its heyday as the end of the trail from Texas was still ahead of it.

But Dodge City was no saint's paradise in the late winter of 1875. The railroad had arrived in '72 and

Hays City -1871- North Main St.
Court House built in -1871-
Tony Drums famous Saloon -1868.
Freaucnted by Wild Bill, Buffalo Bill, General Custer, & Officers.
Burned out in 1896.

Doug Philip Collection

Hays, Kansas in the early days. Scotty was here in 1874.

brought the usual load of riffraff that followed men wherever they opened new country. The only law then was at Fort Dodge, which had been established on the Arkansas River in 1864.[1] When a teamster had built a sod house to use as a stopping place for freighters and buffalo hunters, he set it five miles upstream from the fort, making sure he was off the military reservation surrounding the fort so he'd be free to sell liquor. When the construction gangs came through in the summer of 1872 building the grade and laying steel for the Santa Fe, they pitched their camp by the teamster's soddy and the town was suddenly born.

The town was first called Buffalo City, but that quickly changed to Dodge City. Late in the fall of '72, the first passenger train came into Dodge City, and the banks of the Arkansas were never the same again. The iron horse brought gamblers, prostitutes, card sharps and every kind of human parasite.[2] Buffalo hides were

big business, and already men were saying that Dodge
City could be the biggest of all shipping points for
Texas cattle because of its location. The town had a
future.

Jimmie, however, was unimpressed by Dodge City
as he rode down the cold empty street. The biggest
business house he saw was Rath and Wright, General
Outfitters. Most of the other business places seemed to
be saloons and gambling parlors. The saloons didn't
interest Jimmie for he didn't care for liquor; it only
befuddled a man's mind. Gambling had a certain appeal for him because he had grown up to respond
quickly to a dare, and "I'll bet you" were challenging
words. Right now, however, he had no money to spare
for gambling.

Old whiskey barrels, filled with water, were standing along the edges of the board sidewalks. They were
the only defense the town had against fire. A sheet of
ice covered each barrel now.

Looking for a place to spend the night, his eye fell
on Beebe's Iowa House. If it hadn't been so cold, he
would have rolled up in his blanket outside town or
stayed in a barn loft somewhere, but he had to part with
some of his meager reserve of money for a warm place
to sleep. He had spent one cold night on the prairie
between here and Hays City, and he didn't relish the
thought of another like it.

Jimmie began looking for work, walking up and
down the long block of slapped-together shacks that
made up Front Street. He noted that a sign over the
door of the marshal's office proclaimed that Billy Rivers was marshal now. He decided that only a man with
plenty of money and a love of the high life found in the
saloons and brothels could enjoy Dodge City in the
winter.

There was just no work to be found this time of year,
and Jimmie doubted if there would be much when
spring opened up. This was a town built to handle the

buffalo hide trade, and that was about over. The mighty buffalo was almost gone. The destruction of this magnificent animal that was so uniquely American stirred a resentment deep inside Jimmie.

The cattle trail from Texas to the northern markets crossed the Arkansas just four miles west of town. But so far, most of the northbound herds had ignored Dodge City. If the cattle didn't stop, there would be few new jobs here this summer. Jimmie couldn't foresee that this year, 1875, would bring a tremendous increase in the number of cattle shipped from Dodge City.[3] The land to the north was beginning to sprout farmers and fences. The Texas cattlemen would find it more convenient to ship from Dodge City than to fight their way through the fences to Hays or Ogallala.

Jimmie's disappointment in Dodge City caused him to turn his attention elsewhere. So after a short stay, he saddled up and headed north and west, his goal Cheyenne.

The cold fingers of winter were just beginning to lose their grip when Jimmie rode into Cheyenne. With spring so close, Jimmie reasoned that there just had to be some work here that a husky sixteen-year-old boy could do to earn a living.

If Jimmie expected Cheyenne to be another Dodge City, he was mistaken. The railroad had passed through Cheyenne almost eight years ago, while it had been in Dodge City only a little over two years. Cheyenne was much bigger, and it looked solider. But the real difference was something almost intangible. While Dodge City was locked in the doldrums of winter, Cheyenne was warmed by an undercurrent that Jimmie felt as soon as he turned into 17th Street.

He crossed the intersection of 17th and Ferguson and saw the post office on the corner, reminding him that he must write to his brothers back in Victoria and let them know where he was. Then, among the business houses, he spotted a small restaurant. A cup of hot

coffee would take the edge off the chill that the cutting
March wind had driven into him.

The restaurant was half full of men drinking coffee
and eating or just lounging around talking about the
gold that had been reported in the Black Hills. Now
Jimmie knew why this town had seemed so different.
Rumors of gold can send an electrifying charge through
men any time, anywhere. It was sparks from that
charge that Jimmie had felt when he first rode into
Cheyenne.

Jimmie ordered a cup of coffee, and the man next to
him grinned and asked if he was ready to head for the
Black Hills when the snow melted. Jimmie informed
him that he was only looking for a job. The man winked
at his partner.

"Well, Scotty, my boy, you'll have no trouble finding work. Most young bucks will be heading for the
Hills come spring, and the cowmen are going to be
hiring anybody who can fork a horse."

"Even a Scotchman," the other man added with a
grin.

Jimmie didn't resent the fun being poked at him.
He knew that he had a Scottish burr on his tongue, but
no one had noticed that back at Victoria. Jimmie didn't
consider his speech odd; it was these men with their
flat western drawl that sounded queer.

When he left the restaurant, Jimmie had reached
two conclusions. One was that from here on among
these cowboys who had nicknames for everything, he
was going to be Scotty. The other was that this gold
fever that was gripping the town was contagious. Already he had a touch of it. To hear men talk, gold was to
be had in the Black Hills just for picking it up.

Of course, a man would run the risk of losing his
scalp if he went into the Hills now. The treaty of 1868
had given complete control of that land to the Indians
and barred all white men. But plenty of white men here

Sixteenth Street in Cheyenne, Wyoming, 1868.

in Cheyenne were dreaming about the gold in those hills, and Scotty dreamed, too.

He rode down to 14th Street and looked at the depot beside the tracks then turned back toward the main part of town and found himself on Pioneer Street. Over half the business places were saloons, he decided.

It was too cold to be riding around sight seeing, so he found a livery barn and led his horse inside. The owner was a talkative man enthusiastic about the growth of his town. Cheyenne had three thousand permanent residents, he said, with five churches, three grocery stores, three blacksmith and wagon shops, hardware stores, bakeries, a confectionery store, jewelry store, boarding houses, tailor shops, barber shops and dozens of saloons and cigar stores.[4]

Scotty grinned and asked about a place to stay. He was told about Dyer's, Planter's House, the American House, the Railroad House and the newest, the Inter-Ocean Hotel, owned by B. M. Ford on the corner of Hill Street and 16th.

Scotty asked about the soldiers he had seen and was told that Fort D. A. Russell, just three miles out of town, had fifteen companies stationed there. Camp Carlin, two miles out along the tracks, was a government supply depot.

Scotty had already seen some of the big hotels and decided they were too elegant for his modest means. He'd settle for one of the cheaper boarding houses. Even if he got a job, he wouldn't waste his money on a fancy hotel; he'd use it to outfit himself for a trip into the Black Hills.

After finding a place where a bed was only twenty-five cents a night, he got some supper and started looking for a saloon where talk would be flowing about the gold in the Hills.

Walking down 16th Street, he saw a place called the

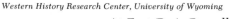

Western History Research Center, University of Wyoming

At Fort D. A. Russell, Wyoming.

View from the southwest of Fort D. A. Russell, Wyoming, 1870.

Parisian Varieties and went inside. He was astonished at the size of the place. A stage show was in progress. There was room there for nearly three hundred people in front of the stage and the area was full. Cowboys, loafers and soldiers from the fort out on Crow Creek mingled with each other.

Although the army had been given the job of keeping white men out of Indian country, talk about going to the Black Hills didn't dwindle in the presence of the soldiers. Talk didn't break any treaty.

Scotty learned that Pease and Taylor, the leading grocers in town, were stocking up heavily in anticipation of a rush to supply outfits heading for the Hills. I. C. Whipple, mayor of Cheyenne, and a big grocer himself, had rebuilt his store after it had burned six months ago and he was also ready for the rush.

There was talk, too, about the big reception to be held the next day for John M. Thayer, former senator from Nebraska, who was coming to succeed John Campbell as governor of Wyoming Territory.

Scotty wasn't interested in the reception. But the stage show did hold his attention. There was a dance on stage performed by scantily clad girls. Scotty had never seen anything like that before. When the girls

had finished their high kicks, a tight rope walker tried
his hand at holding the audience's attention. A ballad
singer followed the tight rope walker and had better
luck holding his listeners. Clog dancers and Negro
minstrels followed.

Scotty left the variety show and went over to the
gambling tables. Many of the dealers here were
women dressed in silks and wearing more diamonds
than Scotty knew existed. This was indeed a strange
world to him.

Scotty found himself standing beside a rancher at
one table watching the action, and he struck up a conversation. When he mentioned the gold in the Hills, he
got an angry response because the rancher was going to
lose some of his hands when the rush began this spring.

Scotty lost no time in asking for a job, and he was
hired on the spot after promising that he wouldn't head
for the Hills, too, as soon as the thaws came. Scotty
knew he wouldn't be able to make the trip into the
Hills until he had earned some money. He didn't
guarantee how long after the spring thaws he would
stay on the job.

Two men from the Gordon stockade in the Black
Hills arrived in Cheyenne with samples of the gold
they had found. Gold fever hit a hysterical pitch in
town. Mayor Whipple telegraphed Washington, plead-
ing for an opening of the Indian lands. The reply he
received said that consultations were beginning.
Cheyenne newspapers took that response to mean that
the land would soon be open.[5]

J. Newton Warren from the Gordon stockade on
French Creek in the Hills gave a talk that night in the
court room, and Scotty was there. It seemed to him that
every man present was ready to go the next morning.
Warren said he was going to head back in twenty days
and asked for volunteers. If Scotty had had the money,
he would have been one of those volunteers.

However, before the Warren party could get outfitted, word came from the army that nobody could go into the Hills until the present treaty was changed. Some men from the Gordon party had been intercepted and forced to guide the army back to French Creek, where the entire Gordon party was to be arrested and escorted out of the Hills.

Before heading out to his job on the ranch, Scotty wrote a letter to his brothers back in Victoria, telling them where he was and asking them to write to him.

There wasn't much work to do on the ranch when Scotty first got there. But by calving time, the rains had started. Wyoming experienced one of its wettest spring seasons. For three weeks the sun barely showed itself. Moisture of some kind fell every day for over sixty consecutive days. It was miserable work on the ranch. Scotty kept thinking about the prospectors trying to get to the Hills, miring down in the mud and having to watch for soldiers because the order was still out to keep the whites out of the Hills.

The branding was finally completed and the cattle turned loose on the open prairies to get fat during the summer. With less work to do, Scotty thought more and more about the gold in the Hills. On a trip into Cheyenne for supplies, he found that many of the men he had known had gone north.

When Scotty got back to the ranch, he did some calculating and decided that by the end of July he should have enough money to buy the supplies he'd need. He'd quit his job then, draw his wages, and head for the gold fields.

III

WHEN THE END of July came, Scotty left his job on the ranch. He had liked the work, although he had grown homesick occasionally for his old home in Scotland or even his brothers' company in Victoria. He had passed his seventeenth birthday back in April, and though he looked older to the men working with him, there was still a lot of boy bottled up inside him.

Scotty had made some friends while working on the ranch. One was a rancher, Hi Kelly, who had a fine ranch up on the Chugwater about fifty miles north of Cheyenne. Scotty had been up there a few times. Kelly had a Sioux wife, and they raised a big garden every summer. This year, with such a wet spring, Kelly's garden looked wonderful. Scotty's friendship with Hi Kelly would last as long as they both lived.[1]

Kelly had good buildings on his ranch and had already begun fencing in hundreds of acres for his stock. He had fifteen hundred head of cattle, some of which he kept in his pasture. He had several Shorthorn bulls that he valued at over five hundred dollars each.

Kelly operated a station for travelers on their way between Cheyenne and Fort Laramie and was doing a good business. He told Scotty that he figured over half the people going from Cheyenne to Fort Laramie intended to go right on to the Black Hills if they could.

Scotty was determined to get to the Black Hills some way. If others had made it, he could, too. He was convinced that a fortune was waiting for him here in this land if he could only find it. Perhaps it was in the gold fields of the Black Hills.

In Cheyenne, he found men who were quietly planning to make the journey into the Hills in spite of the tales coming back of soldiers running out the miners. The men Scotty talked to were convinced that the soldiers would never find them once they got to the Hills. Scotty shared that conviction.

Scotty began buying the things he thought he would need in the Hills. He found prices sky high in Cheyenne and realized that the merchants were anticipating buyers just like him. There was little talk about men going to the Hills, but every merchant and man in the street knew that was what the men were outfitting for. Scotty bought a heavy coat in spite of the high price asked. He knew he'd need it. He didn't expect to come back until he had made his fortune, and that might take part or all of the winter.

One man who had been to the Hills once helped Scotty pick out what he would need. Instead of buying a pack horse, Scotty paid one of the men with a wagon to haul his stuff. Among the men assembling to make the trip was another young fellow. Although older than Scotty, he and Scotty agreed to stick together and pool their resources.

Scotty bought a horse and saddle and filled his saddle bags with personal things he didn't want to put in the wagon hauling the rest of his equipment. He tied his bedroll on behind his saddle.

Plans were made to leave early on the morning of the 28th of August. Scotty got everything ready, his excitement mingled with misgivings. They were going into Indian territory where they had no right to be. Both red man and white soldier would be against them.

Scotty worried some about his chances of getting scalped instead of getting rich, but it didn't weaken his resolve to have his try at finding his fortune. But as the hour for leaving Cheyenne drew near, homesickness edged in on him. Before he went to sleep the last night before his departure, he wrote to his brother, George, back in Victoria, Kansas.

Cheyenne, Wyo.
Aug. 27, 1875

My dear Brother:

On the eve of starting out. Once more I did not get the box you sent, but if it comes within a week there is a man that will bring it.

I am taking with me 250 lbs of flour, 25 bacon, 6 of powder, 20 of sugar, salt, etc. 7 dollars worth of coffee and tea, 18 for hauling it out there, 35 for a pony, 5 for ammunition. Me and another fellow are paying 16 dollars for a whip-saw for sawing boards, 4 for stricknine, an overcoat and that is all my means. I don't know whether I am right or not. However if this is my last letter, good bye all.

You need not write any more till you hear from me. Tell them at home that I am well.

With love to all I remain,

Your loving brother
Jamie.[2]

Early the next morning, the caravan started out, swinging to the east of the army road between Fort D. A. Russell and Fort Laramie, eighty miles away. Soldiers were certain to be somewhere along that road, and they'd ask questions that couldn't be answered. The best way to get through was to avoid running into soldiers. Scotty had hoped to get a look at Fort Laramie, since he had heard so much about it but that would have to wait.

As the crow flew, it was just a little over two hundred miles from Cheyenne to the section of the Black Hills where gold had been discovered. The company Scotty was traveling with moved fast because they didn't like the idea of being exposed out on this prairie any longer than absolutely necessary. When they pulled into Discovery Gulch, both horses and men were tired, but the men were too excited to care.

They found a camp already set up in Discovery Gulch, and some shelters built. Even though the new group from Cheyenne meant competition for the gold claims, the established colony welcomed the new-comers. The more there were in camp, the less the risk of being overrun by an Indian attack.

Scotty and his partner set up their tent quickly. They agreed that they would build a small shack or possibly a lean-to against a rock wall somewhere before winter set in. But there was plenty of time. Right now they intended to find a likely looking spot to stake a claim then try their luck at getting rich quick.

Scotty made a decision that night. He was not going to be panicked into staking his claim on the first ground that showed signs of gold. He was going to search these hills thoroughly and find a place where the gold was plentiful. When he staked his claim and settled down to work it, he expected to get rich in a hurry.

Scotty and his partner roamed to the north of the camp where the hills seemed more rugged. Along the creeks, they found traces of the yellow dust but never enough to get Scotty overly excited.

When his partner grew tired of looking without finding a rich strike, Scotty went on alone. For several days, he searched but did not find what he was looking for. He considered it his personal misfortune to be back in camp the morning that the soldiers came.

There were more prospectors in camp than there were soldiers, and Scotty thought they might decide to defy Captain Pollack's order for them to pack up and leave. But they didn't, and Scotty knew he had to knuckle under to the order, too, although it went against his nature to yield so meekly. He had accomplished nothing on this trip, not even staking a good claim.

At Camp Robinson, Captain Pollack turned his prisoners over to civil authorities since none of them were military personnel. Then he took his men back toward the Hills to look for more white intruders on Indian lands.

Post Sutler's store, Fort Robinson, Nebraska.

Scotty expected the authorities to put the prisoners on trial, but they merely released them without bail after confiscating most of their supplies so they could not return to the Hills without restocking. That was the same as dismissing the charges because few of these men would return to Camp Robinson unless brought here again under military guard.

Most of the men headed for Fort Laramie and Cheyenne. A few turned right around, retracing their tracks back into the hills even without supplies.

Scotty went southwest with the main body of prospectors. He didn't have enough supplies left to get him through a winter in the Hills. There was none of the urgency driving the men now that had brought them into the Hills in such haste. It was seven days after they left Discovery Gulch before they reached the North Platte River at Fort Laramie. The river was low, and they forded it close to the mouth of Laramie River.

Scotty gazed in wonder at the nearly completed

new military bridge across the Platte.[3] It looked strong
enough to hold up the heaviest military loads or withstand the floods that raged down the river almost every
spring. The fact was that that bridge would be used by
the military for over three quarters of a century.

They camped on the military reservation just outside the fort itself.[4] Scotty went down to the post
trader's store for a while, then made a quick tour of the
fort. The indignity of being escorted out of the Black
Hills by the army was still too fresh in his mind for him
to enjoy mingling with the soldiers now.

The fort was an impressive sight to Scotty. There
were two new concrete barracks, two stories high;
eleven officers quarters, six frame buildings, four
adobe and one concrete; a new concrete hospital; two
guard houses, one stone and one adobe; six frame store
houses; stables with room for nearly one hundred fifty
horses; a stone magazine; three adobe laundress's
quarters; adjutant's office, school house, post office,
bakery, and workshops. To Scotty, it was quite a show
of military strength out here in the middle of nowhere.

Four days later, the party reached Cheyenne.
Scotty already had his mind set on returning to the

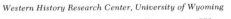
Western History Research Center, University of Wyoming

Fort Laramie, Wyoming, 1870.

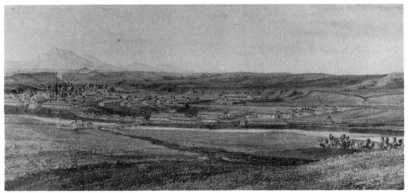

Hills. He'd had no trouble with Indians, and that fear, which had ridden him so hard before starting out last month, was greatly diminished.

There was a lot of building going on in Cheyenne. The town had three bad fires that year of '75, and many of the new buildings going up were of brick construction.

By the first of October, Scotty was laying plans for his return to the Hills. He wouldn't go with a big group this time. He decided that his chances of escaping the prying eyes of the army were better if he wasn't with a lot of people. He knew his way around now, so all he needed was one partner. Of course, his danger from Indians would be increased considerably, but he was willing to risk that.

Early in October he wrote to his brother, George, again.

Cheyenne, Oct. 8

My dear brother:

I got your note of the 3rd today and was glad Mrs. Philip was sending me some clothes as I will need them if I go to the Black Hills. There is no treaty made yet but there is some going to now.

— — — — —

(A part of the letter here is no longer readable.)

—Custer Creek of park is first and 17 miles north is Spring Creek and 20 miles from Spring is Castle Creek.

I am very much obliged to Jane for sending my clothes tho I haven't got them yet and for her long letter. Upon my word I expect to make a big thing in the Hills, and if I do I will pay her someday. I do want to go but I don't want to be taken out by the troops again.

I see Alex is working for Grant for good wages. I wouldn't be surprised to see him head shepherd yet.

The Black Hills is a good place but then although the Government would treat for it I wouldn't advise you to go for I think your fortune is in Victoria. I will write before I start. I don't think I'll start till the last of the month. I have nothing more to say. I remain your loving brother.

James Philip

P.S. You said you sent me a letter from Bob in one of yours but I never saw it. I would like you to send me all the home letters. I

have not written Bob since a long time before I left Victoria. I
return you my father's letter.[5]

Bob, of course, was a brother, the only one of five,
who stayed in Scotland with his parents. David was
now in Canada and George and Alex were in Victoria.
Scotty was the adventurer. The clothes for which he
thanked his sister-in-law never did arrive, and he had
to start for the Hills again without this added winter
apparel.

True to his decision not to return to the Hills with a
large group, Scotty looked around Cheyenne until he
found the partner he wanted for his new venture. Boston Smith was older than Scotty but no more experienced in the ways of the land. Although Smith didn't
admit it, Scotty guessed that he might be an army
deserter. Scotty didn't know his real name or even if he
came from Boston, although his accent suggested a
New England background.

It was late in October when the two boys started for
the Hills. They slipped out of Cheyenne one morning
before it was light. Scotty led the way because he knew
where he was going; Boston Smith didn't.

They rode in an arc to the northeast to avoid the
Fort Laramie military road. They had no pack horse.
Everything they owned was in their saddle bags or tied
in their bed rolls behind their saddles. There was
plenty of game and both boys had good rifles.

By swinging away from the military road, however,
they moved into the territory of the Sioux and
Cheyenne. The Indians were even more determined
to keep prospectors out of the Black Hills than the army
was.

IV

SCOTTY'S COURSE led the boys northeast where they forded the North Platte River close to the Nebraska line. Each night they picketed their horses where they could get good grass, then rolled up in their blankets close by.

Here Scotty was given another hard lesson in frontier life. He woke up one morning with frost on his blankets and the ground around him and looked immediately for the horses. When he saw nothing, he jumped up in alarm. Running to the place where they had picketed the horses, he found the picket pins still anchored in the ground with only a short piece of rope on each pin.

Scotty's yell brought his partner out of his blankets, reaching for his gun. Then he saw Scotty holding the end of a rope that had been sawed in two with a knife and he scrambled to his feet for a better look.

It took only a moment to realize that Indians had taken the horses. The boys didn't have to remind each other how lucky they were to be alive. The Indians who had sneaked up so close to cut the ropes and led the horses away could just as easily have come on into camp and used their knives on the boys.

Scotty and his partner were faced with a serious problem now. They still had their supplies and saddles but no way of moving anything. Without horses, they couldn't survive long out here on these prairies. It

would be a mighty long walk back to Cheyenne. Fort
Laramie was closer, almost due west, but neither boy
wanted to go there, even if he could make it, and admit
to the army that he'd been trying to reach the Hills.

"Let's get our horses back," Scotty said grimly.

"Even if we have to kill a couple of dozen Indians,"
Boston Smith added.

They set out with more courage than plan. They
had no trouble following the frosty tracks in the grass
close to camp. The Indians had headed north northeast. That was almost the direction the boys had been
traveling. But if they failed to recover their horses,
they'd be stranded farther from civilization than ever.

As the sun came out, the frost melted and the grass
dried. The tracks almost disappeared. Scotty, however,
had already decided from the tracks that there were not
many Indians. They were in no hurry and making no
effort to hide their trail. They obviously didn't expect
two men on foot to follow them.

These Indians were probably a small raiding party,
and they'd take their stolen horses back to the main
camp and brag about their bravery and skill. Scotty
knew that the only hope he and Boston had of recover-
ing their horses was to find the Indians before they
reached their main camp.

For three days the boys tramped over the prairie to
the northeast. They didn't make much headway but
Scotty occasionally saw signs of unshod ponies
mingled with a couple wearing shoes. They were
never far ahead of them. The two shod horses could be
his and Boston's. They'd had their horses shod just
before leaving Cheyenne because the rocks in the
Hills would soon make a horse's feet sore if he wasn't
shod. He guessed there were less than a dozen Indians
in the party.

"They're sure taking their time if these are the ones
we're after," Boston said as they stopped and examined

the tracks around a little lagoon that had caught and held the rain water running off the hills around it.

"They think anybody would be a fool to follow them on foot," Scotty said. "If we can surprise them, we might get our horses back."

The evening of the third day, the boys came to the Runningwater in northwestern Nebraska.[1] The stream was small here, but Scotty knew it would be a good place for the Indians to go into camp.

Scotty moved along the bank of the creek looking for tracks. Not far downstream, he found them, unshod ponies and a few shoe marks in the mud where the animals had come down to drink. At almost the same time that he discovered the tracks, Boston grabbed Scotty's arm and pointed farther downstream. Scotty looked and his eyes popped. A half dozen Indian ponies were grazing on the hillside not far away. Scotty's eyes swept the hills and soon spotted an Indian guard on the highest rise above the river.

The Indian hadn't spotted the boys yet, and Scotty sank down in the tall grass, pulling Boston down with him. They kept their eyes on the guard, who seemed interested in something downstream. Scotty decided the camp must be in that direction.

"Suppose this is the main Indian camp?" Boston asked nervously.

Scotty shook his head. "Don't see enough ponies. These are probably just the ones who stole our horses."

With the Indian's attention held by something downstream, the boys rose into a crouch and moved silently along the river bank. They came to a curve in the river and from there they could see a small camp where nearly a dozen Indians were squatting around a small fire. The ponies were scattered to the south and west over the hillside.

"There's my bay gelding," Scotty whispered, trying to hold down the excitement that swelled inside him. "There's your horse, too."

Boston nodded. "Now how do we get them?"

"We'll have to wait till dark," Scotty said. "Look, they're both still wearing their neck ropes. We should be able to catch them without trouble. I'm sure I can get up to my horse."

"The trouble won't be with the horses," Boston said, staring at the Indian camp.

The boys settled down in the grass to wait. Scotty kept an eye on his bay so he'd know exactly where he was when it got dark enough to go after him. Just before dark, four soldiers rode down the slope from the south into the Indian camp. Scotty wondered at first if there was going to be trouble, then he saw that there wasn't.

"Checking with the Indians to see if any whites have passed by here on their way to the Hills," Boston guessed.

Scotty nodded. "Sure. The soldiers and the Indians are together on this."

"I sure don't want the soldiers to see me," Boston said, sinking lower into the grass.

Scotty looked at his companion, surer than ever that he must be a deserter. "Me, either," he agreed. "They ran me out of the Hills once."

It wasn't until many years later that Scotty learned that his guess was right. Boston Smith was a deserter, and he would rather have tangled with the Indians than to be taken back by the soldiers to stand trial for desertion.

Dusk descended on the river, and Scotty kept his eye on his bay as long as he could see him.

"We'll be on our own once we start after our horses," Scotty whispered. "If we get them, we'll head north. Let's swing a little to the west of north because I think we're almost directly south of Camp Robinson. We don't want to cross trails with the soldiers there or the Indians at the Red Cloud Agency."

"We'll have to arrange a meeting place."

"We'll meet on the White River west of Camp

Robinson," Scotty said. "I'd guess the White is about twenty miles north of here."

After wishing each other luck, the two boys began creeping through the grass toward the hillside. The horses obviously liked the short grass up on the side of the hill better than the tall grass along the creek.

Scotty's horse was closer than Boston's, although farther up the hillside. Boston's horse was down nearer the Indian camp. Scotty moved as quietly as possible, but the Indian ponies shied away from him as he approached. He moved more slowly as he came near the spot where he calculated the bay should be.

Scotty was carrying very little with him except his rifle and a revolver in a holster strapped around his waist. All his other equipment, including his saddle and bridle, were back at the camp where the Indians had stolen the horses.

Scotty spotted a horse ahead. He couldn't identify it, but it was about where he thought his bay ought to

Ralph Jones Collection

Crossing the White River.

be. If that wasn't his horse, he wouldn't know which way to turn to find it. Gripping his rifle in his right hand, he held out his left, speaking softly to the horse, hoping he would recognize his voice.

The horse nickered a welcome to the Scottish voice of his master. Scotty held his breath. Would the Indians hear that and realize what it meant? But no Indian materialized out of the darkness, and Scotty moved forward again, speaking softly to the horse.

Catching the trailing neck rope, he made a hackamore of it and slipped it over the horse's nose. With a leap, he landed on the animal's back.

At that instant, a rifle cracked down the slope in the direction of the camp. That was about where Boston Smith should be trying to catch his horse. The Indian ponies around Scotty broke into a run and Scotty's bay went with them.[2]

Scotty let him run, using the rope only enough to guide him at an angle toward the river. Surrounded as he was by the pounding of hooves, Scotty couldn't be sure that some of those horses didn't carry Indians or soldiers.

As he edged away from the other horses, Scotty heard shouts from the camp and realized that not all the Indians, at least, were pursuing him. Still he kicked his horse into his fastest speed and clung to his bare back like a bur.

They came to the creek at a place where it was wider than normal and the water was running slowly. Without hesitation, Scotty sent his horse into the shallow water. At the first plunge, the horse sank to his knees.

A wave of horror rolled over Scotty as he realized that his horse had plunged into a bed of quicksand. He'd had very little experience with the treacherous sand, but he had heard plenty about it. The Platte to the south was full of quicksand bars, but he hadn't expected any here in this small stream.

Scotty lost his grip on his rifle when his horse came to such a sudden stop in the sand, and it went spinning into the creek. The horse lunged forward, trying to break the suction of the sand. Scotty gave little thought to the loss of his rifle; his concern at the moment was getting out of the sand.

Behind him, he heard the howling of the Indians then the pound of more running horses. His partner, Boston, was surely either captured or dead by now. Scotty would be in the same fix if he didn't get out of this sand. He kicked his horse in the ribs, and the bay struggled harder than ever.

The horse finally got his front feet on solid footing and dragged himself out of the sand in a series of hard lunges. Once on the north bank of the creek, Scotty urged the bay into a run again, heading north.

Scotty listened intently as he rode, but he caught no sound of pursuit. He finally decided that the Indians must have thought there was only one thief in their horse herd and had not heard Scotty ride off to the north.

After riding until midnight, Scotty grew so tired that he slid off his horse, tied the end of the neck rope around his wrist, and slept on the prairie without blanket or pillow.

He woke with the first light of day. He had nothing to eat for breakfast. Food, however, was not his greatest worry. He'd have to keep moving until he was sure he was beyond the reach of the Indians. On these plains there was no really safe place for a man traveling alone.

He saw some game, but he had no rifle to kill it. He finally came on some prairie chickens that were not alarmed at his approach. He got within easy pistol range, so he had wild chicken for dinner.

Reaching the White River well west of Camp Robinson, he lingered for a few hours in the vain hope that his partner might show up. As the afternoon wore on, his conviction grew that Boston Smith had been killed by the Indians.[3] Scotty was alone. There was no point in waiting any longer for a partner who wouldn't show up.

He considered riding into Camp Robinson, getting supplies and a saddle, then heading back to Cheyenne because he couldn't go on toward the Black Hills once the soldiers knew he was here.

But Scotty had a stubborn streak. He had been run out of the Hills once by the military, and he had promised himself he'd go back and find some of that gold. He wasn't going to let a few little things like having no supplies, no rifle, and no saddle keep him from accomplishing what he had set out to do.

Keeping well to the west of Camp Robinson and the Red Cloud Agency, which was just to the south and east of the military post, he rode north toward the Nebraska border.

Somewhere well to the north of White River, Scotty stumbled onto a camp of a half dozen wagons. At first he thought these were travelers camping for the night. But as he rode closer, he saw that these wagons had been here for a while.

The people welcomed him and explained that they were heading for the Black Hills but were uncertain where they were or how to get to the gulch where the gold had been found. Scotty could scarcely believe his good fortune. Within five minutes, he had made a deal with the men to guide them to the best gold fields in the Hills in exchange for a grubstake.

Now Scotty had company, a place to sleep and plenty to eat as he made his way back into the Hills. He had resolved not to travel with a group, but after his experiences traveling alone, he welcomed the company. However, food and companionship didn't guarantee success in the gold fields, as he well knew.

V

SCOTTY WAS flabbergasted when he led the wagons into Discovery Gulch where he had been earlier this fall. The gulch was swarming with prospectors. There were several buildings scattered over the area. A town site had been laid out not far from the place where the buildings had been last September. This colony had the atmosphere of permanency, but remembering how the soldiers had pushed the prospectors out before, Scotty doubted if it was.

Custer, South Dakota, in pioneer days.

Scotty sold his horse and bought mining tools from some prospectors who had extras and began walking over the hills and down the gulches. He looked over some of the most promising areas he had searched before and probed into new areas, finding some gold but still not the big strike he was looking for.

More prospectors poured in, and the new town site took on a name, Custer City. In order to be fair about the distribution of lots, a drawing was scheduled. Scotty lined up with the others and took his turn drawing a lot.[1] According to the plat laid out, the lot that Scotty drew would be in one of the best residential districts or maybe even in the business district if the

South Dakota State Historical Society

Custer, Dakota Territory, in 1876.

town grew like the planners thought it would. Scotty was very pleased with his luck and decided he might make some money on his lot even if he didn't find his fortune in the ground.

Then it happened, just like it had back in September. The soldiers came again. General George Crook had been assigned the task of clearing the prospectors out of the Black Hills, and he had sent small companies of soldiers over all the area to carry out his order.

There was a lot of grumbling among the prospectors but nothing more. There was a difference this time, however, from the way it had been back in September. The captain's decree said that the prospectors could store their tools here if they wished in the hope that the government would work out an agreement soon with the Indians to allow white men to take gold from the Hills.

Scotty found a place to leave his equipment where he could pick it up sometime later. He was sure the government would find some way to open up these Hills to the prospector. If not, there was going to be a nasty three way war here between the Indians trying to hold their ground, the soldiers trying to uphold a treaty that was most unpopular with the white men, and the prospectors who were willing to face both the Indians and the army to search for the precious yellow metal.

The prospectors were taken south to Camp Robinson and turned over to the civilian authorities. Once again, the authorities released the prisoners without bail and with only a warning not to return to the Hills. Some of the prospectors barely waited until the authorities had turned their backs before heading north again.

It was November now, and winter was descending on the Hills. It took a hardy soul to head north and begin all over again. Prospectors, however, were both a hardy and an irrational lot. Winter weather that would

W. H. Over Museum, University of South Dakota (Morrow Collection)

Custer City as it looked when Scotty arrived the second time.

keep them off most jobs didn't daunt them in their search for gold.

Scotty was as hardy as any, but two disappointments were enough for him. He hadn't found anything resembling a paying strike. He decided he'd wait until the army took off the pressure. It was an expensive waste of time to battle the army, the Indians and the elements and come up with nothing as he had done so far. When the Hills were opened up to the white man, he'd return.

Back in Cheyenne, he found things as bleak as they had been when he had first arrived here late last winter. There was more activity now, for there were more men waiting for their chance to get rich in the Hills. Some of the more impatient began their trek to the Hills in the dead of winter. Unless they were extremely lucky, they'd only prove their own foolishness, Scotty decided.

There wasn't half enough work around Cheyenne

through the winter for the number of men looking for jobs. Scotty didn't find any steady work, but he managed to locate odd jobs around town, and he saved every penny he could.

During the winter he wrote to his father back in Scotland and the letter revealed an optimism that his own lack of success did not bear out.

—The opinion of all the men who were in the Hills when I was there that this will come up to California for riches. We could find gold in any creek by digging, but maybe not in paying quantities as far as we could see in the time the Government would let us stay. As soon as the treaty is signed there will be a grand rush. There are five or six hundred miners and others ready to start at a minute's notice, and I shall be with them.

I do not like the British Government and I shall always be an American. The people are generous to a fault, respect all men for their worth and not for birth.

Some of the letter is damaged with wear and age until it is illegible. Later in the letter he told more about the Hills.

—are about 250 miles from the placer N.E. There was about 1500 people in the Hills when I was there. We have laid out a city on one of the creeks and named it Custer, after the General who had charge of the expedition.

After another damaged part of the letter, he says:

—discovered gold first and it is the opinion of all that it will be the first and largest city in the Hills. I have a lot in the City and I shall hang on to it, and I think I have some good mining ground. I will hope for the best.[2]

By spring Scotty had saved up enough money to outfit himself for a return to the Hills, but the treaty everyone expected still had not been signed. The impatient prospectors could not understand the slow progress of the negotiations between the government and the Indians.

Although Scotty had resolved to wait until a treaty had been signed with the Indians that would open up the Hills to prospectors, he forgot that resolution when word reached Cheyenne that a new strike, much richer than the one in Discovery Gulch, had been made farther north in Deadwood Gulch. Those still waiting in Cheyenne ignored all warnings now and headed northeast. Scotty was right with them, as eager as any.

Arriving in the northern Hills on the 16th of July in 1876, Scotty struck out immediately to find a likely spot to stake a claim. He forgot about his disappointments down in Discovery Gulch where the glowing prospects had barely yielded Scotty enough gold to pay for the time it took to get it. Deadwood Gulch would be better. Everybody said so. There were enough people here now that Scotty was sure that the soldiers couldn't

South Dakota State Historical Society

Deadwood, Dakota Territory, with pack donkeys in the foreground.

run them out. It would take a full army to move this many people, and certainly no Indians were going to tackle this big a settlement.

Such a large number of people worked to Scotty's disadvantage, too. Everywhere he turned looking for a place to stake out a claim, he found people already there. And once a man staked a claim, he had to watch that someone didn't jump it. There were always some people who would rather take something someone else had found than to go out and find something for themselves.

It took Scotty only three days to get settled and stake a claim. He found a partner and they began digging a hole on their claim. On the 19th, Scotty wrote to his brother, George.

> Arrived here on the 16th, looked around, took a claim, and went to work today, I and another young fellow working together. We commenced a hole today 10 by 6 feet. I intend writing a little every day until I get a chance to send it.[3]

For six days he kept his promise, adding a little to his letter each day. But he had little to write that was exciting. The digging was hard and the progress slow.

At the end of three days of work, they had their hole down eleven feet, and it was becoming wet in the bottom. When water started seeping into the hole, they began a drainage ditch to carry off the water.

Their claim was in a beautiful area with forests stretching away in every direction and wild gooseberries and strawberries right on their own land. This beauty did little, however, to cheer up Scotty and his partner. They hadn't found a trace of gold in three days of work. The fourth day was spent in digging the drainage ditch which had to be nine feet deep.

Scotty's last nickel had gone into this venture, and he either had to find some gold or go hungry when his supplies ran out. Two more days of hard work produced nothing. Scotty's partner became discouraged

Frontiersmen of Dakota Territory during the early years. James B. Hickok is second from the left and William F. Cody third from left.

and quit. As he headed for home, he took Scotty's letter with him to mail at the first post office he saw.

Scotty was discouraged but not ready to quit. He had been dreaming of finding gold for over a year. A week's failure wasn't going to make him give up that dream. He still had a hundred pounds of flour and as long as that held out, he'd stay and keep digging.

After another few days, however, he had to give up and look for a better location. He prospected up and down the gulch and into side canyons but always with the same luck. He saw men on claims close to the places where he dug bring out enough gold to make them rich men, but he came up with nothing but rocks and dirt. Bitterness set in.

Scotty was only eighteen now, but he felt that he was a veteran in these hills. This was his third venture up here and all he had to show for it was experience.

He spent some time in Deadwood, the shack town that had sprung up in the gulch like a mushroom after a long rain. When he came into town shortly after his partner had gone home, he heard that Wild Bill Hickok was in town. Scotty had never met Hickok, but since everyone back in Hays, Kansas, had seemed to know him and had opinions, either good or bad, about him, Scotty felt that he could almost claim him as home folk.

Scotty received quite a shock when he came into town on Thursday, the third of August, and learned that Hickok had been killed in a saloon the day before by a man named Jack McCall. Other men had been killed in the new town, but Scotty had paid little attention to the recounting of their deaths. But it seemed almost like a personal loss when Hickok was killed.[4]

South Dakota State Historical Society

The trial of Jack McCall.

South Dakota State Historical Society
"Wild Bill" Hickok.

Through the fall months, Scotty worked the ground in several places both near to Deadwood and out at the fringe of the so-called rich area. Neither paid off for him. Cold weather set in and Scotty found himself without money or anything to show for all his work.

It was a tough winter for Scotty. There were jobs to be had in Deadwood, but there were literally hundreds of men like Scotty, broke and desperate, who were vying for those jobs. The one salvation for those who had failed to find gold was that the few who had struck it really rich were willing to pay high wages for the simplest chore. They were above doing menial work.

Scotty worked at any job he could get. His chief employment was cutting firewood. The wealthy had built fine cabins, but they had no intentions of blistering their hands on an ax handle. They gave men like Scotty the work they had to have to survive.

In February of 1877, the treaty was finally signed that legalized the presence of the prospectors in the Black Hills. There were more white men in the Hills then than there were in the towns around the edge of the Indian reservation.

By the time spring came, Scotty had his fill of Deadwood Gulch and its glittering promise of wealth. He could legally stay now, but the luster was gone. He had decided that his fortune was not to be found in the gold fields. There had to be something else.

With the snow melting off the hills, those prospectors who had not stayed on their claims all winter left Deadwood and went back to their claims. Scotty left Deadwood, too, but he went south.

At Camp Robinson, he paused to look around, then moved on to Fort Laramie. It was hard for him to bury his distrust of the army. Ever since the soldiers had put an abrupt end to his first venture into the Hills, he had tried to avoid the men in uniform. They had come to symbolize his failure to get rich quick. But now that he'd had a fair chance in the gold fields and still had failed to get rich, his anger at the army began to fade. If he had taken the advice of the soldiers and stayed out of the Hills, he'd have been a year ahead now.

He arrived at Fort Laramie dead broke. Swallowing his pride, he went to the commanding officer at the fort

Deadwood, South Dakota, in the early days.

to ask if the army was hiring any civilians. He found that the army needed teamsters. Although Scotty hadn't driven teams other than two horses on a plow or a wagon back in Victoria, he took the job, convincing the hiring officer that he could handle as many mules as he wanted to hitch together.

Scotty found that he got along with the mules better than the sergeants and lieutenants. He had a natural way with animals, but he didn't like the regulations under which all army work must be done.

Still he didn't complain until he had built up a small stake. Then, just at pay day, he had a run-in with a sergeant about the way to handle a loading job. He was informed, as every new soldier has been informed since the army began, that there are three ways to do things — the right way, the wrong way, and the army way — and he was working for the army now.

Scotty took a special delight in letting the sergeant know that he wasn't working for the army as of that moment. He drew his pay and began looking elsewhere for the place to earn the fortune he was still convinced this land held for him.

VI

SCOTTY HEADED back northeast. There was something about that country close to the Black Hills that fascinated him. The hills themselves had lost much of their appeal for Scotty, but the rich grassland on every side intrigued him with its potential.

Raising cattle was a profitable business down around Victoria, Kansas, and the grass here looked better to Scotty than it did back where his brothers lived. This was a land of endless oceans of grass, and few people here to take advantage of it.

There could be no rich ranchers here, however, as long as the Indians roamed freely over the area. To an Indian, stealing from another man was not a crime but rather a mark of achievement. It would be easier to kill a rancher's cow than hunt down one of the vanishing buffalo, anyway.

When Scotty reached Camp Robinson, he was surprised at the size of the Indian camp surrounding the Agency to the east of the army post. On his way to the Black Hills over a year ago, Scotty had been uneasy because of the rumor that the Indians who had just wiped out Custer's command up on the Little Big Horn would be roaming the prairies in search of more whites to kill. But they had seen no hostile Indians that trip, and during the winter the army had waged a harsh campaign against the Indians, issuing an ultimatum for them to come in to the agency and surrender or be

Officers' quarters at Fort Robinson, Nebraska.

Red Cloud Agency near Fort Robinson, Nebraska, 1876.

hunted down like wild dogs. Only now did Scotty realize how successful that campaign apparently had been.[1]

At the army post, Scotty was assured that the Indians were peaceful. The only job available was that of teamster to haul in supplies from the railroad at Sidney. Scotty had just quit a similar job and wasn't ready to tackle another with army regulations stifling every move.

Then Scotty learned that the army needed hay for its horses for the coming winter. Not enough had been put up, and the army would pay fifteen dollars a ton for hay delivered to the post.[2] Scotty inquired about the price of horses, mower, rake and hayrack. He was sure he could find good meadows where he could cut hay.

When he left the post, he rode past the agency. Most of the Indians were friendly, but there was a sullen undertone in some that gave Scotty a chill. He saw a band of about a hundred Cheyennes, tall and proud. Scotty doubted if he had ever seen a company of men that were better physical specimens. The agent told him they had just arrived from the Powder River country to surrender their arms and be registered.

Scotty also learned from the agent that most of the Indians were peaceful, especially Red Cloud's band. The greatest potential danger seemed to lie in Crazy Horse's band. Early in May, Crazy Horse had come in with over two hundred braves and their women and children. They had surrendered their guns and registered as scouts. But the agent had been hearing rumors that Crazy Horse was only waiting for the right opportunity to break away.

Scotty left the agency and began his search for a good hay meadow. The hay would be ready to cut within a week and he had no time to lose.

Down the creek from the agency, he found a Frenchman named Joseph Larabee with an Indian squaw.[3] Larabee was apparently making this his permanent home. He had a large family, including some good looking grown daughters. The oldest daughter, Helen, was in Crazy Horse's camp now, the wife of the Oglala chief.

At a spot about eight miles north of the Red Cloud Agency and the Black Hills road, Scotty found just what he was looking for. Here were acres of tall grass that would make fine hay for winter feed. He made camp and decided immediately that he would establish a ranch here. He didn't have any cattle and only this riding horse. But he had to have horses for his haying. And soon he could buy cattle with the money he'd make selling hay to the army.

He rode back to Camp Robinson and signed an agreement to deliver hay to the post. Then he went down to the agency and bought a mowing machine and some horses that the agent had for sale. This pretty well depleted the savings he had accumulated from his teamster job at Fort Laramie.

While he was at the agency, Scotty found a man down on his luck looking for work. After talking to him for a while, Scotty suggested that they go partners in the haying business. The man, George Clark, readily

Nebraska State Historical Society

Distributing goods at the Red Cloud Agency. Copied from a drawing in "Harper's Weekly," May 13, 1876.

agreed to Scotty's proposal and used his money and credit to buy a hayrack and a rake.

With two men to do the work, Scotty's ranch quickly took shape. They started building a small house. Scotty realized that it wouldn't be anything to brag about when he thought of the fine houses back at Victoria where he had stayed the first summer and winter he had been in America, but it would keep out some of the cold of winter. He and George Clark would be so busy they wouldn't have much time to spend loafing around in a house, anyway.

Scotty began cutting the hay, and George Clark took the other team and raked the hay as soon as it was cured. On the second day of mowing, tragedy struck at Scotty. His best mare, hitched to the mower, stepped in a hidden hole in the hay meadow and broke her leg.

Nebraska State Historical Society

A sketch showing the Indians receiving their food allotments at the Red Cloud Agency. Published in "Harper's Weekly" November 13, 1875.

There was nothing Scotty could do except shoot the horse to put her out of her misery. That left him with only one horse to pull the mower. He had already spent all his money. Now he had to ride back to the Agency and buy a team of mules the agent had, promising to pay for the mules when he delivered the hay to the army.

It was a subdued Scotty who rode back to his ranch, leading his mules. He had prided himself in always paying his way as he went. But now he was in debt. There had been no other way. But at least, he knew where he was going to get the money to pay for his mules. However, the profit from his hay that he had planned to use for buying cattle would first have to cover his debt to the agent. He'd buy cattle with what was left.

Hauling the hay to the army post was going to be a slow job, so Scotty stacked most of the hay, either in the meadow where it was cut or up close to the house where he felt he could watch it better.

He couldn't afford to delay putting up the hay to haul it very far. If it rained on the hay when it was in the swath or bunch, the hay would have to lie there until it dried, and this cycle of rain and sun bleached the hay until it wouldn't be good feed. The army might refuse to accept it. So Scotty stacked the hay as soon as it was ready.

On one trip to Camp Robinson, Scotty learned that the Cheyennes had been taken to a reservation in Oklahoma. Mrs. Larabee, in complete sympathy with the Cheyennes, was very distressed. Joseph Larabee told Scotty that he thought it was a bad mistake to move the Cheyennes south where they were not used to living.

Scotty also heard stories of trouble among the Indians. An agreement late in July had given the Indians permission to go on a buffalo hunt in the fall. A feast to celebrate the coming hunt was planned. However, when it was announced that the feast would be held at the camp of Crazy Horse, Red Cloud and his band refused to go.

This caused dissension between the camps. Red Cloud accused Crazy Horse of looking for a chance to escape from the agency. Agent Irwin believed Red Cloud and prepared for trouble, fearing that once the

South Dakota State Historical Society

Red Cloud as an old man.

hunt began, Crazy Horse would escape and head north
to join Sitting Bull in Canada. He cancelled the hunting trip.

All the Indians resented being deprived of their
chance to go on a hunt. Scotty realized this could erupt
into trouble that would engulf him and his partner on
their little ranch. There were plans, Scotty knew, to
move the Red Cloud Agency to the Missouri River in
Dakota Territory, but he wondered if the move would
be made before a general outbreak occurred.

Scotty and his partner were cutting and putting up
the last of the hay crop when word reached them that
there was trouble at the agency. Chief Joseph was
making his break far to the west of them, and Camp
Robinson had been alerted to send troops to help capture the Nez Perce chief as he led his tribe from their
Oregon home northeast toward central Canada.

Colonel Bradley, post commander at Camp Robinson, had called for Indian scouts to help in the campaign against Chief Joseph. Crazy Horse had been
asked to go since he had signed on as a scout, but he
refused because he thought the soldiers were going on
a campaign against his friend, Sitting Bull. Finally he
had been convinced that the campaign was just against
the Nez Perce, and he had agreed to go.

However, his statement that he would fight until
there was not a Nez Perce left was mistranslated by the
interpreter and came out in English that he would fight
until there was not a white man left.[4] This word spread
quickly. General Crook, assembling troops and scouts
for the campaign against Chief Joseph, feared that
Crazy Horse would turn on his soldiers in the field. He
ordered Crazy Horse brought in for questioning.

A cavalry battalion from Camp Robinson was sent
to bring in Crazy Horse. Several Indian scouts went
with the battalion, among them No Water, the personal
enemy of Crazy Horse. The battalion captured the

camp of Crazy Horse but the Oglala chief slipped away and headed for the Spotted Tail agency to the east.

Scotty stayed close to his ranch to keep watch on his stacks of hay because he knew that the trouble that would come from this could sweep over his little ranch like a prairie fire. When he did leave his ranch, he went only as far as Joseph Larabee's place. J. E. Utterback, the blacksmith at the army post, was there describing the happenings of the night before.

Lieutenant Lee, acting agent at the Spotted Tail Agency, had brought Crazy Horse back to Camp Robinson the day before, apparently convincing him that he would not be mistreated if he returned. Lieutenant Lee tried to get Colonel Bradley to talk with Crazy Horse and clear up the misunderstanding. But none of the officers at Camp Robinson trusted Crazy Horse, and the order went out to put the Oglala chief in the guard house.

When Crazy Horse saw the cells in the building where they were taking him, he turned on his captors with a knife and one soldier ran him through with a bayonet. Little Big Man, Crazy Horse's friend in past years, tried to restrain the Oglala chief and was injured himself.[5] Utterback had been there and seen the whole thing.

He graphically described the howling of the Indians when Crazy Horse was taken to the adjutant's office next to the guard house where he died later in the night. Every white man at the post and the agency, whether soldier or civilian, expected a pitched battle before the night was past but nothing came of it. Chief Red Cloud was given most of the credit for preventing an uprising over the death of the Oglala chief.

Scotty and his partner stayed close to their little ranch for a few days, watching developments. Scotty was only nineteen now, and he had been in America only three years, but he was sure he knew the Indians

Little Big Man.

well enough to know that they weren't likely to allow
the death of a great chief like Crazy Horse to go un-
punished.

But as the days went by and no battle broke out,
Scotty began to realize how submissive the Indians
had become. In a way, he felt sorry for them. He had
seen the Indians in their pride, such as the Cheyennes
who had been at the agency when he arrived from Fort

Nebraska State Historical Society

*Red Cloud Agency, 1876. Trader establishment and corner
of Agency building.*

Laramie. It was sad to think that their spirits had been
broken so badly.

Scotty cut and stacked over a hundred and twenty
tons of hay before he finished. He sold about forty tons
of it to the army for fifteen dollars a ton. He and his
partner spent several days hauling the hay to the post.
The six hundred dollars they received looked like a
fortune to Scotty.

With the haying done, Scotty and George began
looking for other means of making money. Scotty heard
that the Black Hills merchants were paying six cents a
pound to have their freight hauled out from Fort Pierre
on the Missouri River in Dakota Territory. That looked
like a big profit to Scotty. He already had some horses
and mules. He'd need more plus a good wagon. They
got a small order from the agency for goods to be
brought from Fort Pierre, then George Clark set out for
the Missouri to bring his first load. Scotty figured the

Sitting Bull and his favorite wife.

profits from a couple of loads would pay off what they owed.

Scotty bought a sow and litter of pigs. It didn't seem right for a ranch not to have something besides horses

Ziemann Collection

Haying crew at Fort Bennett.

on it. Besides, Scotty figured he could raise his pork cheaper than he could buy it.

In October, the Indians were moved off the agency toward the Missouri River where a new agency was prepared for them at the mouth of Yellow Medicine Creek. Scotty wasn't exactly glad to see them go. He had made a lot of friends among the Indians. With them gone, ranchers would swarm into this country. Scotty might find himself squeezed in by ranchers bringing in great herds to eat the grass. He was glad that the Larabees were staying. He had become good friends with the family.

Scotty discovered that not all the Indians had left the country when fire burned one of his hay stacks farthest from the house.[6] Every few nights another stack was burned. Scotty had stacked some of his hay close to the house. Now he began moving the farthest stacks closer to the house until he had about forty tons of hay stacked within a few yards of the buildings.

He wasn't sure that even these precautions would save his hay. If the Indians came close enough to fire these stacks, they might burn his house, too. These were renegade bucks setting the fires, and they would destroy anything that belonged to a white man.

Many of the Indians resented being moved from their familiar land around Camp Robinson. Scotty heard from the soldiers that a big band of Indians had broken away from the march and were thought to be heading for Sitting Bull up in Canada. The soldiers estimated that a thousand to seventeen hundred had broken away.[7]

Scotty knew that not all those Indians who had broken away had gone to Canada. Some of them were right close to his ranch, and their presence made the days and nights very uneasy for him.

VII

SCOTTY AND his partner had worked hard to put up that hay, and it hurt Scotty to see it burned, but all he could do was stay close to the house and protect the hay he had stacked nearby. The Indians didn't venture close enough to burn that.

Scotty wrote often that fall to his brother, George, back in Victoria, Kansas. One of those letters was dated November 4, 1877 at Camp Robinson.[1]

My dear brother:

I received your welcome letter last night and was glad to see you were all well. I wrote a long letter two months ago, but don't think you got it. It is snowing heavy just now.

You have likely heard the Indians have left Red Cloud. They have gone down to the Missouri.

My partner has gone with a load of freight. We get 6¢ a lb. He will be gone a month.

I don't think the Indian war is over yet. The Sioux were very dissatisfied at moving, and I think the Gov. officers are trying to make them break out again. I can talk a deal of the Sioux language. I think if they don't break out in the winter they will in the spring.

The Black Hills is getting better, rich men putting in quartz mills, and I think it will make a good country yet.

Enclosed you will find a sample of the Black Hills gold. It isn't big enough for a pin but it is the best I could do.

Your loving brother,
James Philip.

The month of November wore away before Scotty's partner got back from his freighting trip to Fort Pierre.

The weather got worse. Snow piled up, and Scotty lost the sharp edge of enthusiasm he had acquired for this country.

Stage coaches were running steadily now between Sidney on the Union Pacific Railroad to the south and the Black Hills. Camp Robinson was one of the main stops along the way. Every few days Scotty heard that one of the coaches had been held up. Usually the bandits were after the gold being shipped out of the Black Hills, but occasionally a north bound stage was stopped and the passengers robbed of everything of value they carried.

There were no more hay stack burnings. Cold weather and snow might have put a stop to the sport, but Scotty believed the Indians had moved on. Game had been scarce while the Indians had been at the agency. But now Scotty occasionally saw some within a mile or so of his ranch.

He began to feed his sow and pigs on meat because the price of grain at the post trader's store was five or six cents a pound, and Scotty decided he could hunt game for his pigs cheaper than that.

On the last day of November, he wrote his brother, George, again.[2]

Dear Brother:

I received your very welcome letter a few days ago and was glad to hear you were all well about Victoria. We have fearful rough weather here.

Just now you ask where is my ranch. It is eight miles north of the Red Cloud Agency and Black Hills road.

My partner has gone to the Missouri about 350 miles trip. He has been gone a month and I haven't heard anything of him.

Tell me if you hear anything of Africa. I would like to go anywhere south. At any rate I won't stay another winter in this northern country. There was a barrel of water froze solid at the door last night. But still it is a real good country too, plenty of game.

The Deadwood stage.

You ask me to give you a sketch of my travels. Well, you know I am not much of a composer. Besides there is nothing in it very romantic or adventurous. I never killed any animal but what would run from a man, only a bear, and a bear will try to get out of your way until he is wounded.

Your last letter — there was no news in it. Tell Mrs. Philip to write me. I remain your loving brother,

James Philip

The weather continued cold with plenty of snow, and Scotty's determination not to winter here again remained steadfast. But that determination was destined to fade into oblivion with the coming of spring. In the meantime, George Clark returned from the Missouri, and life took on a brighter outlook for the lonely Scotty.

Most of the soldiers who had been assigned to escort the Indians to their new agency grounds on the Missouri returned to Camp Robinson with the word that the Indians had balked. They had gone into camp for the winter less than seventy-five miles from their old agency on the White River and made it clear they intended to remain right there.[3]

Freighting business came to a virtual halt. It was too cold to make the long trips, and the danger of getting lost in a blizzard was too great.

Scotty rode into Camp Robinson one day in January and found a big change. Camp Robinson had become Fort Robinson.[4] Scotty could see no outward change unless it was that the soldiers walked with just a bit more pride.

On this trip, Scotty underwent a bigger change than the post had. He was asked to be a civilian scout and courier for the army, working out of Fort Robinson. He

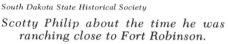

South Dakota State Historical Society

Scotty Philip about the time he was ranching close to Fort Robinson.

Indian burials, either on the Cheyenne River or the Bad River.

wouldn't have to quit his little ranch but would be on call when the army needed him. The added income prompted him to accept.

So in January of 1878, Scotty became scout and courier for the army, a job that he didn't expect to require much time or energy. But in that, he was mistaken. His own prediction that the Indian trouble was not over proved only too correct.

Through the remainder of the winter, he had little to do. The few chores at the ranch could be handled by his partner when Scotty wasn't there. A few times the army sent him with messages to the Indian villages. Seeing how the Indians survived the bitter winter with inadequate shelter, and in Scotty's opinion, a bare minimum of food, deepened his respect for the red man. They had a right to resent the way they had been treated. He couldn't condemn them too much for burning his stacks of hay last fall. In their place, he probably would have done worse.

In early spring, a man named Edgar Beecher Bronson came in from the Platte Valley with a big herd of cattle and claimed all the land from the head of the White River downstream twenty miles to Fort Robinson and from the White River down to the Niobrara or Runningwater, fifteen miles to the south.[5] His cattle carried the Three Crows brand. His cowboys pushed them out on the rich buffalo grass that only the year before had been the camping grounds of the Sioux and Cheyenne.

Bronson had been in the country only a short time. But he had just wintered his big herd along the Platte River where the weather had been almost as bad as it had been up here. No tenderfoot could have done that.

Scotty liked Bronson, and before the day was over, he had agreed to work for him in his spare time with the understanding that the army had first call on him.

Bronson's headquarters was on Dead Man's Creek, only five miles from Fort Robinson, so Scotty was actually closer to the fort when he was at the Three Crows headquarters than when he was on his own little ranch.

Bronson's choice of headquarters proved to be most fortunate. The Indians called the place Ghost Creek because at one time a band of Indians had camped there, and some fast acting disease had struck them. So many died that there were not enough survivors to bury the dead. After that, the Sioux would not venture into this canyon at night. In the following years, the Sioux raided many ranches in the area, but they never came near Bronson's headquarters.

Although Bronson's Three Crows was the first ranch in the area, before the spring was gone, others moved in. Newman's ranch far down the Niobrara close to the sandhills was the biggest of the newcomers.

Scotty helped Bronson build his house and the corrals to handle his cattle. In a short time, the place took on the air of a prosperous ranch.

With the coming of spring, Scotty forgot his decision to leave the country before another winter set in. The hills looked like the slopes of Paradise to the cattleman. Green grass carpeted the countryside, and the early flowers poking their heads up through the new grass dotted the prairie with yellow and white.

Still Scotty's first home in America at Victoria held its grip on him. Family ties were strong in Scotty as his letters proved.

May 13, 1878[6]

My dear Brother:

I received your note yesterday and was surprised you never get my letters. I think things will be pretty lively this summer if the Indians break out, as they are pretty certain to do. I have no news, but hoping this will find you all in good health as this leaves me enjoying that blessing.

Your loving brother,
James Philip.

Scotty suddenly found himself a very busy man. Not only did he have his own little ranch to manage while working in his spare time at Bronson's ranch, he was subject to call at any time by the army. In addition to this, he and his partner, George Clark, were continuing their freighting business. In fact, Scotty was realizing more profit from his freighting than from any of his other ventures.

Although Scotty had bought some cattle now, he still had more horses than cattle on his ranch. He needed horses and mules in his freighting business. Besides, he got a chance to buy horses cheap as he described to his brother in a letter.[7]

There is a great many captured from the Indians and sold at Government sales at from 3 to 10 dolls. each.

There was a great War Dance here, the best I ever saw. General Crook and all the officers were there.

Mrs. Philip said Annie Hardie is coming out to see you. Could you not persuade father and sister to come, too. It would be a great deal better to be in Victoria than in Dallas (Scotland).

I will send you some money — 110 dollars. If you get a chance I wish you would buy some heifers with it.

I see Philip and Co. are driving a great trade. I will send the half sovereign I got from Garrow to hang at your chain.

You spoke of a ¼ section of land you will file for me. Do it if you can for I intend to home. This is what I call Victoria.

Love to you all,
James Philip.

Like most men who went west, Scotty wanted land of his own. He had claimed the land where his little ranch was, but claiming it and getting legal title to it were entirely different things. There was no land office close, and it would probably be impossible to describe his land so he could get legal title. Anyway, nobody was contesting his claim to the land.

Scotty suddenly found himself with enough time to make one of the freighting trips himself. Bronson didn't need him for a while, and the army had no work for him. He decided he could do best with a load of freight from Fort Pierre into the Hills. A trip this time of year appealed to him.

Taking his team and Studebaker wagon north up the Sidney-Deadwood trail, he cut off to the east before he got to Deadwood, hitting the Bad River just north of the Bad Lands. He followed the Bad River right to Fort Pierre. Scotty had never seen better grazing land. It was all on the reservation, and the Indians weren't using it. In fact, he didn't see an Indian all the way across the reservation.

The Red Cloud Agency that had set up new headquarters on the Missouri River had given up the idea of moving the Indians to it. Chief Red Cloud had stopped only about seventy-five miles from Fort Robinson, and he was still there.[8] Since most of the land west of the Missouri was reservation land, anyway, the government moved the agency back to the west where the Indians were.

After loading at Fort Pierre, Scotty headed due west

for Deadwood. The road was well marked by the many freight wagons that had already gone over it. The Black Hills received much of its freight from the east, where it came up the Missouri River by boat to Fort Pierre then straight west by freight wagon to the Hills. Most of the rest came by rail to Sidney, down in Nebraska, then north over the Sidney-Deadwood road. Some came

Nebraska State Historical Society

The Sidney-Black Hills trail.

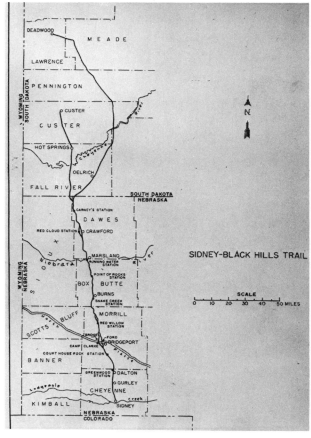

South Dakota State Historical Society

A bull train at Fort Pierre, South Dakota. Bull trains such as this were on the road when Scotty freighted.

down from Bismarck, and the remainder came from the railroad at Cheyenne over the Cheyenne-Black Hills road.

When Scotty arrived in Deadwood, he looked around for familiar faces. Most faces were new to him, and those he recognized belonged to rich men now who had found the gold that spelled the difference between success and failure. The failures had left the Hills long ago.

Scotty didn't envy these men so much now. He had a good freighting business with two wagons and teams. George Clark ran the other wagon. He had the beginning of a good ranch down by Fort Robinson, and he was convinced that there was big money in raising cattle.

He had only started to unload the merchandise he had brought for delivery at Deadwood when somebody brought a newspaper that was a couple of weeks old and shoved it into his hands. There he read of the death of C. Phillips, shot right here in Deadwood.[9]

South Dakota State Historical Society

Typical mule freighting team.

"What's this got to do with me?" Scotty wanted to know.

"A lot of people thought it was you," the man said.

The sheriff found Scotty shortly after that to tell him that he had a letter from Scotty's relatives in Victoria, Kansas, asking if it was true that Scotty had been killed here in Deadwood.

"Just what did you tell them?" Scotty demanded.

The sheriff, who was a stranger to Scotty, shrugged. "I described the man who had been killed. He was a fair-haired, blue-eyed man." He looked at Scotty. "I reckon that should set them at ease. That sure don't describe you."

Scotty nodded in agreement. He had black hair and brown eyes and was anything but fair in complexion. He had known C. Phillips and was surprised that his relatives could possibly confuse him with C. Phillips. Of course, Scotty had no way of knowing what his relatives had heard. Maybe there had been no first initial given, and they could have thought that the last name had been misspelled.

Scotty guessed that his brothers back in Kansas probably thought that he was living with one foot in the grave up here, anyway. There were times when that was closer to the truth than Scotty cared to admit.

VIII

TAKING THE stage road south out of Deadwood, Scotty hurried back to his ranch close to Fort Robinson. There he found everything in order, his pigs and few cattle doing well.

He lost no time in writing to his brother, George.[1]

June 13, 1878

Dear Brother:
I have just got home from a four weeks trip to the Missouri River and the Black Hills. Never found your letter of May 15th. I don't know how you don't get my letters as I answered everyone.

St. George chapel in Victoria, Kansas. Grant, the leader of the English colony was buried in front of the chapel in April, 1878.

*George Grant's "Villa"
south of Victoria, Kansas.*

And you thought I was dead. It is all foolishness to think of that, not but what I can be killed, but I think I can take care of myself as well as anyone. And it is one thing sure, I never will be killed for a prostitute as C.P. was.

And old Grant is dead, poor fellow. He wasn't a bad man.

I am glad you are getting on so well, but sorry you lost money in the bank. Well, if you were like me you wouldn't lose nothing. We have very wet weather, raining most every day.

The rest of the letter is missing. Although he seldom mentioned his financial circumstances, he let his brother know this time that surplus money was not a problem with him.

With things going so smoothly at the ranch and neither the army nor Bronson having any special work for him to do, Scotty decided to hitch his big mules to the Studebaker wagon and head for Sidney to bring in a load of supplies. In Deadwood, it seemed that every store and every individual was crying for goods. The winter had been a hard one and the spring very rainy. Not many freighters wanted to buck the muddy roads to bring in supplies.

If Scotty brought in a load of goods now, he could get five or six cents a pound for hauling. Later, when the rains stopped and the roads were dry, he couldn't expect more than two or three cents a pound. The extra money encouraged Scotty to make the trip now.

Scotty headed south with his empty wagon, making close to thirty miles a day. Each day he met a couple of stage coaches heading for the Hills, and at least one passed him on its way south. Scotty wasn't surprised to see the north bound stages loaded to capacity, but he was astonished to see that the south bound coaches were also full. Evidently there were almost as many discouraged miners heading back where they came from as there were hopeful men moving in.

Of the four trails leading into the Black Hills, the Sidney trail was the one with the heaviest traffic. It was a little shorter than the one from Cheyenne, and there was less danger from renegade bands of Indians. There were many reports of Indian trouble on the Cheyenne-Black Hills road, especially along Hat Creek.[2]

Also, there were soldiers at Fort Sidney and Fort Robinson on the Sidney-Deadwood road, and often soldiers were stationed at the north end of the bridge spanning the North Platte River. This encouraged a constant stream of traffic that made an isolated raid such as would fit the style of a few renegade Indian bucks almost impossible.

The roads leading from Fort Pierre and Bismarck were not so popular because the river traffic getting the prospectors to their jumping off place was slower than the trains taking them west out of Omaha. In the winter, the trails to the northeast and east of the Black Hills were usually buried under snow. Snow also blanketed the plains to the south of the Hills, but it was seldom so deep nor did it last so long.

Scotty even met one herd of cattle being pushed north. He could only guess whether the cattle were headed for the new Pine Ridge Indian Agency to feed the Indians or to the Black Hills to supply meat for the hungry miners.

He met two long trains of freight wagons belonging to Pratt and Ferris, the biggest freighting company hauling out of Sidney. All their wagons were pulled by oxen or mules. The bull trains were slow, but those big oxen could move huge loads at a steady pace. There were twenty-three wagons in each train. In most cases, each wagon was pulled by eight yoke of oxen.

That was big business, Scotty thought. If he owned the wagons and oxen in just that one train, he'd consider himself rich. Pratt and Ferris had a good many such outfits. One of the drivers told Scotty that he had eight thousand pounds of freight on his wagon. Scotty didn't expect to haul nearly that big a load behind his four mules when he came back.

Scotty had planned to cross the North Platte River at a ford and save the toll charge at Clarke's Bridge. But the rains had made the river too high so he turned upstream from the ford to the bridge.

Henry Clarke had built the bridge two years ago in 1876. Clarke had been a bridge builder for the railroad as it stretched its rails across the continent so he had asked the railroad company to help him build this bridge across the Platte. Through several months in the spring of the year, the Platte ran too high for freight wagons to ford it safely, so it was to the advantage of the railroad to have a bridge across the North Platte to allow freighters to haul from Sidney to the Black Hills any time of the year.

The bridge was solidly built, well braced with trusses.[3] It was nearly two thousand feet long, made of sixty-one spans. It had to be solid to withstand the ice jams of late winter and the floods that invariably followed, plus the heavy traffic that passed over it every day. Proof of its durability is the fact that it stood for twenty-five years.

Pratt and Ferris freighting train on the way to the Black Hills from Sidney, Nebraska.

At the bridge, Scotty paid his toll, two dollars for wagon and driver, fifty cents for each animal. It would cost Scotty another four dollars to cross back on his way north with his freight, but it would be well worth it. Fording the Platte when the water was high was a risk few freighters wanted to take.

At the north end of the bridge was Fort Clarke,[4] a two-story blockhouse over thirty feet square. Soldiers were usually stationed here to discourage Indians or white renegades planning to attack freight wagons or

Camp Clark bridge.

Nebraska State Historical Society

*Camp Clark, 1876, showing the end of the bridge with the store and post
office in the foreground.*

stage coaches crossing the bridge. So, instead of being
the spot along the Sidney-Deadwood road where
travelers were most vulnerable to attack, it became the
safest.

At the south end of the bridge, Clarke had set up a
post office, and miners heading into the Hills often
mailed letters from there. Many had the feeling that
once they crossed that bridge, they'd be severing all
ties with civilization as they knew it.

Clarke also had a supply store and a feed and livery
barn here. Often the army stationed a small detach-
ment of soldiers here, too, to protect the buildings and
the south end of the bridge.

At Sidney, Scotty found the town struggling to control its tremendous growth since '76 when Clarke put
in his bridge. Before that, miners heading for the Hills
usually went on west by rail and left the tracks at
Cheyenne, crossing the Platte on the ferry at Fort

Laramie. The bridge crossing the treacherous Platte north of Sidney changed the picture.

The flow of miners into the Hills was slowing up. But the need for supplies was even greater because of the number of people already there. Freighting business was better than it had ever been before.

Pratt and Ferris had enlarged their warehouses at Sidney. So had McCann and Company. McCann reported shipping out as much as three hundred thousand pounds of freight a day. Scotty wondered

Nebraska State Historical Society

Sidney, Nebraska, in 1876. Fort Sidney is in the upper left corner.

how much Pratt and Ferris sent out. They were a bigger outfit than McCann.

Much of the freighting was done, however, by "shotgun" freighters. These were the independent freighters like Scotty. Some had two or three wagons; others just one. Many hoped to make enough off their freighting to buy the needed equipment for prospecting; others intended to make freighting their business.

If a freighter with an unassigned cargo arrived in one of the gold towns in the Black Hills when commodities were scarce, he could command fantastic prices. Scotty had been in the Hills when flour was selling for sixty cents a pound and potatoes for fifteen cents.[5]

Scotty loaded his wagon with products he knew he could dispose of quickly in Deadwood — flour, bacon, shirts, pants and boots. He added miners' tools and other hardware until he had all he wanted to haul behind his mules. He knew that those last few pounds that overloaded a wagon were far from profitable. They slowed the freighter's progress and worked his team too hard. However, the rains had stopped, and the roads were drying out rapidly.

Scotty pulled out of Sidney before the sun came up the next morning. His mules were in good shape and ready to travel. He had barely gotten out of town when the stage coach whipped past him in a flurry of color and noise. It was polished until it shone in the rays of the rising sun.

Scotty admired the brilliant colors on these coaches.[6] There were bright red panels along the sides, new leather curtains at the windows, and flashing yellow wheels that dazzled people as they streaked past them on the road. High stepping horses pulled these new Concord stages at a rapid clip.

Scotty felt that he had been fortunate to get to see the stage coach he had heard so much about. "Old

The Pratt and Ferris freight house at Sidney, Nebraska, circa 1876.

Ironsides" had been put into use just a couple of weeks ago to frustrate the highwaymen who made a business of robbing coaches coming down from the Hills loaded with gold.[7]

Old Ironsides had been especially made by Abbot and Downing in New Hampshire where they made all their other Concord coaches. The entire inside of Old Ironsides was lined with half inch steel. The windows in the sides and doors were much smaller than windows on regular coaches. They looked like portholes. A section of the roof could be lifted out or bolted down from the inside. Even if the outlaws stopped the coach, they would have a difficult time getting inside. And once inside, their troubles were far from over. An eight hundred pound safe was bolted to the floor. The safe was tough enough to withstand the assault of most robbers.

To add to the security of Old Ironsides, six or eight armed guards rode with the coach from Deadwood to Sidney. The cost to the shippers was one dollar for each one hundred dollars worth of gold. That was a high rate, but most shippers considered it money well spent. Their losses from shipments on regular coaches had been staggering.

The cargoes in Old Ironsides usually ran from one hundred to two hundred thousand dollars. In all the years that the special coach ran from Deadwood to Sidney, it was successfully robbed only once, in September of 1878. That time the robbers guessed wrong because they picked a time when the cargo was only forty-five thousand dollars. Shortly after the robbery, most of the stolen gold was recovered, and the robbers caught and sent to the penitentiary. The heyday of the highway bandit was about over.

Scotty let his mules pick their own ground-covering pace. The trail led straight north from Sidney for fourteen miles.[8] There was a water hole at this spot, and Scotty paused here for noon to let his mules rest and crop a little grass. Then he hitched up again and angled to the north and west for a little over seven miles. North again for another seven miles brought him to Greenwood Station where he unhitched for the night.

He made Court House Rock Station at noon the next day. That was ten miles northwest of Greenwood Station and was situated a mile south and a mile west of Court House Rock itself. From there it was only nine miles to Clarke's Bridge, and Scotty reached it in time to cross the bridge before dark, paying his four dollars toll again.[9] Just beyond Fort Clarke, he found a campsite where his mules had good grass for the night.

The road led straight north from Clarke's Bridge to Red Willow Station twelve miles away, then angled toward Snake Creek Station eighteen miles to the northwest. Scotty spent the night at a stage station between Red Willow and Snake Creek stations. The stage company maintained stations about every fifteen miles, with fresh horses for the coaches and a place where passengers could get something to eat or drink.

Courthouse and Jail Rock.

Beyond Snake Creek Station the trail turned straight north again for thirteen miles to Point of Rocks Station. From there it turned slightly to the northwest for fourteen miles to Running Water Station on the Niobrara River. Twenty-two more miles brought Scotty to Fort Robinson.

Scotty spent a day at his ranch, making sure everything was all right and giving his mules time to rest and eat. Then he pushed on toward Deadwood.

He reached Carney's Station at noon after leaving his ranch, then nine miles farther north, he hit the forks of the trail. The west fork went on to Custer while the right fork swung to the northeast, avoiding the roughest hills and coming into Deadwood from the southeast. The stage line claimed that the distance from Sidney to Deadwood was two hundred and sixty-seven miles.

Scotty had no trouble disposing of his cargo at a

good profit. But he heard some disturbing news. A
newspaper man from down along the Missouri was in
town, and he said he had been talking to some army
men who had come from Indian Territory. Disease had
struck the Cheyenne Indians who had been taken
down to Fort Reno the year before. Unrest among them
was growing, and the army feared bad trouble.

Scotty tried to tell himself that this wouldn't affect
his life here along the Nebraska-Dakota border, but he
couldn't get thoughts of the Cheyennes' troubles out of
his mind.

He didn't linger in Deadwood but headed back for
his ranch.

IX

SCOTTY BOUGHT a few more cattle and put them on his ranch, then spent some time fixing up his house and corrals. He had completely forgotten his resolution never to spend another winter in this country.

The army called on him to carry dispatches occasionally, often to the Pine Ridge Agency, seventy-five miles to the northeast. Everything seemed peaceful enough, but sad stories about the Cheyennes down in Indian Territory continued to filter into the Indian camps of the north. Mrs. Larabee was sure they would all die down in that hot damp country.

Scotty didn't know what the Indian Territory was like, but he told himself that the soldiers would take good care of the Indians there. Then he remembered things that had happened when the Sioux were at the agency close to Camp Robinson, and he wondered. Joseph Larabee and his wife vividly recalled their shock at the death of Crazy Horse, probably because he was their son-in-law.

Scotty made a deal with the army to supply hay for winter feed again. When haying time came, Scotty turned his full attention to his work. He didn't expect any trouble this fall from Indians burning the stacks.

He hired a man named Dan Powell to help with the haying. While working one day, Powell spotted a buffalo and shot it. It was the last wild buffalo ever killed in the area. Scotty and Dan Powell were destined to remain good friends as long as they lived.

The army needed hay more than it needed messengers, so Scotty was excused from courier duty while he was working in the hay. On one occasion near the middle of September, when Scotty hauled a load of hay in to the post, he found the place buzzing with excitement.

A telegraph wire had been strung from Sidney up to Fort Robinson and a message had come over that wire, reporting that Dull Knife, the Cheyenne chief, had escaped from the reservation down at Fort Reno and was heading north with his band.[1]

General Bradley, in command at Fort Robinson, was ordered to keep every man at the post on the alert, awaiting further orders. Scotty was placed on active call again. Since his haying was about finished, this didn't disrupt his working schedule to any extent.

General Bradley showed no alarm because it seemed impossible that a little band of Indians could come all the way across Kansas and Nebraska and threaten the security and safety of people in the vicinity of Fort Robinson.

Scotty listened to the reports coming in that Dull Knife's band was plundering and killing on its way north. Some high authorities believed Dull Knife had been in communication with Sitting Bull up in Canada and was trying to rendezvous with him now, so they could make a last great stand together.

Scotty couldn't believe that. How could Dull Knife get in contact with Sitting Bull, a thousand miles from Fort Reno? Of course, if Dull Knife's entire band could slip out from under the army's watchful eye, one messenger could surely have sneaked out and made the round trip to Canada. If Sitting Bull did come to meet Dull Knife, they would likely meet somewhere around Fort Robinson or the Black Hills. But it was all just too fantastic to believe.

General George Crook astride a saddle mule.

Scotty knew he wouldn't get much work done around his ranch until Dull Knife was captured. General Bradley was keeping all men on the alert until he got further orders.

Scotty remembered those tall powerful Cheyenne braves he had seen when he first came to Fort Robinson and how their spirits had been broken before they had been sent to Fort Reno. If the tales he had heard about how disease was killing the Cheyennes like cattle around a poisoned water hole were true, he didn't blame Dull Knife for making a run for life and freedom. In his place, Scotty would have done the same thing.

Scotty realized that his thinking might be influenced by the Larabees. His contact with the family was mostly through Sarah, the fourth daughter. Sarah didn't say much, but her sentiments were clear, and Scotty's sympathies were in agreement.

News reached Fort Robinson daily on the telegraph wire. General Crook had taken command of the effort to stop Dull Knife's flight.[2] He had troops pursuing the Indians from Fort Reno and Camp Supply in Indian Territory, but Scotty knew Indians and Indian ways well enough now to know that it wasn't likely that soldiers already behind the Indians would ever catch up with them. Only those waiting in their path had a chance to stop them.

A line of soldiers was thrown along the railroad running east and west of Dodge City, hoping to catch the Indians as they crossed the rails there. But the Indians crossed those rails with only one small battle being fought close to Dodge City. Several Indians

Doug Philip Collection (taken from Beougher Collection)

Officers' quarters at Fort Hays in the 1870s.

were captured, but the main body escaped to the north, burning ranches and farms as they went. Smoke from those fires was clearly visible in Dodge City.

General Crook now made preparations to stop Dull Knife's band along the Kansas Pacific Railroad, the next barrier the Indians would have to cross. Soldiers from Fort Hays and Fort Wallace were put on patrol along the rails, hoping that, as soon as the Indians revealed where they were going to cross, the waiting companies of soldiers could be rushed in by train and the Indians brought to bay for a decisive battle. Few soldiers expected to stop the Indians without a battle to the death. The Indians wouldn't have left their reservation in Indian Territory if they hadn't been prepared to die if they couldn't escape.

On the twentieth of September, General Bradley received orders to prepare his men for possible action against the Indians. It seemed a bit ridiculous because on that same day, Fort Robinson had received a report of the battle two days ago close to Dodge City. But it pointed up the respect General Crook had for the wily chief, Dull Knife. The Indians were still hundreds of miles away, but General Crook was setting up defenses along the Kansas Pacific, the Union Pacific on the Platte, and now at Fort Robinson, a hundred and twenty-five miles north of the U.P. Line.

Early in October, reports reached Fort Robinson of a battle fought with the Indians in Kansas in a canyon called Famished Woman's Fork (close to the present Scott County Park) in which Lieutenant Colonel W. H. Lewis of the Nineteenth Infantry was killed. Colonel Lewis had taken command of the cavalry troops from Fort Reno and Camp Supply when they reached Kansas. Other soldiers were wounded, but only one Indian and some ponies were killed by the soldiers. Again the Indians escaped to the north.

The Indians crossed the Kansas Pacific Railroad without being intercepted and melted into the prairie to the north. Excitement grew at Fort Robinson as the dispatches came in, reporting the progress of the Indians and the army's complete inability to stop them.

After the battle at Famished Woman's Fork, Dull Knife's band moved north. The young bucks fanned out, raiding ranches, killing the men and stealing the horses. Eighteen ranchers were killed, most of them from the Beaver and Sapa Creeks in Kansas.[3] In Nebraska, George Rowley was killed near Stinking Water Creek while trying to get to his home on Frenchman Creek.

Still the Indians were not stopped. Excitement was changing to alarm at Fort Robinson now. If Dull Knife managed to slip through the soldiers guarding the Union Pacific, only the men at Fort Robinson would stand between the Indians and the Red Cloud Agency. So far, Chief Red Cloud had shown no sympathy for Dull Knife and his struggle to escape to the freedom of Canada. That was no guarantee, however, that he wouldn't suddenly become hostile to the soldiers around the reservation if Dull Knife actually reached him with tales of the treatment he had received down in Indian Territory. If Red Cloud's warriors joined with Dull Knife, there weren't enough soldiers between here and Canada to keep them from reaching Sitting Bull beyond the Canadian border.

Major Thornburg, on a scouting expedition south of the Platte, reported on October 3rd that he had sighted the Cheyennes on the Frenchman River. At least sixty of the estimated two hundred and fifty he had seen were armed warriors.

At noon on the next day Dull Knife defiantly led his entire band across the Union Pacific tracks less than a mile east of Ogallala. The news was wired to Major Thornburg at Sidney, and he brought his troops by train to Ogallala and set out in pursuit of the Indians.

Now orders came to Fort Robinson for action.[4]

Major Carlton took five troops of the Third Cavalry to the edge of the sand hills to intercept Dull Knife if he came through the hills. His orders were to prevent Dull Knife from joining Red Cloud at the Pine Ridge Agency until Major Thornburg could catch up with the Indians from the rear.

Scotty had never been down in the sand hills, but he had heard terrible stories about the drifting sand with no landmarks and only an occasional lake for water.[5] Many stories were told of men who had gone into those hills and never come back. Scotty had no desire to explore those hills himself, and he knew the soldiers shared his lack of enthusiasm for that desolate country.

Although it was generally conceded that the sand hills were too dangerous for white men to venture into, no one doubted Dull Knife's ability to cross them. The soldiers' main concern was for Major Thornburg's command, pursuing Dull Knife right now across that ninety mile wide desert between the Platte and the Niobrara.

A message finally came on the wire from Major Thornburg. He reported that the Indians had apparently split up into tiny groups of two to six and were hiding in the sand hills, resting. The major had found water only in isolated lakes, and uncertainty about what might lie ahead had caused him to turn back to Ogallala, claiming that further pursuit was hopeless.

Scotty, riding as courier from General Bradley at Fort Robinson to Major Carlton out on the Niobrara, took orders to the major to patrol the divide between the Niobrara and White Rivers, and at all costs, prevent Dull Knife from reaching Red Cloud.[6]

The Indians had dropped completely out of sight, and this caused more concern among the soldiers than had the daily news of their steady progress. They could only guess what had happened to Dull Knife's band.

Some speculated that the Indians were wandering aimlessly in that wasteland, dying of thirst and starvation. Others respected Dull Knife's leadership too much to believe that he'd take his people into a place where he couldn't provide for them.

Then, on the night of October 13th, a small band of Cheyenne warriors raided Clay Deer's store.[7] This store was on the old Red Cloud Agency grounds, a mile east of Fort Robinson. Deer had kept the store open after the Indians had been moved into Dakota Territory. The raiders got away with all the horses Deer had. All rumors that Dull Knife's band had starved to death in the sand hills were squelched.

Major Paddock, the post trader at Fort Robinson, took extra precautions to guard his supplies. Even though the fort was right at his elbow, most of the soldiers were out on patrol looking for the Cheyennes.

Word reached the post that the Indians were a part of Little Wolf's band, and that they had camped on Crow Butte, an isolated peak only a few miles from the fort. The butte could be climbed on only one side. Some of the soldiers still left at the fort went after the Indians and threw a ring around the butte, certain that they had some of Dull Knife's band trapped at last.

However, when morning came, the soldiers discovered that the Indians had come down off the butte and slipped through their lines. It wasn't until later that the army learned Dull Knife's strategy in this move. Little Wolf had taken the young strong warriors with him. They were to lead the soldiers in a chase to the north as they went to meet Sitting Bull. Dull Knife and the older and weaker members of his band were hiding in the sand hills, hopeful that the pursuing soldiers would leave an unguarded rear through which Dull Knife and the older people could escape to Canada. Little Wolf successfully carried out his assignment, reaching Sitting Bull in Canada, safely beyond the reach of the U.S. soldiers.

Nebraska State Historical Society

Crow Butte from the west, near Crawford, Nebraska.

Major Carlton, however, didn't follow Little Wolf's band. His soldiers continued to patrol the divide between the White and the Niobrara. A week after Little Wolf's raid on Clay Deer's store, he became impatient waiting for Dull Knife to come out of the hills and ordered some of his troops into the hills.

Two days later the troops, under Captain Jack Johnson, located a camp of sixty Indians. The Indians were in rags with nothing to eat and ponies so worn down they could barely travel. They surrendered without a fight. Among the captured chiefs were Dull Knife, Wild Hog and Old Crow. The other segments of Dull Knife's band were rounded up and Captain Johnson headed them north and west toward Fort Robinson.[8]

A heavy snow storm hit them on the 24th, and the captain went into camp on Chadron Creek. With the weather so bad and the Indians in such poor physical shape, he let them seek their own shelter without placing a heavy guard on them.

Morning disclosed the Indians dug into shallow rifle pits, ready to do battle.[9] They had been on army rations for two days and had regained some of their strength, enough to make one last effort to gain freedom.

For two days the Indians held out. Captain Johnson refused to waste lives trying to overrun their poor fortifications when the end of the siege was inevitable.

On the second day, Lieutenant Chase brought a field gun from Fort Robinson and fired a couple of rounds at the Indian positions. This quickly brought the final surrender of Dull Knife. After disarming his prisoners, Captain Johnson marched them, one hundred and forty-nine men, women and children, into Fort Robinson. The only weapons found were some old rifles. The captain couldn't understand how the Indians had put up such a good fight with only those poor weapons.

It was snowing again when the soldiers reached Fort Robinson and shoved their prisoners into an empty barracks and locked the door. The next day, they went into the barracks and searched the Indians thoroughly for weapons but found nothing. They neglected to look under the floor boards of the barracks, just as they had neglected to look under the long dresses of the squaws the day before when they had disarmed the warriors out on Chadron Creek.

X

WITH THE INDIANS imprisoned, Scotty was relieved of much of his army duty. Everyone knew that nearly half of the Indians had escaped to Canada with Little Wolf, but nothing could be done about that now. The army's current problem was deciding what to do with Dull Knife and his band.

Scotty found things at his ranch in good shape, considering how much he had been gone the last two months. His cattle had weathered the two snow storms in good condition and were out searching for grass as soon as the sun began melting the snow.

There was little for Scotty to do after he got his ranch ready for winter. He had reached the conclusion that he had to work for himself rather than hire out to others if he expected to make much money. This little ranch was his own; so was his freighting business. But what about the army? This fall his job as courier had kept him away from his own work a long time. Still, the wages were pretty good, and with winter coming on, there wasn't a lot he could do around the ranch. In winter, freighting was more of a hazard than a profitable business. He might be smart to stay with the army until spring, at least.

When Scotty visited the Larabee place, he found the family more and more withdrawn. He knew it was because the Cheyennes were shut up in the barracks at the post. Little was said about them, but the unspoken words were almost tangible. Scotty was at the Larabees' often these days, and he expected to continue the visits unless Sarah told him not to come.

Scotty went to the army post every day or two and kept up on the progress of the debate on what to do with Dull Knife and his followers. Some wanted to send them back to their reservation at Fort Reno down in Indian Territory. Others wanted them tried for the killings they had committed on their flight up from the Territory. The Sioux at the Pine Ridge Reservation wanted them released to settle among them.[1]

The army had no intention of letting Dull Knife settle among the Sioux, but with rumors that the Sioux were liable to rise up in revolt with the coming of grass in the spring, they didn't want to cross Chief Red Cloud and his Council too sharply, either.

In December, several Sioux chiefs, among them Red Cloud, American Horse, Red Dog, and No Flesh, came over from the reservation and held a council in the prison barracks with Dull Knife and his lesser chiefs. The army sent two captains and some non-commissioned officers to the council. The meeting was peaceful, but the officers had no say in the decisions reached.[2]

Dull Knife asked to be allowed to live with Red Cloud at the reservation and promised no trouble if permission was granted. Scotty, hearing the details of the request, was sure what the decision would be. If the decision could be made by the officers in charge right here at Fort Robinson, it might be in favor of Dull Knife's request. But the decision would be made at some high officer's desk far from the Indian country. There the officers would consider the running battle the army had had with Dull Knife and the restlessness of the Sioux. They'd be afraid to let Dull Knife mingle with the Sioux, and the request would be turned down.

The appearance of Captain Vroom and his men to

Chief Red Cloud as a young man.

camp a mile outside the fort seemed to verify Scotty's suspicions. Nobody knew what decisions had been made. If those decisions had been favorable to the Indians, they wouldn't have been kept secret. If Dull Knife was to be moved back to Indian Territory or punished, the army would try to do it without letting Red Cloud know.

Scotty made it a point to keep in close touch with happenings at the fort. Things were bound to break soon, and though he wanted no part of any battle that might be shaping up, he did want to know when to expect trouble.

He arrived at the post early on the morning of the fifth of January and learned that the decision had been announced. Captain Wessels had orders from the War Department, acting on the decision of the Indian Bureau, to march Dull Knife's band back to the reservation at Fort Reno in Indian Territory.[3] Captain Wessels knew the impossibility of such a march this time of year, but his orders left no room for argument.

There were several inches of snow on the ground, and the thermometer dropped below zero every night. No one at Fort Robinson believed that many of Dull Knife's band could survive a six hundred mile march through this weather. But the decision had been made back in the warm offices of the Indian Bureau. Captain Wessels had no alternative but to try to carry out his orders.[4]

The three most important chiefs, Dull Knife, Wild Hog and Old Crow, were brought from the prison barracks and the captain told them of the order. Dull Knife responded with a speech in which he declared that his people would not make the march and if they had to die, they'd do it here, even if they had to kill each other.

Captain Wessels warned them that all food and fuel would be cut off from the barracks until the Indians agreed to return to Fort Reno.[5] Scotty could scarcely believe the order, yet he understood the captain's position. It was the officer's way of trying to squelch the insubordination swiftly and decisively.

The Indians had had no new clothes issued to them since arriving at the fort. Although clothes had been ordered from the Indian Bureau, none had arrived. With no food or fuel in the barracks in this bitter cold weather, the Indians couldn't survive very long.

During the day Scotty listened to the war songs and the death chants in the barracks. He knew these proud

Dull Knife's defiance, from a drawing by Maynard Dixon.

Indians well enough now to know that those chants meant they were determined to die here rather than be taken south again. Scotty expected them to make a break before long. If they were going to die, they'd try to take some of their enemies with them.

Each day when Scotty came to the fort, he heard the chants. The days and nights continued bitter cold. Still no food or fuel went to the prison barracks. Guards patrolled the area around the barracks.

On the ninth of January, Scotty arrived too late to witness the near battle that broke out after Captain Wessels had called for the three chiefs again. The Indians had not allowed their old Chief, Dull Knife, to go. But Wild Hog and Old Crow went. They again refused to lead their people south, and the captain ordered them put in irons. Wild Hog managed to stab a soldier when they grabbed him but both chiefs were put in irons.[6] Wild Hog sounded the war cry, and it was quickly taken up by the warriors in the barracks. For most of the day, their war cries mingled with the death chants of the women. The floor of the barracks was ripped up, and the boards used to barricade the windows. But the outbreak everyone expected did not come.

Scotty was sure the night could not pass without a break. Several of the soldiers agreed, but the officers didn't. They took no special precautions, and when taps sounded at nine that night, only the usual number of guards were patrolling the area around the barracks.

The night was still and very cold. The moon was almost full. Even at his ranch several miles away, Scotty heard the firing when it began. The break had come, but he didn't ride to the fort. He didn't sleep, either. He stayed alert, hoping to protect his horses if the Indians came this way. They'd have to have horses and would do anything to get them. Bronson's Three Crows ranch, only five miles from the post, was the

*Wild Hog, high chief of
the Cheyennes.*

Old Crow.

logical target for the Indians. He had many more horses than Scotty did.

The firing faded away and finally stopped altogether. The Indians had apparently gone the other direction, but still Scotty guarded his ranch. At daylight, he rode to the post to find out what had happened.

A few weary and half frozen soldiers were at the barracks. The hospital was full of wounded soldiers and a few wounded Indians. Post Surgeon E. B. Mosely looked as if he hadn't had any sleep for days. Certainly he hadn't had any since the outbreak began last night at ten o'clock.

At Major Paddock's trader's store, Scotty got the full story. The Indians had used the rifles hidden under the barracks floor to kill all the guards at the barracks, then made a run for the hills. The Indians with the rifles had formed a skirmish line and fought back the soldiers while the women and children ran. The Indians fought much better than anyone expected them to.[7] Nearly starved and frozen, they still put up a good battle, a fact proven by the wounded and dead soldiers.

The army estimated that nearly half the warriors had been killed. They crossed the White River, apparently headed for Bronson's ranch to get horses. But the soldiers were too close behind them, so they recrossed the river and climbed into the bluffs where the cavalry couldn't follow. Dull Knife's son, Buffalo Hump, was found among the dead, but Dull Knife himself had escaped. The soldiers had given up the chase last night when the Indians got into the bluffs, but Captain Wessels had taken out four troops of cavalry at dawn and expected to have the Indian survivors back at the fort by nightfall.

Princess, Dull Knife's daughter, had been killed last night by Captain Vroom's men at the foot of the bluffs where she had been fighting with the warriors in the rear guard. The soldiers had killed several squaws who had grabbed up rifles dropped by fallen braves and continued the fight. Many of the soldiers in the hospital were nursing frozen feet and legs, for they had turned out last night in their bare feet to stop the break-out.

Scotty soon discovered that every scout and courier was needed today. He caught up with Captain Wessells about ten miles from the post, having followed the soldiers' trail along the summit of the ridge between White River and Soldier Creek. The trail was plain to see in the snow.

Seventeen miles from the post, Scotty was riding with the troops when the Indians' trail came around a bluff and disappeared over a ridge half a mile away. It was clearly discernible, so no one expected an ambush.[8] But the Cheyennes had doubled back, and now they opened fire on the column. A few soldiers were killed and wounded, and the rest dashed for the safety of trees some distance away.

Each side was well protected, and it settled into a long range battle. The soldiers could not get near the Indians without exposing themselves to the enemy rifles. Captain Wessells considered such a charge a waste of manpower. The starving Indians couldn't hold out long. He had them surrounded and expected them to surrender before nightfall.

Scotty was sent back to the fort with a report to General Bradley. At nightfall, Captain Wessells came in with his men but without any prisoners. The Indians had not surrendered, and the soldiers had not been prepared for a night out in such bitter cold weather.

During the afternoon, other troopers had found and captured fifty-two wounded and weak Indians and brought them in. Sixty were still unaccounted for. Scotty was sure that most of them had been in that band that had ambushed Captain Wessells.

The soldiers went out the next morning, still without packs or rations, certain they could end the battle before sundown.[9] They found the Indians in the timber just below the area they had held the day before. But once again their position defied any attempt to overrun it. This day the only casualty was a soldier's horse the Indians managed to kill. The trooper escaped, but the soldiers could not get to the horse to bury it. At nightfall, they had to return to the post, knowing the Indians would feast on horse meat.

Scotty was kept busy, usually as a messenger between the troops in the field and the post. On the thirteenth of January, the soldiers found the Cheyennes six miles farther west, well entrenched on the Hat Creek Bluffs. Again they held a position that made a charge the equivalent of suicide.

The troops had brought rations and packs this time, and they surrounded the Indians' position to keep them pinned down until they surrendered. They were close to cattle range now, and Captain Wessels feared the Indians would get food if the army allowed them to move around at night.

During the first night of the siege, however, the Indians slipped through the guards and moved on. Day after day, the troops caught up with the Indians, who always dug into some well protected place, and the soldiers surrounded them. But at night, the Indians managed to slip through the most heavily guarded lines the captain could devise.

Scotty continued to carry messages, especially now that Captain Wessells stayed in the field day and night. The trail of the Indians was always easy to follow, but the places they chose for their daily defenses were impossible to overrun.

But the running battle between the well provided soldiers, and the starving, freezing Indians had to come to its inevitable end.[10] On the twenty-second of

January, twelve days after the escape attempt began, Captain Wessels, supported by Lieutenant Dodd and his Sioux scouts, cornered the Cheyennes in the Hat Creek Bluffs, forty-four miles west-southwest of Fort Robinson. There in a five foot deep ravine, the Cheyennes made their last stand.

When the battle was over, nine were left living. Only two of them, both women, were unwounded. Those nine, plus the dead that had been counted over the last seven days, accounted for all the sixty missing Cheyennes except six or eight who had been cut off from the main band in their initial dash for freedom and had escaped to the Pine Ridge Reservation to join Red Cloud. Among those making the escape was Dull Knife himself.

Sixty-four or sixty-five Indians were killed during the long drawn-out battle. Many more were wounded. Eleven soldiers were killed and ten wounded. Among the army's wounded was Woman's Dress, one of the best of the Sioux scouts.

It had been a busy, danger-filled two weeks for Scotty.

XI

THE COLD WEATHER that had plagued both Indian and soldier during the outbreak loosened its grip some, but winter clung to the snow covered plains. Scotty didn't venture far from his ranch and the care of his horses, mules and cattle.

He had plenty of time to reflect on the dreams he'd had when he was a boy back in Scotland. He had thought then that he could become a rich man quickly if he could only get to America. Once in Kansas, he'd been sure his fortune was waiting for him just over the horizon.

He had gone over that horizon. Neither the wild towns of Dodge City or Cheyenne nor the gold fields of the Black Hills had yielded that fortune to him. But still the dream persisted.

Looking around him now, he realized that he had the foundation on which a fortune could possibly be built. He was free of debt. He had a little ranch, a good Studebaker freight wagon with mules to pull it, horses to operate his ranch and handle his hay crop, and a few cattle. Besides, he was still drawing his pay from the army for scouting and courier duty.

He had often joked with other young fellows that the thing a man needed to get ahead in this country was a wife. Scotty would be twenty-one this April, and he was beginning to think that this wasn't such a joke, after all. A wife would give a man a permanent home, children, a goal to work for.

Scotty's frequent visits to Joseph Larabee's place helped convince him that a wife was exactly what he needed. Larabee's fourth daughter, Sarah, had caught his eye the first time he had seen her.

Sarah had been married before to a man named Moran, but Scotty had never seen him. In fact, so little was ever said about him that he might have doubted that Moran had ever existed, if it hadn't been for Sarah's little son, Louis. They called him Posey. Scotty had plans for adopting the little boy as his own if he and Sarah should get married. But he soon learned that the custom among Sarah's people was for someone else, usually the grandparents, to take the child of a previous marriage so that the new marriage wouldn't be encumbered with the remnants of the old.

George Clark, the man Scotty had teamed up with in the freighting and ranching business when he first came here had moved off by himself, so Scotty would have his little ranch house for his own living quarters if he did decide to take a wife.

He made up his mind that he would quit scouting and carrying messages for the army before his wedding. He'd have a full time job then just making his ranch grow into the fortune he had dreamed of so long.

A bad blizzard in March brought all plans for the summer to a halt.[1] Scotty had his hands full taking care of his stock. He had shelter for his animals, and they came through the storm in good shape.

Another blizzard struck on April fifteenth and didn't let up until the seventeenth. This was much more damaging because some cattle had already begun to range out looking for the first green shoots of grass. These cattle drifted from their home range with the storm.

Scotty managed to keep his horses and mules in his

little barn and corrals but his cattle drifted. He considered himself very fortunate when he located his cattle two days later in the canyons and bluffs not far from his ranch. Most cattlemen were not so lucky.

It was some time after this that he was swapping tales with some other cowboys about the blizzards when one cowboy from the Newman ranch, the N Bar well to the east of Scotty on the Niobrara, caught Scotty's attention with his stories of the storms. He talked with a southern drawl that marked him as a man from somewhere far to the south.

Scotty got a chance to visit with this cowboy later, and he learned that his name was James Dahlman from Texas, and he had never seen ice or snow until he came north this last March to work on the N Bar. One of his first jobs had been to go with a dozen other N Bar men into the sand hills looking for cattle that had drifted south with the blizzards. Like Scotty, Dahlman had heard many tales of men and animals that had disappeared in these sand hills never to be seen again.

Dahlman hadn't been too eager to go. But the cattle they found there were the fattest ones the cowboys found anywhere on the range. They found four-year-old mavericks there that had never been branded that were as fat and sleek as pen fed cattle.

Scotty took an instant liking to Jim Dahlman, and they became life long friends. In later years Dahlman spent ten years in public office in Dawes County, eight years as county sheriff and two years as mayor of Chadron. After that, he moved to the eastern edge of the state and became mayor of Omaha, sitting in the mayor's chair for twenty-one years.

Long after Scotty's and Dahlman's friendship had blossomed on the Nebraska plains, Mayor Jim Dahlman of Omaha was reprimanded in the papers for being very un-mayor-like in riding a horse up and down the streets of Omaha, roping pedestrians.[2]

Nebraska State Historical Society

James C. Dahlman

Scotty was in his real estate office in Fort Pierre when the discussion among Scotty and one of his partners, Warren Young, of Young, Philip & McPherson, and a man named Matthew Brown turned to this incident involving the Omaha mayor. Scotty stoutly defended Dahlman's actions, but when he failed to convince anyone, he stopped the argument suddenly by slamming a fist on the arm of his chair and shouting, "Jim Dahlman is my friend."

It was about the time that Scotty met Jim Dahlman in the spring of '79 that Scotty wrote one of the last letters on record to his family back in Victoria. This, too, was directed to his older brother, George.[3]

I got my picture taken in the Hills. It is a horrible looking thing, but it is all I could do.

You say you could throw me but I don't know. It takes a good man to do that tho' I do say it myself. I weigh 194 lbs so you can see you better not threaten me too much.

No, George, you cannot expect much news for there is nothing going on that would interest you, so I will conclude with love to you all.

Your loving brother,
James Philip.

Scotty neglected to tell his brother about his marriage which was coming up soon. If there were more letters after his marriage, they were few and far between, and none seems to have been saved.

Scotty ran into problems when he began to plan his wedding. A month before the scheduled ceremony, he resigned his civilian post with the army.[4] But getting a marriage license was simply out of the question. Fort Robinson, where Scotty intended to be married, was at that time a part of Holt County. O'Neil was the seat of Holt County, and it was approximately two hundred and fifty miles east of Fort Robinson. There weren't enough settlers west of O'Neil to organize a county, so everything along the Dakota border to the Wyoming Territory line was attached to Holt County.

Flora Ziemann

Sarah (Sally) Philip, Scotty's wife, taken when she was about 40.

Not having a marriage license didn't worry Scotty much. He rode to the Pine Ridge Reservation and brought back the missionary there, J. Robinson, to perform the ceremony. Scotty had plenty of friends who would serve as witnesses.

The French voyageur, Joseph Larabee, who was to be Scotty's father-in-law, had once worked for the Hudson Bay Company. He had married an Indian woman to the south and west of Fort Robinson and had drifted up to the White River to settle. He had a big family. The oldest daughter, Helen, had married Crazy Horse and had gone on with the Oglala tribe of the Sioux when they moved to their new reservation in Dakota Territory.

Scotty would come to be good friends with two other brothers-in-law, Mike Dunn, who married the second daughter, Susie, and J. E. Utterback, a blacksmith at the Fort Robinson post, who married the third daughter, Zoe. Both Dunn and Utterback became big ranchers, although they never reached the cattle king status attained by Scotty.

Scotty never called Sarah by her real name. To him, she was Sally. Her name even appears on the marriage certificate that way.[5]

Scotty had a flare for doing things in a big way, and his wedding was no exception. For the ceremony itself, he got two good friends, Joseph Eldridge and George Stover, to sign as witnesses. But the ceremony was just the beginning of the festivities.

Scotty arranged for a dance to celebrate the occasion. He engaged Richard Boesl to furnish the music for the dance that went on through the night. Boesl was known through the area as Zither Dick.[6]

The missionary, J. Robinson, stayed overnight before going back to his Protestant Episcopal Church on the Pine Ridge Reservation. To the Indians he was known as Black Bear because of his heavy black beard.

South Dakota State Historical Society

J. E. Utterback, Scotty's brother-in-law, with his granddaughter.

With the wedding and the celebration over, Scotty took his new bride to his ranch north of the post. Then he turned his full attention to the task of carving a fortune out of this land. He had complete confidence in his ability to do it.

Scotty took stock of his circumstances. He had more cattle than before the wedding because his father-in-law, Joseph Larabee, had given him several head. Larabee had done well and had a big herd. He obviously approved of his new son-in-law.

The additional cattle made Scotty think more and more of expanding his ranch. There was still room. Edgar Bronson, for whom Scotty had worked, was a good example. He was expanding rapidly.

But Scotty knew this couldn't go on long. With the Indians gone, land hungry ranchers would move in. Soon even this vast area would be crowded. If he intended to spread out, he'd have to do it soon or it would be too late.

Scotty still had his freighting business, and he planned to work hard at it. Supplies were needed as much as ever in the Black Hills. The profit from his freighting would help him build up his herd faster. This freighting wasn't going to last forever, either, although there were men running the bull trains who absolutely refused to admit there would ever be a change in their business. Scotty had heard rumors already of railroads coming into the Black Hills to tap the riches there. Once they reached this area, the day of the bull or mule train freighter would be over.

Scotty had practically forgotten his plans to get a homestead and settle down back at Victoria. Sally was a part of this country, and when he married her, he married the country. He had no regrets. He liked Kansas, but he loved the wide open spaces here along the Nebraska-Dakota border.

After making sure his cattle were doing well on their range, Scotty headed for Sidney to bring back a load of freight. He took this load to Custer City, and there he found some freight consigned to Fort Pierre. He took it east to the Missouri River. There he loaded up with more freight for the miners in the Black Hills

A freighting outfit used by the Northwestern Company.

and brought it back to Deadwood. Each time he loaded
or unloaded consigned freight, he picked up wages for
his labor.

At one time this money might have meant a big
night on the town. But that was all past. He saw cattle in
the money he was earning. Every dollar he could spare
would go toward building a herd.

It was not all easy going for Scotty. Storms caused
him plenty of trouble on the trail. Not only did a hard
rain render life miserable for him and his mules, but it
turned the road into a quagmire that made moving a
loaded wagon almost impossible. Scotty lost a day now
and then in his schedule because the mud slowed him
from twenty-five miles a day to less than half that.

Flooded creeks, that normally could be forded
without getting anything wet but the mules' hocks and
the felloes of the wagon wheels, forced him to make
camp and wait for the water to go down. Then the
approaches to the stream were slick and as the wagon
left the water, the mules had to struggle up the grassy
slope covered with slime deposited by the flash flood.

But Scotty worked tirelessly at his job, knowing that
when he had trouble with flooded creeks, the other
freighters were having the same difficulties. When he

Nebraska State Historical Society

Bull trains en route to Deadwood, South Dakota, 1876.

arrived at his destination, the merchants would be just that much more eager to buy any unconsigned freight that he had.

Often he carried passengers on his freight wagon. He charged less than half the fare of the stage coach, so he got many passengers who couldn't afford to ride the coach. The money they saved was more valuable to them than the time they lost. He also picked up some impatient passengers, for when the coach was full, the travelers had to wait for the next coach or catch a ride with a freighter.

Scotty welcomed these passengers for it gave him a chance to visit during the long miles that could become most monotonous. The small fare they paid was just that much more to be used for buying cattle.

More ranchers were moving in around Fort Robinson, and they worried about Indian trouble since Red

Cloud's territory was still close by. But Scotty didn't look for any more trouble. The defeat of Dull Knife's band marked the end of the Indian wars, he thought, unless something new stirred up the tribes. Besides, Scotty had a half Indian wife now. Under Indian law, that made him practically immune to trouble from them as long as he behaved himself.

However, too many men who had made their fortunes elsewhere, were moving big herds of cattle into the area in the hopes of getting richer. Scotty could see that he was going to be crowded out before he got big enough to hold his own against them.

XII

WINTER STOPPED the freighting and Scotty concentrated on caring for his livestock. Then with the coming of spring, his little herd became independent again, finding plenty of grass and water without his help. Scotty turned his full attention once more to his freighting. As soon as the spring rains let up enough to make the roads passable, he prepared for a trip to Fort Pierre for a load of freight for the Hills.

He didn't like to leave now because Sally would present him with their first child before long. But that was all the more reason for him to bring home more money. He had a good herd of cattle now with a fine crop of calves on the ground, but his ambitions far exceeded his possessions. This was a big land, and he wanted to be a big man in it.

Sally assured Scotty that she would be all right on the little ranch, so he hitched his mules to his wagon and headed for the Missouri River.

There was an unusual amount of activity in Fort Pierre. Across the river, the town of Pierre, which had a population of two hundred ninety-eight this spring of 1880, was bustling in preparation for the coming of the Northwestern Railroad, due this summer. The railroad would speed up the delivery of goods from the outside world which came now by river steamer. But it presented a problem for Fort Pierre and the freighting business to the Black Hills. The river boats could dock and unload their freight on the west bank of the river, but the trains would halt on the east side. All the freight destined for the Hills would have to be ferried across the Missouri River.

Scotty didn't worry about that now. The freight he was to haul was in Fort Pierre, and he loaded his Studebaker wagon as quickly as he could. He wanted to get home to Sally.

Before he finished loading, a big bull train pulled out for the Hills. Scotty figured he would soon pass the bull train because the oxen moved slower than his mules.

His second afternoon out from Fort Pierre, he came in sight of the bull train. He stopped a mile short of their camp, so there would be no chance of interference between the camps. The next morning he pushed his long legged mules past the slower moving oxen. The bull train had actually gotten an earlier start than he had because they usually moved early in the day, then rested through the heat of the day and plodded forward again in the later afternoon and early evening.

As Scotty moved past the bull train, he looked it over,[1] thinking that perhaps he should go into the freighting business in a big way such as the owner of this outfit had. There were ten teams in this train, each team consisting of ten yoke of oxen pulling three wagons coupled together. A bullwhacker had told Scotty once that his lead wagon usually hauled about seven thousand pounds, his swing wagon about five thousand and his trail wagon about three thousand. That added up to about seven and a half tons of freight for each ten yoke team. This man had ten such teams. Seventy-five tons of freight would bring a fortune in Deadwood. Scotty's load, less than four tons, would look pretty puny in comparison.

Scotty could move faster, however. Not only did the mules walk faster, but they didn't have to depend entirely on grass along the way for a living. Scotty carried grain for the mules, although that did cut into the total amount of paying freight he could haul. The oxen were lucky to cover fifteen miles a day. Often it was nearer twelve. Scotty would put his mules over twenty miles easily, sometimes twenty-five, and still leave time for them to graze a few hours on the rich grass.

A mile wide strip to be used by the freighting trains had been set aside from Fort Pierre to Deadwood through the heart of the reservation. The Indians had agreed not to molest anything in that strip. But often a freighting outfit wandered out of the strip, perhaps by accident, but more likely to find better grass for the animals or a trail that was unrutted.

In wet weather, the loaded wagons cut into the prairie sod almost to their hubs. The soil was a sticky gumbo, and this mud, matted with balled-up grass, lodged between the wheels and the sides of the boxes and made the wagons almost impossible to move. Then the freighter had to stop and clean out the mud to allow the wheels to turn freely again.

Scotty was very familiar with the trail now, but he still felt a tingle run down his spine when he caught his first glimpse of the Black Hills to the west. At a spot about a hundred miles from the Hills, the trail topped a ridge called Reno Hill.[2] From here, Scotty could see a low black line on the horizon that looked something like a summer thunder cloud rising in the west. Those were the Black Hills, and he could understand why the Indians called them black.

Scotty always gave his mules an unusually long rest here while he admired the view. This was wonderful country in his opinion. The Black Hills were to the west and the Bad Lands about sixty miles to the south.

But it was the rich grazing land that he was standing on that really attracted him. If a man could claim a few thousand acres of this grass, he'd be independently wealthy in a short time. This was Indian land now, but the white men would get rights to it someday like they got everything they wanted that the Indians owned.

Scotty passed another bull train before he reached Deadwood. The weather was good, and he didn't have to fight the mud. He turned a handsome profit from the goods he sold to the merchants, then headed his mules toward home.

His first child, a daughter, was born shortly after he reached home. He and Sally named her Mary. Scotty intended to write to his family back in Victoria and tell them about Mary, but right now he just didn't have time.

With Sally back on her feet and she and the baby both in good health, Scotty headed his freight wagon south to pick up a load of freight at Sidney. He had orders from Deadwood merchants for all that he could haul.

The load he pulled out of Sidney was different from anything he had ever hauled before. The front of his wagon was full of flour and winter clothing for the miners. But the back half was piled high with crates of live chickens. Poultry brought a fantastic price in the Hills. The chickens required a lot of attention that Scotty usually didn't have to give to his loads of freight, but they didn't weigh much compared to the space they occupied. Still the merchants paid enough more for their transportation that Scotty made just as much as he would have from a heavier load.

Through the late summer and early fall, Scotty continued to haul from Sidney and Fort Pierre. He stopped only long enough to put up the hay on his meadow. He sold some of the hay to the army post and stacked the rest close to his barn for winter feed for his own mules and horses and cows during storms when they couldn't forage for themselves.

His last trip before winter took him to Fort Pierre in late October. The rails had reached Pierre across the

Pierre Street with streetcar, 1887, Pierre, South Dakota.

river and the Northwestern Railroad was working out
an agreement for a right-of-way for a railroad to the
Black Hills.[3] They had bought a section of land across
the river from the end of the track at Pierre for three
thousand two hundred dollars, and talk was rampant in
Fort Pierre about the railroad that would soon be there.
The truth was that it would be twenty-six years before a
railroad bridge would be put across the Missouri at this
point.

Scotty arrived in Fort Pierre just after the railroad
had put a ferry into operation across the river. Goods
arriving in Pierre by rail destined for delivery west of
the river were freighted across the river on the steam-
boat, "Jim Leighton." There were also other ferries,
the "Pearl," the "Elk," and the "City of Fort Pierre,"
all owned by Captain Ed Senechal and sons. Passengers could ride across on the boats with the freight.
Scotty was tempted to ride across and back just for the
trip, but with winter so close, he knew he didn't dare

South Dakota State Historical Society

"Jim Leighton."

tarry in Fort Pierre. He couldn't risk getting caught in an early winter storm on these trackless prairies.

He reached home without incident and with money in his pocket. He settled down to work through the winter improving his place and taking care of his growing herd. During the long evenings he discussed the future of his ranching with Sally while he played with his little daughter. More and more ranchers were pouring into the area around Fort Robinson, partly because of the good grass and partly because of the proximity of the fort. Not many white men trusted the Indians yet, even though they had been moved north of the border into Dakota.

Already Scotty was beginning to feel squeezed in.

He had visions of expanding his holdings into a great ranch, and room for that expansion was disappearing every day.

He kept remembering that wonderful grassland between the Black Hills and the Missouri River. It was part of the Pine Ridge Reservation now, where white men were not allowed. But the Indians were not interested in raising domestic meat. If they couldn't chase down their meat and kill it on the open range as they had done for centuries, then they'd wait until the Great White Father brought it to them. And all those millions of acres of wonderful grass on the reservation were not being used.

To Scotty that seemed like an unholy waste. That grass grew lush and tall during the summer and usually ended up in the inferno of a prairie fire in the dry fall or winter months. Not only was that a waste, but it was a hazard to everyone living near that prairie.

Scotty had been thinking about that grass ever since the first time he had seen it. Now he felt it was time to act. He was being squeezed in by his own people. His wife's people had nothing but room on their reservation. Not only that, Sally had an allotment of land up there on the reservation, and she could take her husband with her when she claimed it.

The glamor of the freighting business was beginning to wear off for Scotty. He still made good money at it, but the talk of the coming of the railroads made the future too uncertain. Besides, he had decided that his future lay in cattle, not in staring at the tails of his mules from the seat of a freight wagon.

When spring came, however, he was still on his little ranch north of the old Red Cloud Agency. Scotty was offered the job of driving a team of oxen in a bull train freighting goods into the Black Hills. The wages were good, and Scotty decided to make a few trips while he reached a final decision on whether to move to the reservation.

The first trip was to Sidney to bring a train load of freight to the Hills. Shortly after a brief stop at his ranch on the way north to the Hills, he was surprised to notice a rider coming up to the train from the south. Scotty didn't pay a great deal of attention to the man until he came toward the team he was driving. Then he recognized his older brother, George.

Scotty was amazed. He hadn't ever expected to see George up here. When he learned why he was here, he

The Philip brothers (left to right): George, Alexander, Scotty.

felt guilty. Scotty hadn't written to anybody for months, and his brothers at Victoria, Kansas, had become worried about him, so George had come north looking for him.[4]

George explained that he had gone to the Pine Ridge Agency and inquired about him, but nobody there knew James Philip. Finally one man there suggested that he might mean the man they called Scotty who lived out on White Clay Creek.

George had ridden over to the ranch and found Sally and her little daughter, Mary, there. Sally had told him that Scotty had just left with the bull train for the Black Hills, so George had hurried to overtake him.

Scotty told George to go back to the hotel at the Pine Ridge Agency, and he would come there and see him the next morning. George left, and Scotty made arrangements that afternoon for someone else to handle his team, then he headed for the agency.

Early the next morning he was at the hotel in a brand new suit to see George. They had a grand visit, and Scotty enjoyed that day more than any since his marriage to Sally. George told him all about things back at Victoria and what he had heard from their father back in Scotland. Their mother had died six years ago, barely a year after Scotty left home. Scotty hadn't had a recent letter from his old home because he hadn't answered the last ones he had received.

Scotty resolved never to let his ties with his family break again. He told George about his little herd of cattle and of his plans to expand. He also told him that he might move up on the reservation where Sally had been given an allotment of land. George agreed that Scotty was doing all right here in the northland, but he had no intentions of leaving Kansas himself.

At the end of his freighting trip, Scotty drew his wages and refused to sign on for another trip. Instead, he rode out into the grassland of the reservation. Once again, he marvelled at such wonderful cattle country. He headed south of the road between Deadwood and Fort Pierre to look at the land along the creeks and rivers. For miles he rode along the banks of Bad River. Every inch of it was good cattle country. Well down the river, at the mouth of a little creek called Grindstone Butte Creek, he came to the land that was Sally's allotment. This was good land, a wonderful place for a ranch with plenty of room to expand in all directions.

When he got back home, he told Sally they were going to move to Bad River on the reservation. Sally said nothing to dampen his enthusiasm.

Scotty loaded their possessions in his Studebaker Wagon and let Sally drive the mules hitched to it. He herded his cattle and loose horses and mules along ahead of the wagon. There was nothing left behind but a little house and a lot of memories. Scotty had no time to waste on these. His thoughts were already far ahead on the glowing promise of the future.

But on the way to Bad River, little Mary took sick and died. The blow was almost more than Scotty could bear.

XIII

SCOTTY WISHED he could bury his daughter in an established cemetery but that was impossible. The best he could do was pick a pretty spot along the trail. There wasn't even time to linger at the place and mourn his loss. He had to get on to the mouth of Grindstone Creek and establish his home before cold weather descended again on the land.

Scotty guided the herd down Bad River, letting the animals graze as they went. When they arrived at the mouth of Grindstone Creek, eighty miles from the Missouri River, the cattle and horses were in better shape than they had been when he left his little ranch close to Fort Robinson.

In this area where Grindstone Creek ran into Bad River, the valleys were wide, and they were buried in a sea of western wheat grass that the cattle waded through like a boy wading across a stream. Even the gullies running into the creek were wide and more often than not well grassed over. Back in Kansas, Scotty remembered that the gullies running into the streams were usually stripped bare of vegetation. He had thought Kansas was a wonderful place for raising cattle. This looked even better.

Bad River was not a big stream, but there were many deep holes in it where water was always plentiful. A strong underground flow kept the holes filled with fresh water. Even the tributaries running into Bad

River were pitted with deep holes. To Scotty that meant there would always be water for his cattle and horses in those holes, even in dry weather. There were trees along the river thick as a forest, and every creek and most draws were heavily timbered, but out on the prairie away from the streams there was nothing but rich grass.[1]

Scotty selected a bend in Bad River for his house. There were no neighbors except the very few white men with Indian wives who were settling on the land allotted to the Indian women. From there, these white men could range out on both sides of Bad River with their cattle. This was truly a cattleman's paradise.

There were many ranchers on the fringes of the reservation who would give their eye teeth to run their cattle on this great expanse of the best grazing on the continent, but without Indian wives, they were legally barred.

Shortly after Scotty had a house built for Sally, their second daughter, Emma, was born. She appeared to be healthy and strong, and Scotty resolved that if it was in his power, he'd let nothing happen to this baby to keep her from growing into a healthy young lady.

With unlimited range for his cattle, Scotty felt at last that he had found the place to make his fortune. With all the grass his cattle could eat and the trees along the river for protection from storms, he couldn't see what could prevent him from making this into a cattle empire.

Then late in the fall, all the white men on the reservation were notified by the Indian Bureau that they would be evicted from the reservation if they couldn't show proof of their marriage to the Indian women with whom they were living.

At first, Scotty thought this was a stroke of good fortune for him. He knew several white men who were living on the reservation with Indian women who were not their wives just to get the use of this great ocean of

grass. Scotty doubted if they would marry these Indian
women even to save their privileges on the reservation. They'd have to move off which would leave even
more room for expansion for the few squaw men who
were legally married.

Then it struck Scotty suddenly that he might have
trouble qualifying himself. There was no doubt in his
mind that he was legally married to Sally. Nor was
there any doubt in Sally's mind. But there was no legal
document declaring that James Philip and Sarah
Larabee were man and wife.

Scotty pondered this for a while, then decided
there was no point in risking the possibility of getting
thrown off the reservation just for the lack of a piece of
paper. It irked him to have to go to so much trouble just
to prove something that everybody who really mat-
tered already knew. Nevertheless, he went down to the
Pine Ridge Agency and asked the missionary there for
something he could show the government officials to
prove that he and Sally were married.

The missionary willingly complied, filling in the
blanks as Scotty supplied the information. The missionary remembered the wedding but he had forgotten
the details. Then Scotty had to find his friends, Joseph
Eldridge and George Stover, and get them to sign the
certificate as witnesses.

Scotty returned home with the legal looking document which certified that Scotty and Sally were married. Scotty didn't even notice until later that his name
was spelled Phillips, instead of Philip. And Sally's
name was Sally, not Sarah as it legally should have
been. Scotty blamed himself for that. He had probably
told the missionary her name was Sally.

It didn't worry Scotty; not even the fact that the
certificate was dated January 1, 1882. That was the day
the certificate was made out, not the date of Scotty's
wedding. If the government wanted to make some-

thing of that, it could just try. Scotty had considered himself legally married since back in '79. If the government insisted that he'd been legally married only since January 1, 1882, that was all right, even if he did have one child peacefully laid to rest and another one a few months older than the certificate he held.

Scotty's cattle came through the winter in fine shape. Cattle prices at terminal markets were higher than Scotty had ever known them to be. He hoped to cash in on that high price this fall with some of his bigger stuff.

From an occasional visitor on his way from the Hills to the Missouri, Scotty heard stories of the restless ranchers in the Hills. There were more cattle there than there was range on which to run them. The ranchers were calling for the government to open the Sioux reservation to the white man's cattle.

One man gave Scotty a three week old copy of the March 11 issue of the Black Hills *Daily Times*.[2] Scotty's eye was caught immediately by an announcement.

PUBLIC NOTICE

'There will be a mass meeting of citizens of Lawrence, Pennington and Custer Counties in the courthouse at Deadwood, Wednesday, March 15, 1882, at 2 p.m. for the purpose of taking such steps as may be deemed advisable to secure and utilize the 45,000 square miles of grazing land in southwestern Dakota known as the Great Sioux Reservation, unequalled in America for its nutritious grasses, sufficient to sustain one million head of stock. The benefits to be derived from this must be obvious to all. It will attract stockmen from all of the northwest. It will bring capital to our midst and give employment to a large number of people. It is the great inducement to the building of the railroads to the Black Hills. Let everyone who is interested in the greatest welfare of the Black Hills attend and assist in the movement.'

The notice was signed by 'the committee' but gave no names. It didn't matter to Scotty who had put that notice in the paper. It did matter to him what had happened at that meeting. If enough people worked together to persuade the government to open up the reservation, then cattlemen would swarm in around Scotty like bees in a clover patch.

Whoever had written that notice wanted forty-five thousand square miles of the reservation opened up. That would be almost all of it. Scotty wondered what they expected to do with the Indians. Of course, most of the Indians did stay close to the agency and ninety percent of the reservation was unused. But some men like Scotty and his two brothers-in-law, Mike Dunn and J. E. Utterback, were making full use of all the reservation land they could. This committee in the Black Hills would put an end to that. Scotty wasn't at all certain that it couldn't be done.

Scotty's calf crop was good and his big steers were filling out, ready for market. Prices remained high, and Scotty planned to sell all his big steers to take advantage of those prices. He made infrequent trips to Fort Pierre for supplies and crossed the river once to Pierre to make arrangements to ship out his cattle.

On these trips, he usually heard stories about the ranchers trying to open up the reservation. When the Pettigrew bill[3] passed Congress and became a law on August 7, he realized how strong this organization was. This new law would limit the Indians to five small reservations with only a fraction of the acres they now controlled. They would get cattle in exchange for signing over the land.

Dakota territorial governor, Newton Edmunds, appointed a commission to negotiate with the Indians, and this commission made its way around among the tribes, talking to the chiefs. They got a favorable response from the chiefs, and the ranchers celebrated. But Congress insisted that the commission proceed according to the Laramie Treaty which said that any such agreement must have the approval of three-

South Dakota State Historical Society

The stockyards at Pierre, South Dakota.

fourths of the adult males of each tribe. Scotty knew
that his worries were over for the moment. No white
man would ever get three-fourths of the Indian braves
to agree on anything, especially when it meant giving
up so much land.

Scotty drove his fat steers to Fort Pierre in September and crowded them onto the ferry, the "Jim
Leighton." On the east bank of the Missouri, the cattle
were driven into the shipping pens and loaded on the
train.

Scotty's steers were in excellent shape and they
brought top price of nine dollars thirty-five cents a
hundredweight at Chicago.[4] Scotty had never had so
much money in his possession at one time as he had
when he got back from Chicago.

With his money, Scotty bought more heifers. He
had none of the worries he'd had back at Fort Robin-

South Dakota State Historical Society

The first streetcar in South Dakota. Looking south on Pierre St., 1888.

son. While the ranchers around the edge of the reservation might expect the Indians to steal a certain percent of their cattle for meat, they wouldn't bother Scotty's herd. The Indians didn't steal from their brothers. And Scotty was considered a brother because his wife was half Indian. He found the Indians good neighbors. A few of them had small herds of their own ranging out on this great ocean of grass.

Spring brought still higher prices for cattle. Scotty was tempted to sell some of his herd but he resisted the temptation. There was only one way he could build up a big herd and selling anything but marketable steers would defeat his purpose.

At Fort Pierre, Scotty heard about the controversy over relocation of the territorial capitol.[5] Nearly a dozen cities wanted it, including Pierre. Pierre insisted it should have it because it was near the center of the population. Yankton, which was the capitol now, claimed that it should keep it, pointing out the expense

South Dakota State Historical Society

A cattle drive.

and turmoil of moving it. But Bismarck, farther up the Missouri River, seemed to have the inside track in the race.

Scotty paid little attention to the struggle, even when Bismarck was awarded the capitol and some men contested the ruling, saying there was fraud in the governor's office. The price of cattle was more important to Scotty now.

As Scotty had expected, the men who had pushed through the bill to open up the reservation to white ranchers and settlers had no luck in getting the men of the Indian tribes to sign the bill. Even though each Indian was promised some cattle in exchange for his signature, very few would sign. Scotty was certain they would never break up the reservation until they put through a law that didn't require three-fourths of the Indian men to sign it.

Scotty had several neighbors now. Some of them had come in about the same time he had; others had drifted in later. All had one thing in common — they were white men with Indian wives. One brother-in-law, J. E. Utterback, who had married Sally's sister, Zoe, had some land on Bad River and ranged his cattle south toward the White River. His other brother-in-law, Mike Dunn, who had married another of Sally's sisters, Susie, had his land over on White River.

Just a mile up Bad River from Scotty's place on Grindstone Creek was the allotment of Dan Powell's wife, Mary Charging Eagle. She was a niece of Chief Red Cloud.[6]

Four or five miles below Scotty on the south side of Bad River was the big Jarman ranch, and just a little farther downstream was George Waldron's ranch, also on the south side of the river. Nearly twenty miles downstream from Scotty on the north side of the river was Louis LaPlant's ranch. LaPlant was one of the biggest ranchers along the river, and Scotty often stopped there on the road to or from Fort Pierre.[7]

Although there were several bigger ranchers than Scotty along the river, he no longer felt like poor relation. His herd was growing rapidly and he was expanding his claim on the grass north of the river.

Scotty's third child, another daughter, was born on December 3. They named her Olive. Like most fathers, Scotty had hoped for a son, but a strong healthy daughter was something to be proud of.

Scotty tried to ignore the persistent rumors that the reservation would soon be opened to settlement or lease. He knew that eventually one or the other would happen. The white men always got what they wanted from the Indians in time. But until that happened here, Scotty had all the land he could use, and he intended to take full advantage of it.

Rheborg Collection

Clara Philip, Scotty's daughter.

XIV

SCOTTY KEPT a close eye on the maneuverings to open
the reservation to white settlement. A senator from
Massachusetts, Henry L. Dawes,[1] had followed the
Edmunds Commission into the reservation in 1884 to
try to discover why the Indians hadn't agreed to the
terms of the Pettigrew law. He went back to Washington, convinced that the offer to the Indians had been
too low. He introduced another bill, liberalizing the
payments for the land the Indians would release.

Scotty read the bill carefully when it was printed in
the papers and discovered that Dawes was falling into
the same trap that had kept the last law from becoming
effective. He insisted that the Indian men sign the
agreement before they could get their pay for the land.

Scotty relaxed. The only things he had ever known
three-fourths of the Indian men to agree on were plans
for a hunt or a war.

That spring Scotty received word that his brother,
Robert, the only brother to stay in Scotland, had died
on April 30, leaving a young widow and one son less
than four years old.

Prices for cattle remained high, and Scotty did very
well with the steers he sent to market. But he kept all
his heifers and young cows. He was rapidly becoming
recognized as one of the bigger cattlemen along Bad
River. Wet summers and mild winters were keeping
his gains high and his losses low. If ever there was a

Mitchell Collection

Robert Philip, Scotty's brother and the only brother to stay in Scotland.

time for a rancher to get ahead in Dakota, this was it, and Scotty was taking full advantage of it.

A call went out for ranchers from every corner of the country to attend a convention in St. Louis in November of 1884, but Scotty ignored it. He was sure one of the main topics would be the leasing of reservation land, and that was one thing he was not in favor of. The presence at that convention of a rancher from the reservation would be like waving a red flag at a bull. He watched eagerly for reports from the convention, however. The Black Hills *Pioneer*, printed at Deadwood, said that thirteen hundred delegates attended, but that the cattlemen of the northwest were defeated in their attempts to get the convention to demand that reservation land be opened for lease by ranchers.

Scotty was relieved. Still, he knew that the cattlemen would continue to hammer at the door until the reservation was opened. Bigger and bigger herds were crowding the edges of the reservation, and many were secretly pasturing great sections of the reservation now, without paying anything for the privilege. The Indians seldom went far from their headquarters and didn't even realize what was happening. They probably wouldn't have done anything about it, anyway, except perhaps steal a few extra head for beef.

At Christmas time, Scotty heard that his father had died in Scotland on December 8. He was seventy-one years old.

Early in 1885, another daughter, Hazel, was born to Scotty and Sally. Four girls, three of them living, and still no son.

Cattle prices dipped to about six dollars a hundredweight, but that was still a good price, considering the cost of putting a hundred pounds of beef on a steer, so Scotty tried not to worry about the drop.

When the territorial legislature met in Bismarck for the first time, it voted to move the capitol of the territory again, this time to Pierre, but the governor vetoed the bill.[2] Scotty was disappointed at the veto because he felt it would have been good for the country around Pierre, including Bad River, to have the capitol so close.

Scotty also watched the argument raging in the papers over whether the territory would be admitted to the Union as one state or divided into two. There was no doubt in Scotty's mind but that the territory would join the Union, but he couldn't see that it would make a lot of difference whether it came in as one or two states.

The winter of 1885-86 was unusually mild with very little snow. Scotty's cattle came through in fine shape, and he looked forward to another prosperous year. But cattle prices continued to plunge below their decline of the year before. By fall, good steers were bringing only three dollars a hundredweight at the markets.[3] With plenty of range, Scotty decided to hold his steers. Another year's growth would add more weight, and the price was bound to come up. Even if it didn't, the added weight would bring more money than he'd get by selling now.

His herd was growing rapidly. He branded Seven Bar L (7-L) and S Bar 7 (S-7) on the left side of his cattle; L Bar Seven (L-7) on the left hip of his horses. He would later use the L-7 on cattle, too.

Hazel Philip, Scotty's daughter.

The first train reached Rapid City from the south on July 3 that summer.[4] It was the occasion for a huge celebration that carried over into the regular July 4th festivities. It was one of the biggest things to happen in Rapid City since the city's founding.

Scotty heard about the arrival of the first train and it brought a bit of nostalgia to him. He had freighted goods into Rapid City and Deadwood from Sidney and Fort Pierre for four or five summers. Now those days were gone forever. The railroad would be a boon to the Black Hills ranchers because they would no longer have to make a long trail drive to market.

Scotty was closer to the Missouri than he was to Rapid City. If he drove to Rapid, he could eliminate the ferry across the Missouri to Pierre. But he'd have to cross the Cheyenne River on his way to Rapid City. The Cheyenne didn't present any real hazards except in flood time, but crossing any river with fat steers was not a pleasant prospect.

When Scotty saw his father-in-law that summer, he learned that he had traded for a magnificent gray stallion, the fastest horse in the country. Scotty loved fast horses and the gray stallion was just that. Scotty was interested in hearing how Joseph Larabee had come to get him.

Larabee and a partner had heard of some unusual springs in the southern area of the Black Hills that spewed out hot water. The Indians claimed that this water could cure sickness. So the partners had moved in and claimed the springs and the land surrounding them.

When they got what they considered a good offer to sell the springs, they took it. They received six hundred dollars and a thoroughbred gray stallion in exchange for the springs and the land around them.[5] Joseph Larabee felt that he had made one of the greatest trades of his life. In later years, he might have doubted the wisdom of his trade could he have seen the magnificent town of Hot Springs that grew up around the mineral springs he had once owned.

But the gray horse was magnificent in himself. Larabee had his quota of sporting blood. Living so close to the Indians, he had also adopted their love for racing horses. He raced his horse against the best the Indians had and never lost. The Indians loved to bet on their favorite horses, and they often won or lost blankets and even horses and cattle on their bets.

Word spread through the reservation that Jim Dahlman, who had gone to Texas to help bring a herd back to Ogallala, had also brought with him a red bay horse that was unbeaten in a matched race. He was coming north from Ogallala and a race between Dahlman's bay, called Fiddler, and Joe Larabee's gray was inevitable.

Scotty had his share of sporting blood, too, and often promoted races between fast horses he owned and those of his neighbors. This race promised to be the greatest race the country had ever seen. The reservation was buzzing with talk about it. Scotty had no trouble keeping up with the progress of the arrangements for the race.

Since the race involved his father-in-law and one of the best friends he had made while living close to Fort Robinson, it took on special interest for Scotty. The date and the place for the race were finally set. It would be run just a couple of miles south of the Pine Ridge Agency at Deer's Trading Post at White Clay.[6] This was just across the border in Nebraska where Deer had moved his trading post from the old Red Cloud Agency close to Fort Robinson.

It was apparent to Scotty that very few people within a hundred and fifty miles of Deer's Trading Post were going to miss that race. Scotty decided he couldn't afford to miss it, either.

When he arrived at the trading post just across the Nebraska line, he found hundreds of people camped there although the race was still a day away. Betting was rampant. The Indians were betting beads, blankets, guns, even their horses on Larabee's gray. They had seen him beat the best horses on the reservation, including some fast government horses. They were convinced that no horse living could outrun him.

Jim Dahlman also had a lot of followers. Some cowboys were here who had come up the trail with him from Texas, and they had seen the blood bay, Fiddler, run away from every horse he had met. An army of ranchers and cowboys had gravitated to the horse as he came north to the reservation line from Ogallala. There was plenty of money to back up their admiration.

Scotty listened to the growing excitement. When Big Bat Pourier put a thousand dollars on Larabee's gray, the confidence of the cowboys sagged a little.[7] Then word filtered around that some of the more hot tempered cowboys had threatened to shoot the man who rode the gray in the race.

Buckskin Jack Russell, a well known horseman and scout, had been working with Larabee's horse. He usually rode the gray when he raced. Russell was no coward, but he was married and had some children. He believed the threats and backed out of riding the gray. Nobody blamed him.

It appeared for a time that the race might have to be forfeited if no one could be found to ride Larabee's horse. The half drunk cowboys came out openly now with a threat to kill anyone taking the job. But not everybody was scared off. A small man named Tom Brady, a good rider, stepped forward and volunteered. Some said he had an eye on one of Joe Larabee's younger girls, and this was his way of proving his love for her. Whatever his reason, his bravery was not questioned.

That night and during the early hours of the day of the race, Indians poured into the area from the reservation just across the Dakota line. Scotty was sure there were more Indians at White Clay now than there were left on the reservation. The crowd numbered into the thousands.

Two acres had been set aside to hold the bets placed on the race. The Indian style of placing a bet was to throw down his wager at the betting post, and anyone who wished could cover it with something of equal value. The betting post was surrounded by hundreds of little piles of guns, holsters, gold, paper money, blankets, beads and trinkets. A row of horses and saddles ringed the piles of wagers at the betting post. Scotty had never seen so much bet on one race in his life.

This could lead to trouble. Most of those who lost would leave here with nothing while the winners would be loaded down with loot. Feelings were bound to run high. Several deputy sheriffs and some Indian police were in evidence, but Scotty doubted if they could control the situation when the race was over and bets had to be paid off.

Fiddler came into sight first, prancing along as Jim Dahlman, not a big man himself, guided him to the starting line. The ranchers and cowboys whooped their approval. The course was to be six hundred yards long, straight as an arrow, with a lane for each horse to run in. That course was now lined ten deep on either side with Indians, cowboys and ranchers.

Most of the Indians were getting their first look at Fiddler, and what they saw made some of them have second thoughts about all the blankets and horses they had bet on Larabee's gray. The blood red bay, Fiddler, was a magnificent horse.

A blanketed Indian pushed his way to the front to watch the long legged bay go past. Then he stepped out onto the course and squatted, doing something with his hands, finally patting the dust. The Indians watched without a sound, but the cowboys hooted. He obviously was making medicine to help the gray horse win.

The Indian was Little Horse. When he had finished making his medicine, he stepped back. "Let him run past here," he said like a benediction.

Again the cowboys hooted but with less ridicule. Nobody living close to the Indians completely discounted the power of their medicine.

Then Tom Brady rode out on the gray. The Indians screamed their excitement. Scotty had never seen two more magnificent horses than the gray and the bay. Both were thoroughbreds and eager to run this race.

Dahlman kept Fiddler under control as they waited the starting signal, but the gray broke under Brady's rein several times before the two stood at the starting line together.

The starting gun cracked and Fiddler, trained to break away like a shot, spurted out ahead of the gray to the dismay of the thousands of Indians. But Brady was a good rider, and he urged the gray to his limit. Inch by inch, he crept up on the bay. The screams of encouragement from thousands of throats was deafening.

Brady whipped the gray with the reins on both sides, Indian style, and brought him up even with Fiddler. Now they ran neck and neck. But Fiddler was noted for his spurts at the finish of a race that pulled him away from all opposition.

Then they reached the spot where Little Horse had made his medicine. The red bay suddenly broke stride, shying to one side. Cursing, Dahlman brought him back on the track but the gray had shot ahead by two lengths. Then Dahlman whipped the bay into the greatest exhibition of speed anyone had ever seen. Fiddler closed the gap to half a length before Larabee's gray crossed the finish line, still in the lead.

Scotty couldn't understand what had happened. Dahlman, returning to his friends who had lost everything they owned, had no explanation, either.

"Fiddler just quit running for the first time in his life," he said, almost in tears.

Probably the only ones at that race who believed they knew what had caused Fiddler to break stride were the thousands of Indians. To them, it was simple. Little Horse had made very powerful medicine.

Scotty waited for things to explode as the cowboys reached the conclusion that somehow they had been cheated. But before that happened, the Indians had collected their spoils and had melted back across the reservation line.

XV

SCOTTY WENT HOME, feeling that he had seen one of the greatest races he would ever see. But the thrill of the race faded as he rode over his sun-scorched range.

For the first time since he had been in this country, there wasn't enough rain to keep the range green. There had been short dry spells before but nothing like this. If Scotty had been confined to a limited number of acres of grass, he'd have been hard pressed to keep his cattle alive. But he shared the whole reservation with just a few ranchers. He let his cattle range as far as they wanted to go. But that wasn't far. The deep holes in Bad River held water through the drought, and the cattle stayed within walking range of them.

When fall came, the grass on the flatland was almost gone. Scotty could only imagine what it was like off the reservation where the ranchers had been crowding each other for years. Nobody put up hay for winter feed. Winters had been open, and cattle had been able to fend for themselves. This year forage was going to be scarce.

An old Indian stopped by one day for a meal, which Scotty always furnished for every visitor, white or red. He said he didn't like the signs. He had come from the west where he had seen the beavers piling up many more saplings than usual for winter food. To him, that meant a very hard winter ahead.

The Indian also pointed out that the birds were

bunching up much earlier than usual. They would soon fly south. That meant an earlier winter. An early hard winter spelled bad times ahead, the Indian predicted.

Just to add conviction to his arguments, the Indian told Scotty and Sally that a rabbit he had killed had the heaviest fur that he'd seen in many years, and he had seen a great northern owl only the day before. Those owls usually stayed farther north, coming this far south only when the weather to the north was going to be so bad the owl couldn't live there.

Scotty was depressed when his visitor left. He had seen some of the same signs the Indian had pointed out, but he had tried to ignore them. Now he couldn't. When he looked at his cattle, which were not fat and sleek like they usually were in the fall, he found it hard not to worry about the months ahead.

But there was still grass in some of the draws. It was mostly coarse grass that the cattle didn't like and had left, but it would be feed for them if snow covered the short grass. The trees also offered his cattle protection from the winter storms. Scotty knew he was better off than many ranchers, especially those not on the reservation.

The first of November, weeks earlier than snow usually came to these plains, a blizzard roared down out of the north, burying the rangeland like pouring a bucketful of sand on a plate. A sharp cold wind blew the snow into huge drifts, sapping the energy from the half starved stock.[1]

Scotty was thankful for the trees along the river. Thin cattle out in that sharp wind would either drift with the wind to distant ranges or go down before it never to rise again.

The blizzard lasted three days. When it ended, snow filled most of the draws level full. The cattle couldn't get to the tall coarse grass down in those draws

now. There was little else to eat anywhere. To add to
the cattle's misery, the temperature dropped below
zero. It was too early for that kind of cold. None of the
stock was prepared for it.

It was the longest winter Scotty had ever seen. One
blizzard followed on the heels of another. It was a
winter in which a man dare not wander far from home.
The threat of storm was in the air continually.

As the new year of 1887 dawned, the thermometer
dropped to thirty below zero and seemed to stick there.
Ranchers watched their cattle slowly starve to death
because they had no hay to feed them. Wolves moved
in and grew fat on the weak cattle they could pull
down.

Ranchers hunted the wolf packs when weather and
work permitted. Much of their time was spent in getting fuel for their own fires. Even the tight houses they
had built on the Dakota plains were not insulated
against the bitter cold that gripped the land. At Bismarck, less than two hundred miles north of Scotty's
ranch, the temperature read 34 degrees below zero on
the 26th of December and 33 below on the 20th of
February.[2] There was very little relief from the cold
between those dates. The cold that gripped the northern section of Dakota also held the southern area in its
icy fingers.

Many of Scotty's weaker cattle died, but most of his
herd survived. There were wolves in the timber along
the creek, but they didn't bother Scotty's cattle as much
as they did those on the flat lands because Scotty's
cattle were stronger and more able to defend themselves. Nevertheless, Scotty felt that he was seeing the
end of his budding empire.

The biggest storm of the winter hit right at the turn
of the year, rolling in on the last day of the old and
staying through the first two days of the new.[3] Blinding
snow made it impossible for a man to see his hand

before his eyes. The wind whipped the breath right out of his lungs.

Behind the snow, paralyzing sub-zero cold settled down over the mountainous drifts. Starving cattle, blinded by the snow and driven by the agony of the cold, wandered aimlessly, keeping that death wind to their backs. They drifted over cliffs and were crushed at the bottom by more cattle falling on them; they broke through the ice on rivers, their frozen bodies damming the water; they drifted into fences and died there until their bodies stacked up so high that those behind could walk over the fence without touching the wires.

When spring finally came, the range was a scene of desolation. Dead cattle and even horses dotted the plains, choked the draws and creeks, and were piled high at the bottom of bluffs and along fences. Many ranchers had tried to salvage something from the disaster by skinning the carcasses. But more often than not, even this proved a failure. Carcasses were frozen stiff and the hides cracked or the skinners found that wolves had torn strips from the hides. With the warming of the prairie sun, the sweet smells of spring were drowned in the rotting stink of decaying flesh.

Scotty counted his losses and felt sorry for himself until he talked to other ranchers. Many of the big outfits in northern Dakota and Montana and Wyoming, even south through Nebraska, Kansas and into the Texas panhandle had lost from sixty to ninety percent of their herds.[4]

Scotty realized then how fortunate he was. This marked the end for many big cow outfits. It wasn't the end for Scotty. But he'd never forget the Big Die-up, nor would he ever go into another winter without hay stacked for winter feed.

Cattle dropped to twenty dollars a head, the lowest price Scotty could remember. Still there was a rush to sell. The plains of Dakota needed restocking, but the

big cattlemen were in no hurry to do it. Many were
getting out of the business completely.

Scotty thought he saw a golden opportunity here.
Cattle prices couldn't stay this low. He had made good
money in the past few years. Now he took some of that
money and went to Minnesota to buy cattle.

He found more cattle there than grass on which to
graze them. Dakota had more grass than cattle. Scotty
bought some cattle and arranged to have them shipped
to Pierre.

At Pierre, Scotty was met by several of his hired
hands. They took the cattle off the train and drove them
down to the landing and put them on the ferry, "Jim
Leighton." On the Fort Pierre side of the river, they
pushed the cattle off the ferry and headed them up Bad
River to Scotty's home range.

Scotty had no way of knowing exactly how many
acres of reservation grass he controlled, but he estimated that his cattle ranged over about ten thousand
acres. No one paid much attention to boundaries because there was plenty of grass for everyone.

That summer Fred Dupree, a French-Canadian
trapper who had turned to raising cattle up on the
Cheyenne River, put on a ten day feast and celebration
to honor the marriage of his daughter, Marcella, to
Douglas Carlin. In later years, Scotty would have deal-
ings with Dug Carlin. Invitations went out to all who
wanted to attend. Scotty would have gone if he could
have spared the time. He heard that a hundred whites
and about five hundred Indians were there for some or
all of the ten days.[5]

Dupree brought in four wagon loads of food to add
to the barbecued meat of thirty fat beeves and four
young buffaloes from the herd he had raised. Fred had
started his buffalo herd from some calves he had captured on the last buffalo hunt on Grand River in 1881.
Now his occasional buffalo barbecues were known

South Dakota State Historical Society

Fred Dupree

from the Grand River to the White. In one of his wagon-loads of food were two ten gallon kegs of whiskey and a cask of imported wine to add to the barrels of wild grape wine that Fred had made himself.[6]

There was music for dancing during the entire celebration. Much of the music was furnished by Fred's son, Pete, who was good with a fiddle. It was a wedding celebration never to be forgotten by those who were there.

The summer was not a wet one, but Scotty saw the cattle he had bought in Minnesota fill out and put on flesh. Although the price was still low when fall came, Scotty shipped the cattle to market. He wouldn't risk carrying over more cattle than he had feed enough to pull through a bad winter. Scotty realized a good profit from the Minnesota cattle in spite of the low price he received.

Although the range was no longer overstocked with cattle, there was still agitation to have the reservation opened up for settlement or at least for lease to the ranchers ringing the boundaries with greedy eyes.

In December, a new bill was brought up in Congress to open the reservation. Twice before such bills had been passed by the Senate only to be turned down by the House. This one, however, passed both houses of Congress and President Cleveland signed it in April.[7]

Still there remained the problem of getting three-fourths of the Indian men to sign the agreement. There had been no change in this from the bill passed back in 1882. Scotty didn't expect any change in the results, either.

There were other things on the minds of the ranchers that winter besides the bill Congress was trying to pass. The blizzard of Jan. 12, 1888 was one that every man, woman and child on the northern plains of America remembered as long as he or she lived. It swept into the Dakota territory on Thursday, and school children caught at school had a bad time getting home. Many teachers kept their pupils at the school house throughout the storm, burning desks and benches to keep from freezing. Some who tried to get home didn't make it. The storm interrupted a fairly mild winter and was equally as intense as the bad storms of the winter before.

The cattlemen didn't suffer as much this time as

they had the year before because they were better prepared. The Big Die-up had caught them with no feed and little protection for their cattle. This time they had feed, and in most cases, some protection for their herds. People died in this storm, too, but not as many as had been lost the previous winter. There was never an accurate count made of the loss in either winter, but it was estimated that Dakota lost about three hundred people in the winter of '86 and '87. Many were simply unaccounted for because they were caught between stopping places, and no one realized they were missing. In later years, when human bones were discovered, it was guessed that these people had been caught, like the cattle, in the Big Die-up.

Rumors ran wild in 1888 that the Dakota Territory was soon to become a state, perhaps two states, and there was confidence everywhere that the reservation would be opened up no later than fall. Homesteaders were poised along the Missouri River ready to rush in and grab the prize pieces of land.

But again they were built up for disappointment. Even the newspapers that were predicting a great homesteader rush were grossly premature, not realizing that only the coming of the railroad could bring in the homesteaders in great numbers.

When the commission appointed by President Cleveland, headed by R. H. Pratt of the Carlisle, Pennsylvania, Indian School, went into the reservation to get the necessary signatures to open up the reservation, it ran into the clever negotiations of Sitting Bull and Red Cloud. The government was offering fifty cents an acre for the land that was to be taken from the Sioux and opened for settlement by the whites. The two chiefs demanded a dollar and a quarter an acre. The negotiators hit an impasse and all went to Washington, including the two chiefs and seventy of their followers.[8]

South Dakota State Historical Society

Clara Philip, left, and her sister Hazel.

President Cleveland refused to see the Indians, and they came home, determined never to sell their land. The high hopes of the whites ringing the reservation were smashed again. Scotty gave it little thought because he had been sure this would be the ultimate result.

There were bitter words spoken by those shut out of the reservation, and many of those words were directed at the squawmen who were growing fat off the profits realized in the limitless grasslands of the reservations.

Scotty knew that he was the target of the wrath of many a fellow cattleman. But the situation was in the government's hands, not his. He certainly wasn't going to give up the great opportunity he had of making his fortune here in this uncrowded paradise for cattlemen, even if his fellow ranchers did fume about it. But he wasn't blind to the trouble this could cause, either.

In November of 1888, another daughter, Clara, was born. Five daughters for Scotty now, four of them living, and still no son.

XVI

BEFORE 1888 was over, still another bill was introduced into Congress aimed at opening the reservation for white settlement.[1] Scotty read about it in the papers, and he was sure that eventually this bill or one similar to it would succeed. This was one effort that repeated defeats would not squelch. When the white man wanted something the Indians had, he persisted until he got it.

Congress took up this bill early in 1889. In February, it passed the House. This time the bill did not contain the requirement that three-fourths of the Indian men had to sign the agreement.

However, in the Senate, Senator Dawes objected to this, and the bill had to go to a conference between the House and Senate committees. When it came out, it once again had the clause requiring the signatures of three-fourths of the adult male Indians. But it also had the dollar and a quarter an acre stipulation insisted on by Red Cloud and Sitting Bull. This was qualified to the extent that only the land homesteaded in the first three years would be paid for at a dollar and a quarter an acre. The land settled in the next two years would be paid for at seventy-five cents an acre. After that, the price dropped to fifty cents.

Congress approved of the bill written in this manner, and President Cleveland signed it on March 2, just before he left office. President Harrison immediately appointed General George Crook to head a commission to get the necessary signatures of the Indians. Few expected him to succeed where others had failed. There was no wild enthusiasm on the fringes of the reservation as there had been in 1882 and again last year. Those ranchers and would-be settlers had been disappointed too many times.

General Crook, however, was well known to the Indians. The Indians respected him, and many signed the agreement. Sitting Bull refused, but his power was not strong enough to keep the other Indians from doing as they pleased. By the middle of August, General Crook had the necessary number of signatures, and a huge portion of the reservation was opened to settlement.[2]

Now Scotty could see the handwriting on the prairie. Most of the ten thousand acres that he claimed were thrown open to the homesteader and rancher. His home, however, was on land allotted to his wife, Sally, and nobody could take it away from him.

Scotty didn't make any drastic change of plans. As long as nobody claimed the land he had been using, he would continue to range his cattle there. He wouldn't yield the land until he was forced to.

Scotty's first son was born this year, premature and not too strong. Scotty gave him the name that was most popular in the Philip family, George. Scotty's father's name was George. Scotty's oldest full brother was George, and he had a son twelve years old now named George. Also Scotty's brother, Robert, the only brother to stay in Scotland, had one son and his name was George. This nephew, George, still in Scotland, although not yet nine years old, was an orphan. His father, Robert, had died before he was four and his mother when he was seven.

Scotty was extremely proud of his only son. But little George lived only six months. Scotty buried him

General George Crook

on his own land, not far from the ranch house and marked that day as the saddest of his life.

Scotty worried about the encroachment of outside ranchers on his grass, but as yet they hadn't come. He had over a thousand head of cattle now under his 7-L and S-7 brands. He also had many horses wearing the L-7 brand on their left hips.[3]

Scotty mingled a great deal with the Indians when they had their celebrations. Sally enjoyed these celebrations immensely, and Scotty usually took her to them.[4] It was at one of these celebrations that Scotty first became aware of the excitement growing among the Indians. Some Indians were openly predicting that they would soon get back all the land that the white men had taken from them.

Scotty learned about the prediction made by a Nez

Perce Indian out in Nevada. According to the vision of
this Nez Perce, a Messiah would come in the spring of
1891 who would help the Indians drive all the white
men from the western plains and mountains, and the
Indians would once more reign supreme over all the
land they had once controlled.[5]

Representatives from every tribe had been invited
to a big council in Nevada where they would learn
what they should do in preparation for the coming of
this Messiah.

These were hard times for the Indians on the Pine
Ridge Reservation. Rations had been short, and the
Indians didn't like the new agent at Pine Ridge. That
added up to certain trouble, the way Scotty saw it.[6]

He said nothing, however. He expected to have
trouble of his own when the grass greened up next
spring, and the settlers swarmed out onto the prairie.

On the second of November that fall, two new states
were added to the Union, South Dakota and North
Dakota. Immediately a battle shaped up for the perma-

Pine Ridge Agency, 1888, with the agent's residence at right.

Beef issue at Pine Ridge, 1888.

nent capitol of South Dakota. Scotty's sentiments were with Pierre because it was near the center of the state and because it was closer to his ranch than any other town vying for the honor.

Scotty began wondering about the future of his ranch here on Bad River since the settlers were certain to come in now. There was land to be had along the river close to Fort Pierre. He liked the river. Huge Stanley County in the new state encompassed a wide strip of land from the Missouri to Pennington County.[7] That was well over half way from the river to the Black Hills and took in Scotty's ranch on Bad River.

There were plenty of land seekers in Pierre and Fort Pierre, but Scotty didn't find the homesteading craze as rampant as he had expected. Scotty located some land he liked about three miles north of Fort Pierre. The eastern edge of the tract of land on which he filed homestead papers was cut off by the Missouri River itself. His land included the site of the original Fort Pierre, which had been a fur trading post.

Scotty and his good friend, Buck Williams, had a

South Dakota State Historical Society

Cheyenne Agency, South Dakota.

long discussion about the changes that had taken place
in the last few months and how it would affect them.
The vast Indian territory had been whittled down into
five comparatively small reservations. The Standing
Rock Reservation was on the border between the two
new states of North and South Dakota. The Cheyenne
River Reservation ranged from the Cheyenne River
north along the Missouri River. The smallest of the
five, the Lower Brule Reservation, was south of Fort
Pierre along the river. South and west of Scotty's Bad
River ranch was the biggest of the reservations, the
Pine Ridge, and to the east of it was the Rosebud. Both
of them bordered Nebraska.

Scotty and his friend decided that the admission of
the states to the Union had opened up an opportunity
they mustn't pass by. New counties, such as Stanley
County, would be carved out of the former reservation
land. A permanent county seat for each county would
have to be established. Pierre was the only town of any
size in this entire area, but it was across the river in
Hughes County. Some town here in Stanley County
would claim the honor of being county seat.

Ziemann Collection

Deadwood Street in Fort Pierre, 1902.

Scotty and Buck Williams recognized the opportunity to start a new town and declare it to be the county seat. Getting the seat of county government would almost guarantee a bright future for a new town. Scotty and his partner decided to do it.

They laid out their town on Scotty's new homestead and quickly agreed on the name of Stanley. That name should give them a psychological edge on any other aspiring town because it would be appropriate for the county and the county seat to have the same name.

Scotty and Buck Williams encouraged people who were coming into the new territory to build homes and business places in the emerging town, arguing that it was wise to get in on the ground floor of a new county seat town. Scotty and his partner put carpenters to work building a hotel. A hotel would add prestige to the new town, and the town would need prestige in the fight ahead. Besides, with a hotel, they could put up land seekers while they were locating their claims, and this would be a good business in itself.

The unrest among the Indians was growing rapidly. But Scotty felt no fear for his family out on Bad River. Scotty spent little time at home that winter. If the new town was to prosper, he had to be there and make sure it became the county seat. Fort Pierre was claiming the right to be the seat of the new county, which was to be officially organized soon. Fort Pierre was an established town but Scotty and his partner declared that their new town was planned to accommodate the county seat; Fort Pierre wasn't. Besides, Fort Pierre was just a footstool for its big brother, Pierre, directly across the river.

In February, the race for county seat between Scotty's town and Fort Pierre began waxing warm. It suddenly came to everyone's attention that Scotty wasn't even a citizen of the United States. Why should he be allowed to try to establish a seat of government in the new county?

On the twenty-third of February, Scotty went across the river to Pierre in Hughes County and made out the necessary papers, applying for citizenship in the United States.

The fight between Fort Pierre and Stanley became very heated.[8] Scotty hadn't expected anything like that. But he wanted the county seat in Stanley, so he and his partner put everything they had into the fight to get it.

The election was set for April 15th and as the date approached, no one who was not strictly partisan would even predict how the election would go. There were many new citizens in the county, people who had just located on their homesteads. That meant a lot of unpredictable votes would be cast.

Scotty was still confident when the polls opened the morning of the 15th. He didn't lose that confidence until the polls closed that night and the votes were counted. It was a close vote but the final tabulation showed that Fort Pierre had won the county seat by a very narrow margin. Although Scotty and his partner hated to give up, they agreed that now their town had little chance to survive.

Ten days after the election, Stanley County was officially organized with the county seat at Fort Pierre. Tex Hemphill was appointed sheriff to fill the office until official elections were held that fall.[9]

Scotty made another trip into Minnesota to buy cattle to fatten out. As yet, no one had crowded him off his land out on Bad River, and as long as he could hold that range, he could make good money fattening out cattle on the rich grass. Now that the reservation was open, he expected huge companies to be formed to manage vast cattle empires. That looked like a sound business practice to Scotty, but he didn't have enough capital for such a venture.

On his return from Minnesota, Scotty found that some of the buildings that had been erected in Stanley were already being moved away, most of them going down to Fort Pierre.

The only thing of value left in Stanley that was owned jointly by Scotty and his partner was the hotel. They talked about what to do with it and finally agreed to play a game of seven-up for it, the winner to be sole owner of the building.[10]

Scotty's luck was better in this than it had been in the county seat election. He won the hotel but after he had won, he wasn't sure just what he would do with it. At least, the hotel was sitting on his own land.

Back at home, Scotty discovered that a few homesteaders were moving in along Bad River, but it was certainly no land rush. This area was simply too far from a railroad or any source of supply.

Many of the homesteaders who had come were also taking pre-emptions. By taking a pre-emption, a settler could claim a quarter of land by actually living on it

South Dakota State Historical Society

Nebraska excursion homesteading near Pierre.

only six days in a six month period then paying out at a
dollar and a quarter an acre. He had to live on his
homestead five years to prove up. A pre-emption, coupled with a homestead, gave a settler a half section of
land.

Some even went a step farther and took a tree claim,
too, under the timber culture law. They could claim a
quarter of land by putting out at least six hundred
seventy-five trees on no more than ten acres and showing proof of their growth within eight or ten years. In
this way, a settler could claim three quarters of land by
exercising all his prerogatives.[11]

Down the river about sixteen or eighteen miles
from Scotty, a new town had sprung up called
Midland.[12] It wasn't much of a town, but it had a store
and it was the closest place to Scotty's ranch where any
kind of supplies could be bought.

The white ranchers around Scotty called the excitement among the Indians the Messiah Craze. The

Ziemann Collection

Fourth of July celebration in Midland, 1909.

representatives from the reservations had returned from the Nevada council with special shirts which they wore like inverted sacks with head and arm holes cut in them. These shirts were supposed to make the wearers immune to bullets.

The sad part of this was, in Scotty's opinion, that many of the Indians actually believed these shirts were bullet proof. That belief could cost them their lives.

XVII

SCOTTY HAD BECOME good friends with many of the Indians on the reservation, and although the reservation lines were now pushed quite a distance to the south of him, he still felt a close kinship to them.

From one of his Indian friends, he learned more about these shirts the tribe representatives had brought back from the big council in Nevada. The shirt looked to Scotty like a white muslin sack with holes cut in it for the wearer's head and arms. It was long, hanging down past the hips. This Indian was one who firmly believed that no white man's rifle bullet could touch him while he was wearing one of those shirts.

Scotty asked him why he believed this. The Indian told him how his friend had seen them tested in Nevada. One of the shirts had been hung on a tree limb, and several Indians had fired at it with rifles. Not a hole had appeared in the shirt. Scotty guessed that the shirt, hanging loosely on a tree limb, was of such flimsy material that the force of the wind created by the bullet had blown the muslin aside and the bullet had passed under it or beside it.[1]

But Scotty said nothing. He knew that a mere white man could not argue an Indian out of his belief in anything supernatural. He would only succeed in making an enemy of a friend.

The tribes had a new dance that they were required to do in preparation for the coming of the Indian Mes-

South Dakota State Historical Society

A rare picture of the "Ghost Dance" at the Pine Ridge Agency in 1890.

siah, who was due in the spring of 1891. The dances were being held at all the reservations but, according to what Scotty could learn, the most frenzied dances were on the Pine Ridge Reservation where Chief Red Cloud was the head.

Scotty had an opportunity to witness one of those ghost dances, and he understood why white men called them that. The Indians, dancing around the open fires in those long white shirts looked more like ghosts than anything possessing flesh and blood.

It was a very restless summer. There was little doubt in anyone's mind that these ghost dances on the reservations would culminate in bad trouble unless a miracle happened. Scotty didn't expect a miracle.

With all the big cattle companies showing up around him, Scotty felt that the little rancher was going to be squeezed out. Scotty's operation wasn't little, but he couldn't compete with the really big outfits. The only way to survive was to become a part of a big company himself. Consequently, he improved on contacts he had made in earlier trips to Minnesota to buy cattle and finally agreed to a partnership that had been proposed to him.

Charles Stuebe of New Ulm, Minnesota, had cattle that he wanted to find new pastures for. Scotty agreed to take the cattle and handle them for a year, and the two men settled on a profit sharing agreement, providing there was any profit. If the cattle wintered and fattened well in South Dakota, then the partners would consider bigger operations.[2]

Scotty shuttled back and forth between his homestead three miles north of Fort Pierre and his ranch out on Bad River. He had to be in Fort Pierre quite often because he had been appointed a commissioner of Stanley County.[3] His fellow commissioners elected Scotty chairman of their board, and Scotty took his responsibility very seriously. A new county had much business to attend to, and Scotty called frequent meetings of the commissioners.

The townsite of Stanley was quickly disappearing. Scotty realized that the hotel he owned would never do any business where it stood, so he accepted an offer from some men in Fort Pierre for the building, and it was moved, parts of it reappearing in several houses down in Fort Pierre.[4]

Since he had to stay on the Missouri River so much of the time, Scotty began to look longingly at the open range in the hills west of the river. He bought some land with buildings north of his homestead and established a headquarters there, running cattle in the hills west of the river. The Minnesota cattle he received from Charles Stuebe went into these hills for the summer, and Scotty brought down some of the men he had working for him on his ranch on Bad River to handle the stock.

Scotty was home when his second son, Stanley, was born on August 3. He appeared to be a strong healthy boy, but Scotty's elation was tempered somewhat by the memory of the short life of his first son whom he had buried just last year.

Stanley Philip at the age of 12.

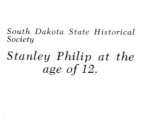

Unrest among the Indians was permeating everything on the plains from the Black Hills to the Missouri. Scotty's Bad River ranch was very close to the main trail used by the Indians in their travels between the Pine Ridge and Cheyenne River Reservations. Traffic on this trail increased as the summer wore away. The ghost dances were growing in size and intensity. Pine Ridge seemed to be the center of the frenzy, but Scotty heard that the dances were rampant on other reservations, too, especially at Standing Rock, Sitting Bull's headquarters, to the north of the Cheyenne River Reservation.

Scotty rounded up all his marketable steers and trailed them to Fort Pierre. There he put them on the

ferry across the river to the loading pens in Pierre and
shipped them to Chicago.

Just after the middle of November a band of Indians
set up camp on Bad River close to Scotty's ranch. Scotty
counted five lodges, and when he went down to talk to
them, he found eight warriors. All were armed with
Winchesters with belts and pockets full of
ammunition.[5]

Scotty saw quickly that they were spoiling for a
fight, but he had no intention of giving them an excuse
to start one here. He made no objection to their camping here, although he had lost several head of cattle
lately, and he blamed traveling bands of Indians such
as these for his losses.

When he asked where the Indians were going, a big
Indian that Scotty recognized as Yellow Thigh, pushed
forward. He said they were going to Pass Creek on
White River. Scotty had heard about the ghost dance
there. It had been going on for nearly a month now, and
some reports said there were a thousand lodges along
the creek with fifteen hundred warriors.

Yellow Thigh was surly and defiant, but Scotty ignored his threatening attitude and asked how many of
his brothers Yellow Thigh expected to find there. Instead of an answer, Yellow Thigh began a tirade against
the white man for starving and robbing the Indians. He
bragged that once he had beaten out the brains of white
children and drunk white women's blood, and the time
would soon come when he would do it again.

Scotty said nothing and Yellow Thigh raved on,
admitting that the range was well stocked now with
cattle instead of buffalo, but it was all meat to the
Indians. He informed Scotty that he was raising horses
now for Indians to ride. Scotty wasn't sure whether he
meant that the Indians would steal the horses, or if he
expected Scotty to give them the horses, since he had
been allowed to live here with his half Indian wife

when this had been part of the reservation and was considered a white brother to the Indians. He didn't ask and let Yellow Thigh rant on until he was tired.

Scotty could see that they had plenty of meat, and he guessed that it was his own 7-L beef they were eating, but he said nothing and went back to the house and left the Indians alone. They didn't intend to bother him, or they would have done it before this.

If there had been even the slightest doubt in Scotty's mind that blood would flow before these ghost dances ended, it was gone now. In the days that followed, more 7-L cattle were butchered, and George Waldron, six or seven miles down Bad River, reported losing some cattle, too.

One night three worried half breed Indians stopped at Scotty's ranch. They had refused to join the ghost dance and were on their way home. They told Scotty that they expected to find their homes destroyed when they reached them. Any Indian or half blood Indian who did not join in the ghost dance was a target of those who did, they said.

Realizing the seriousness of the situation, Scotty rode down the river to George Waldron's place the next day. Waldron agreed with Scotty's conclusions, and the two rode on to Fort Pierre. Crossing the river on the ferry, they went on to see Governor Mellette.

They explained the situation to the governor, and he promised to do something about it. Scotty learned later, after he had been called back into the service of the army, that the governor had written a letter to General Nelson A. Miles that resulted in Scotty's recall to duty.[6]

Nov. 26, 1890

Scotty Philip, who has a thousand head of cattle, and lives at the mouth of the Grindstone Butte Creek, eighty miles up Bad River with an Indian family, and Waldron, the cattle man, seven miles this side of Philip's, left their places at 2 p.m. yesterday to bring me intelligence. Philip is a very cool, courageous man, also a

good scout through the Sioux Trouble of 1875-76 and Cheyenne
Trouble of 1879. He is a reliable man of nerve, good judgment and
good character. He reports that he was never afraid of Indians
before, and thinks there will be an uprising very soon.

Philip says everybody who has been among the Indians any
length of time, outwardly expects that there is going to be an
uprising, and that very quick. The Pass Creek Dance has been
running for a month. Philip and Waldron say it is Short Bull's
headquarters, and they think it is a point fixed for concentration
for all the lodges. They think there are now one thousand lodges,
and fifteen hundred warriors there. Indians claim they won't give
up, and Short Bull will fight when the soldiers try to arrest him.
They say as soon as the fight begins, a hail storm will kill the white
soldiers. The Indians say they have shirts that are bullet proof.
I know Philip well and will take his judgment on the situation
in preference to anybody I know. If you deem this information of
any importance, I can send a messenger to further investigate. I
urgently request however, that you establish a post at Chamber-
lain and at Forest City, both points are reached by rail. I have
requested Secretary of War, and again make the application
through you, for one thousand guns and ammunition to be shipped to me at Huron.

Although Scotty would have preferred to stay out of
this trouble, he felt he couldn't refuse General Miles'
request, made at the recommendation of Governor
Mellette, that he return to the army as scout and
courier. Scotty couldn't see why the Indians, many of
them his friends, should think they had a chance to rise
up and defeat the whites after being corraled for so
many years on the reservations. But the Indians acted
as if they really believed that those ghost shirts would
turn aside any bullets the white men fired at them.

Scotty wondered how he would react if he were
penned up like the Indians were now. Wouldn't he
grasp at a dream like that, even though reason told him
it couldn't come true?

Scotty heard of the army's first move through his
military connections. Major Royer, Indian agent at
Pine Ridge, became so worried that he demanded

South Dakota State Historical Society

The soldiers' camp at Pine Ridge Agency during the 1890 Sioux war.

military protection at the agency. Soldiers had never been stationed there before, but finally the army agreed to send units to watch over the reservation and all the area between there and Rapid City. Military records show that the 2nd, 3rd, 8th, 17th and 21st Infantry; 1st, 5th, 6th, 7th, 8th and 9th cavalry; and the 5th artillery were dispatched to the area to keep things under control.[7]

From his Indian friends, Scotty learned of the Indians' reaction to the appearance of the troops. Led by Short Bull and Kicking Bear, they had fled into the Badlands just to the southwest of Scotty's Bad River ranch.

In Nebraska south of the reservation and along the rivers just to the north of the reservation, white men formed into protective militia groups. Many stayed in hastily erected forts at night and worked their farms and ranches by day.

Word reached Pine Ridge that Sitting Bull had been shot and killed on the Standing Rock Reservation on the 15th of December, and many of his followers

Pine Ridge Agency war scene, 1891.

had fled south to the Cheyenne River Reservation.[8]
The death of Sitting Bull only increased the danger of
major trouble on all the reservations.

It was the Indians who had fled from the Standing
Rock Reservation that eventually became involved in
the Wounded Knee battle. When they reached the
Cheyenne River Reservation, they joined up with
Chief Big Foot.[9] It was Big Foot's band that was on its
way to Pine Ridge to surrender when it was intercepted at the edge of the badlands by soldiers of the 7th
Cavalry, who hadn't forgotten Custer's defeat fourteen
and a half years ago and were eager for revenge.

Scotty was performing his army duties as scout and
courier, but he wasn't with the 7th, so he had nothing to
do with the battle, and he always considered himself
lucky to have avoided it. Major Whitside, in charge of
the units of the 7th that intercepted Big Foot's band,
accepted the Indians' surrender and escorted them
toward Pine Ridge. Seventeen miles from Pine Ridge,

Sitting Bull

they halted for the night. Camp was set up on Wounded Knee Creek.

Colonel Forsyth arrived at the camp with four more troops of the 7th and four artillery pieces. Feeling that it was best that the Indians be disarmed, Colonel Forsyth told his soldiers to take all guns and knives from the Indians the next morning before they began their march to Pine Ridge.

The Indian and soldier version of what happened next differ, but one fact remains starkly evident. Whether it was intentional or accidental, an Indian did fire a gun, and the battle was on. The next few minutes saw over two hundred Indians, men, women, and chil-

South Dakota State Historical Society

Officers of the 7th Cavalry at the time of the Wounded Knee massacre.

dren, and about sixty soldiers killed or wounded. The artillery pieces on the hill lobbed shells into the Indians at the rate of about fifty a minute.[10]

Scotty would never believe that the first shot had been fired intentionally. No warrior he had ever known would have risked starting a battle when Indian women and children were in line of fire as they were here. The soldiers were on both sides of the Indians, which in itself was a poor military tactic. Either Colonel Forsyth hadn't anticipated any trouble or else he hadn't considered the consequences of such a troop deployment. Many soldiers were caught in the fire of their own men. Many, both white and red, were felled by the fire of the Hotchkiss guns on the hill.

The battle was short, but it was costly to all concerned.

XVIII

SCOTTY WAS SENT to Pine Ridge, where Short Bull and Kicking Bear had already come in to surrender before Big Foot's band had been practically wiped out at Wounded Knee. The day after the battle, the weather turned sharply colder, and snow swept in. For a couple of days, it was almost like a blizzard.

Soldiers were sent out to Wounded Knee to bury the Indian dead. All the dead soldiers had been hauled back to Pine Ridge along with the wounded, both white and red. A long ditch was dug on the top of the

The Medicine Man's body at Wounded Knee.

Looking north over the battlefield at Wounded Knee.

Gathering the dead at Wounded Knee.

South Dakota State Historical Society

The mass burial of the Indians at Wounded Knee.

South Dakota State Historical Society

The Indian police used at Pine Ridge Agency in 1890.

hill where the Hotchkiss cannons had been set overlooking Wounded Knee Creek. The Indians, their
bodies frozen solid in grotesque shapes, were buried
in one mass grave.[1]

With the myth of the ghost shirts exploded, the
Indians settled into a sullen silence. Many in Big
Foot's band had been wearing the ghost shirts, but they
had died from the white soldiers' bullets the same as
the others. The Indians' last hope of conquering their
white foe was gone forever.

The despair of the Indians was a pitiful sight to
Scotty. Like the buffalo, the red man's chances for
survival as a race had been dealt a hard blow. Scotty's
race, however, would not try to eradicate the Indian as
it seemed intent on doing to the buffalo.

Ever since Scotty had seen his first picture of the
great buffalo herds when he was a boy back in Scotland, he had admired the huge shaggy animal. Such a
great monarch deserved a better fate than the hide
hunters had given him. Scotty felt that some effort must
be made to preserve the great animal that had furnished food, shelter and weapons for the Indians for
generations.

The winter was hard on cattle on the range, but
Scotty's herds came through in fairly good shape. Some
of the Minnesota cattle were lost, but a high percentage
of them survived and were in good shape when spring
grass greened up. Scotty made his report to his partner
in New Ulm, Minnesota, and in a short time, Charles
Stuebe arrived to look at the cattle.

Scotty met him in Pierre. Stuebe had a banker
friend with him from New Ulm named Mullen. Mullen
was interested in investing in some profitable venture,
and Stuebe had convinced him that cattle ranging on
these open plains of South Dakota was the answer. He
was here to make certain.

Scotty had the Minnesota cattle in the breaks west

Copyright 1902 "Scotty" Philips Herd
By P.H.Kellogg
Rushford, N.Y. Ft. Pierre, S.Dak.

A buffalo from Scotty Philip's herd.

of the Missouri River where the grass was good. Scotty took his visitors in a buckboard on a tour of the herd. Both Charles Stuebe and Mullen were impressed with the good shape of the cattle, and the three men formed a partnership before the two Minnesota men left for home. Scotty was to manage the company, which would be called the Minnesota and Dakota Cattle Company. Stuebe would furnish most of the cattle, and

Mullen would underwrite much of the initial cost. They decided on 73 for their brand.[2]

Scotty was elated over the new partnership. He would be in charge of a big herd now, and huge profits seemed almost certain. Scotty put some men to building new corrals on the ranch north of Fort Pierre. He would keep his ranch on Bad River, and the two places would give him room to range thousands of cattle.

He brought his family up to the ranch north of Fort Pierre for a while during the summer. He wanted them to see the home he expected to move them into someday. He couldn't expect to hold the Bad River range away from the homesteaders indefinitely.

Scotty had asked the government for a post office out on Bad River. Mail had to be brought from a long distance for all the ranchers and homesteaders along the creek. The Post Office Department authorized Scotty to open such an office.

Scotty quickly put up a log building a mile west of his home ranch on Bad River. Dan Powell, his good friend there, was appointed the first postmaster of the new office, called Philip. The office received its first mail on July 1, 1891.[3]

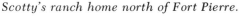
Doug Philip Collection

Scotty's ranch home north of Fort Pierre.

That same month of July, Scotty received ten car-
loads of cattle from Minnesota to put on his ranch
under the 73 brand.[4] They were unloaded at the pens
in Pierre, and Scotty and a dozen of his men were there
to meet them. They were driven down to the river in
small herds, as many as could easily be ferried across
the river at one time on the "Jim Leighton."

The "Jim Leighton" had heavy plank railings
around its sides, and it was divided into pens. The pens
were made of panels that could be moved out of the
way for such cargo as loaded wagons with teams still
hitched. But the pens could also be made solid for
hauling cattle across the river.

The cattle were shoved into the pens, no more than
twenty in each pen. If they had been allowed to bunch
together, they would likely have all crowded to one
side and capsized the boat. The pens kept them from
shifting the balance of the load.

Once the cattle were across the river, Scotty and his
men moved them up to the ranch north of town. There
they were corraled, and the job of putting the 73 brand
on the left hip began.

Scotty ran the 73 cattle separate from his own
brand. He hired Jack Borden as his foreman for the
Minnesota and Dakota Cattle Company. Scotty had
known Borden for a long time, and he trusted him and
his judgment with cattle. Borden's wife, Mabel, was a
sister of Dick Mathieson. Scotty and Mathieson were
good friends and neighbors. Both were ranchers, and
both had been run out of the Black Hills by the army
back in 1875.

More homesteaders had settled along Bad River
during the summer. Scotty wasn't being crowded
much, but some of his cattle were disappearing. The
same thing was happening to other ranchers.

Some accused the homesteaders of stealing the cattle, but Scotty doubted that. Homesteaders might kill a

beef now and then, but the ranchers were losing more cattle than that. It was money, not meat, that the thieves wanted.

Throughout the fall, Scotty talked about the rustling and the need for an association of ranchers to combat it. There had been organizations over in the Black Hills for several years now. Some of them hadn't lasted long, but some were still in existence. Those organizations had done a great deal to curb the cattle rustling in that area.

So far, there hadn't been enough rustling along the Bad and Cheyenne rivers to cause any great alarm, but now it was increasing rapidly, and Scotty felt it was time to act.

A newspaper article that Scotty read that fall made him realize how fast the cattle business was growing. The *Queen City Mail*, printed in Spearfish, reported that in 1890 the assessed number of cattle in South Dakota had been 296,148 head.[5] This fall, 1891, the assessed number was 619,217 head. It had been a boom year for the stockman. So it naturally followed that it had been a boom year for the cattle thief, too.

A meeting was called in Fort Pierre on December 10. Scotty was there. At that meeting, the Missouri River Stockmen's Association was formed with A. D. Marriott as president.[6] George Waldron was elected vice president and J. H. Hallet secretary. Eugene Steere was elected treasurer. The executive committee was headed by Scotty Philip with M. E. Williams, John Robb, and H. A. Scovel on the committee. The president, A. D. Marriott, owned the HAT ranch on Grand River and was destined to become postmaster at Pierre a little more than a year later.

One of the first orders of business of the new organization was to offer a two hundred dollar reward for information leading to the capture of rustlers. W. P. Oakes, who had been elected sheriff of Stanley County at its first official election,[7] welcomed the help of the association in catching the rustlers in the huge county.

Before the organization had really gotten its teeth into the problems facing it, a notice printed in the *Queen City Mail* was brought to the attention of the executive committee. It was a call for representatives from all the cattlemen's organizations in the Hills and the immediate surrounding area to meet on February 20, 1892, for the purpose of organizing one big association. This organization, according to the notice, would "in no way conflict with the local organizations in existence, but will serve greatly to enlarge their work and increase their usefulness. It is earnestly requested that all stockmen who can will be present at the meeting in Rapid City on Feb. 20."[8]

Scotty was chosen to represent the Missouri River Stockmen's Association. Only a few men were present in Rapid City at that first meeting, but it was enough to get the association started. Each delegate was asked his opinion of an organization that would include all the cattle country west of the Missouri River. Scotty gave his endorsement of the plan.[9]

James M. Wood was made president until the first regular meeting of the association, scheduled for April 6. The official name chosen for the organization was the Western South Dakota Stock Growers Association. Scotty returned home, feeling that the meeting had accomplished what it had set out to do.

Scotty's daughters had been getting their schooling wherever they could. He realized what they were missing by not having a regular school with a qualified teacher. There were enough people with children of school age living close to Scotty's 7-L along Bad River now to make a school worth while.

Scotty set about building a school house close to his house. He had only four years of formal education himself; he had acquired the rest of his education the hard way. He didn't want his children to face the handicaps of an abbreviated education similar to his own.

Here in the wilds of his new land, perhaps others would excuse him for not giving his children an education, but he would never excuse himself. Scotty spent a lot of work getting the school house ready for the fall term.

Nanny Whitney was the first teacher, but when she got homesick, Scotty found Jessie Stuart to finish the term. Although the school was meant for the entire neighborhood, Scotty took care of all the details. He had paid for building the school house, and he had furnished it. He made arrangements for the teacher to board at his ranch, and he also paid her a salary of thirty-five dollars a month, which was as much as she could have made in one of the organized districts close to the Missouri River.[10]

When Jessie Stuart arrived, she was amazed to find that the log school house was solid and big enough for all the pupils she would have without being crowded. The building was equipped with a large desk for the teacher and a big blackboard. There were two huge wall maps, one of the United States and the other of South Dakota. And there were plenty of books for the pupils.

Scotty informed the teacher that one of the cowboys would build the fire for her on cold mornings. But the cowboys apparently didn't think it ever got cold. It was very seldom that she found the fire started when she went to the log schoolhouse in the mornings. She knew how to build a fire, however, and didn't complain.

She particularly liked the place where she boarded and grew to admire Sally Philip and even learned to speak some of the Indian language. It was the first time the new teacher had ever been on a ranch, and Scotty was amused at the way she reacted to everything that was so commonplace to him and his youngsters.

Scotty decided to show the new teacher some of the entertainment that the ranching country enjoyed. Usually the neighborhood got together two or three times in the fall, sometimes more often, for a big dance. It wasn't a dance that started at seven or eight in the evening and ended at midnight. These dances began as soon as the crowd could gather at the ranch which was to host the affair on Friday night, and it lasted until sometime on Sunday, giving the merry makers just time enough to get home ready for work on Monday.

Scotty had a big hand in planning this particular dance to be held at Mike Dunn's place over on White River because Mike was Scotty's brother-in-law. Mike had a daughter with the same name as Scotty's oldest daughter, Emma. So Emma Philip was often called Amy to keep from confusing the cousins.[11] Scotty took his entire family to this dance to make a family visit, as well as enjoy the entertainment.

The White River, on which Scotty's brother-in-law Mike Dunn had his ranch.

The ranch home with Scotty and Sarah on the porch in the back, Mike Dunn smoking his cigar on the steps, Emma seated just above him, and Scotty's son Rod and daughter Olive at the right.

Mike Dunn had killed a beef for the occasion. He had also bought a barrel of apples. His wife had cooked a boiler full of hams. There was no shortage of food or music. Every community had its own musicians and this was no exception. The dancing began right after supper Friday night. With breaks for sleeping, eating, and visiting, the dance carried on into Sunday.

This dance was something of a family reunion for Scotty and Sally because J. E. Utterback and his wife, Zoe, another of Sally's sisters, were there. Utterback had just moved down on the White River from Bad River the year before. His brand was the Anvil, a reminder of the days when he had been a blacksmith at Fort Robinson.

It was a weary family and an exhausted teacher that got back to the 7-L late Sunday night. But Scotty was satisfied at the glow in the new teacher's face. It had been a week end she would never forget.

XIX

WITH MORE AND MORE settlers moving into the territory west of the Missouri, Scotty began to feel uneasy
about his homestead. He had papers filed on it, but he
had heard of legal twists that allowed claim jumpers to
hold land they had actually stolen. Scotty's land right
on the bank of the Missouri was the kind someone
might want to steal. Scotty spent much more time up on
his ranch north of the claim than he did on the homestead itself.

He decided the best thing to do was pay out on the
homestead. So early in September, he filed the necessary papers to pay out on his land.

No. 10 Sioux Indian Series.[1]

Receivers Office at Pierre,
South Dakota September 3, 1892

Received from James Philip

The sum of one Hundred and Eighty-two dollars and 88 cents,
being in full for the SE quarter of NE quarter and the NE quarter
of the SE quarter Section 17 and Lots 1-2-3 of Section 16, all in
township No. 5 North of Range No. 31 containing 146 acres and 30
hundreths at $———— per acre.

E. W. Eakin
Receiver

Dated September 6, 1892 — 9 o'clock.

The price in the blank should have been $1.25 but
wasn't filled in by the one making out the application.

Scotty wintered cattle at both ranches. He had

enough men working for him now to divide the crew and have plenty to handle the work at both places. He shuttled back and forth when the weather permitted, checking on the cattle at Bad River where his family stayed and at the ranch north of Fort Pierre. He had moved so many of the 73 cattle down on Bad River that people began to call the Bad River ranch the 73 spread.

Scotty's partnerships were working out very well for him. He still had cattle in partnership with Charles Stuebe that were not part of the Minnesota and Dakota Cattle Company. These cattle carried one of three registered brands, UL or SS on the side or M on the left hip.[2]

The Minnesota and Dakota Cattle Company branded most of its cattle with a 73 but it had also registered the brands, MU and 0/0, both on the left side, and L on the left hip. It was Scotty's job to keep separate records of the cattle under each brand.

Scotty also had some cattle in another partnership with a man named Binder. This partnership had two registered brands, 00 on the left side and 0 on the left hip.

These brands, coupled with Scotty's own five registered brands, gave him more book work than he liked, so many of his records were stored in his memory. Most of his own cattle were branded with a 7-L, L-7, or S-7 on the left side. He had some cattle branded with a 4 on the right hip or X4 on the right side. His horses carried a L-7 or S-7 on the left hip.[3]

In the spring of 1893, another daughter was born to Scotty and Sally. They called this little girl Tina, another family name, but she was not destined to grow up with the family. When eight months old, she died. It was another hard blow for Scotty and Sally. They had lost three children now but still had four girls and a boy living.

Scotty bought a home in Fort Pierre. There would

Scotty's home in Fort Pierre. Left to right: Miss Mortenson (a neighbor), daughters Hazel, Clara, Olive, Emma, Scotty's wife Sarah, and his youngest daughter Annie.

be times, he was sure, when it would be more convenient for his family to live there than on one of the ranches. And he was financially able now to own a home in town.

At the December meeting of the Western South Dakota Stock Growers Association, Scotty applied for membership along with his brother-in-law, Mike Dunn, and a neighbor from down Bad River, Louis LaPlant.[4] Scotty expected most of the members of the Missouri River Stockmen's Association to join the larger organization, but only a few actually did. Scotty maintained membership in both organizations because he saw a need for both of them.

One of the main items of business at this December meeting was the hiring of a range detective to watch for cattle being marketed by someone other than the rightful owners. The choice of Joe Elliott raised some eyebrows among the ranchers at the meeting.[5]

Louis La Plante

Elliott was a well known gunman and had almost come to his end while working for the Wyoming Stock Growers Association. He had been in the Johnson County War and had slipped out of Wyoming when President Harrison had declared martial law in the state.

Elliott was hired at a wage of a hundred and twenty-five dollars a month. Some ranchers were disgusted with the association for hiring such a man. Others thought it was a very wise move because they reasoned that the cattle thieves would think twice before risking a run-in with a gunman like Joe Elliott.

Scotty voiced no opinion. He just hoped that Elliott would put a curb on the stealing. It was growing worse in spite of all the association could do. The reason, he knew, was the number of cattle available to steal. Without the stockmen's association, there would be five times as many cattle stolen. It was because of Scotty's conviction of this that he took a membership in both cattlemen's organizations. It cost him two cents a

head assessment for dues, but he felt it was well worth
it.

In the regular meeting on April 10, 1894, J. E. Utterback joined the Western South Dakota Stock Growers Association, thus bringing in both of Scotty's
brothers-in-law who were ranchers.[6]

It had been a dry winter, and now the usual spring
rains were light and spotty. Some range land didn't get
any rain, and ranchers were facing the summer with
worried faces.

Scotty had cattle spread over a great expanse of
prairie, and the slowness of the spring grass caused
him much concern. But the rains had always come; he
had to believe they would come again.

The Minnesota and Dakota Cattle Company acquired more land for Scotty to run cattle on.[7] One tract
of two hundred acres was to the east of Scotty's ranch
on Bad River and gave him another place that he could
hold against any future encroachment by settlers and
which could be made into a convenient headquarters.

Scotty had many hired hands now. With as many
brands as he had, it appeared to many that his book
work would be staggering. But as most of his neighbors
would attest, Scotty's memory was fantastic. Most of
his records were stored there. When asked for figures,
he would quote them, and very seldom was he wrong.[8]

The Missouri River Stockmen's Association decided to incorporate this spring. Scotty saw little need
of incorporating if the members would join the Western South Dakota Stock Growers Association. But several members of the Missouri River organization had
no wish to belong to the larger group, so the Missouri
River association was incorporated. Twelve men
signed the corporation papers, including Scotty.[9]
Scotty now gave his address as Fort Pierre, although he
still had more land and cattle out on Bad River than
here on the Missouri.

Tom Jones

Although the year was a very dry one, some cattle made good gains by market time. That fall Scotty wrote to a friend, Tom Jones, who had come into the country three years ago and had cattle of his own now. Scotty had liked Tom Jones from the time he had first met him and later would join him in a partnership lease.

The letter was on the stationery of the Minnesota and Dakota Cattle Company which pictured three cows, one bearing Scotty's L-7 brand, one the Minnesota and Dakota Cattle Company's 73 brand, and the other the Philip and Stuebe partnership UL brand.

The letter head of the Minnesota and and Dakota Cattle Company listed Chas. Stuebe, President; M. Mullen, Secy.; James Philip, Manager. The address was given as New Ulm, Minnesota and Philip, South Dakota.[10]

Philip, S.D.
Sept. 26th, 1894

Friend Jones:

I expected to see you yesterday but I did not get in in time. I don't know what arrangements you are making to gather the calves but I hope you will get them in time so as not to be rushed when the snow comes. Dug Lowe will take mine any time you send them to him. Hoping you will bring a big bunch of good beef soon, I remain

Yours truly,
James Philip.

Scotty's third son was born that fall. Roderick appeared to be a strong healthy boy.

The following summer, Scotty helped his friend, George LaPlant, stage a horse race on land just west of Scotty's Fort Pierre ranch. LaPlant had a race track at his ranch about sixty miles up Bad River from Fort Pierre, and in a race there earlier in the summer a Wyoming man had pitted his racer, Two Bits, against a

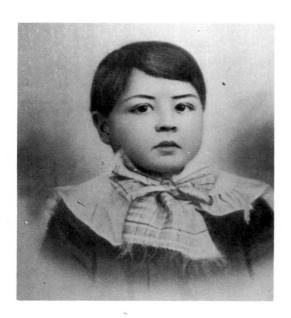

South Dakota State Historical Society

Rodrick Philip

fast horse owned by Missouri's John Massingale. The
Massingale horse had won, and the Wyoming man,
disappointed and broke, had sold his horse to George
LaPlant and Eb Jones. LaPlant had immediately challenged Massingale to a revenge race to be run on
neutral ground. The track west of Scotty's was
chosen.[11]

Over a thousand people, many from Pierre and Fort
Pierre, crowded along the track to bet their money and
watch the race. It was very close, but Two Bits avenged
his earlier loss, and LaPlant made a huge profit off his
bets. Even Sheriff Joseph Root of Stanley County,
elected the fall before, came to watch the fun.[12] He had
his hands full because bitter words flew fast and furi-
ously when the race was over. But the money changed
hands without serious trouble, and the losers went
away, figuring they would get a chance to recoup their
losses when another horse race was scheduled.

Although Scotty had moved his family to his ranch
at Fort Pierre now, he still spent much of his time at the
Bad River ranch because he had so many cattle on the
prairies around there.

It was nothing unusual for the sports lovers of Fort
Pierre and Pierre to travel the sixty miles up Bad River
to George LaPlant's ranch to see one of the special
horse races that he staged on the track west of the ranch
house. One of those races was scheduled the following
summer, and those who had lost money on the race
west of Scotty's Missouri River ranch saw their chance
to regain some of it at LaPlant's ranch.

Scotty went, taking his fastest horse, Skeet. He
hoped to get into a race either before or after the main
event. Usually a big race such as this fostered a dozen
lesser races. Scotty loved to watch fast horses run, and
Skeet was as fast as most of them.

LaPlant was running his Two Bits, which had won
the race the summer before, against a horse that was

*George La Plante,
taken a few days be-
fore his death.*

being brought through the country, racing against the best that could be found. LaPlant had every confidence that Two Bits could beat any horse living.

Before the big race, George LaPlant and Scotty got together and pitted Scotty's Skeet against one of LaPlant's good runners. Scotty collected two hundred dollars when Skeet won that race.[13]

In the main event, Two Bits was nosed out in a very close finish. LaPlant had bet several of his own horses on the race, and he lost them. He managed to buy his horses back from the stranger for four hundred and fifty dollars. But it had been an expensive day for George LaPlant.

Snow came to the prairies the first of November that fall, and Scotty pushed his cattle down closer to the breaks along the rivers for protection. The first severe storm hit on Thanksgiving Day.[14] Scotty's cattle were used to the kind of cold weather this country subjected

them to, and they were fairly well protected so they
survived the storm in good shape.

Down river from Scotty, however, George LaPlant
had brought three thousand head up from Texas. These
cattle had never seen cold weather, and many died in
that first blizzard. In fact, when LaPlant rounded up his
cattle the next spring, he found only three hundred and
sixty-five of the three thousand Texas cattle he had
bought, almost a ninety percent loss. Scotty knew how
to sympathize with him. These South Dakota winters
could be vicious on cattle. Scotty had lost enough in the
Big Die-Up that he would never forget that lesson.

Among the men Scotty had working for him, he
found one that he took a special liking to. Si Hiett was
not the best behaved cowboy Scotty had on his
ranches, but he got the work done when it was assigned
to him. And he had a way of controlling other men
when necessary. Scotty wasn't long in giving him jobs
that carried plenty of responsibility.[15]

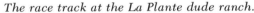

The race track at the La Plante dude ranch.

In spite of the losses sustained by George LaPlant, Scotty felt that the way to capitalize on the booming cattle market was to bring in cattle from the south and fatten them on Dakota grass.

He took a long trip into Texas, and even across the border into Mexico, looking for cattle to buy.[16] He enjoyed the train ride, and since he went when the weather was still cold in the north, he revelled in the warmer climate, too. He bought cattle from several different ranches and arranged to have them shipped north to Pierre. Some of his purchases were for the 73 brand, and some were for his own L-7. There was room for more cattle on the grass that he controlled, and he was making sure that none of that grass was wasted.

Dan Powell had taken over the buildings on Scotty's Bad River ranch, and managed some of his land.[17] This, added to his own ranch work, kept him so busy that, in the summer of 1897, he had to give up the Philip post office, which he had operated since Scotty had gotten it in 1891. The post office was moved west to George Morrison's homestead, and Morrison became the postmaster.[18]

Scotty still maintained big interests along Bad River, but he felt that his future lay in the ranch along the Missouri River. He owned a nice home in Fort Pierre, and it made a good place for his family to live during the winter while the children were in school, as all but Roderick were now. During the summer, he moved the family out on the ranch north of town. He didn't want his children to grow up on the streets of town with nothing to do and there was plenty of work to keep them busy on the ranch.

Scotty felt that the cattlemen were suffering because of some of the laws the state legislature was putting through. His interest in politics had remained high ever since the battle over the county seat and his work as chairman of the County Commissioners of

Stanley County. He continued to keep a close tab on the swing of the pendulum in political circles.

   He didn't particularly want to get back into politics himself, but somebody was going to have to take a stand. Maybe he would have to be the one.

South Dakota State Historical Society

Loading the chuck wagons in the early days at Fort Pierre. Tom Jones is the man on horseback.

XX

IT WAS THIS year, 1897, that Scotty's last child, a daughter named Annie, was born. He now had seven living children, five girls and two boys.

A letter from his brother down in Kansas told him that their nephew, George, orphaned son of Robert, the only one of the Philip brothers who had stayed in Scotland, was here in America now. Scotty wrote to his brother and suggested that his nephew might like to live a while on a ranch in South Dakota. Scotty would give him a good home and plenty of outdoor work. He had to do some figuring to decide the age of his nephew, George, and came to the conclusion that he was about seventeen now.

The trouble with Spain lifted the price of cattle in the spring of 1898, and Scotty foresaw a big profit in the fall for himself and for the Minnesota and Dakota Cattle Company. Scotty pushed over twenty thousand head of company stock out on the grass that spring. Charles Stuebe and even Mr. Mullen of the New Ulm bank came to see how things were going. Mullen tried to give Scotty a tally book in which to keep his records, but Scotty informed him he could keep a better tally in his head.[1]

Scotty bought an interest in a bank and a real estate business in Fort Pierre, feeling that he should be investing some of his accumulating money in something

South Dakota State Historical Society

Sarah Philip with her youngest daughter Annie.

besides cattle. He did buy a little more land close to his ranch along the Missouri.

Scotty was growing more dissatisfied each day with some of the laws the state legislature had passed. Friends now began to urge him to run for the state senate. He was well known over all the area from the Missouri to the Black Hills. They felt that he would be elected easily if he ran. The ranchers were sure they would have a real champion in their corner with Scotty in the senate. Scotty was finally persuaded to make the run for the senate, so he filed as a candidate.

He made a trip back to his old home in Victoria, Kansas, to visit his brothers. There he met young George, fresh out of Scotland. Scotty liked the looks of the boy and he repeated his invitation for him to come up to Dakota to live.

Scotty didn't spend much time campaigning for the

Doug Philip Collection

Scotty's brother Alexander with his wife Anne and son William.

Doug Philip Collection

Alex, Scotty's brother, and his wife in their home in Hays, Kansas.

senate. Everyone who knew him knew where he stood
on the issues. Those who agreed with him would stand
behind him; those who opposed his views weren't
going to vote for him, anyway. He didn't figure there
were enough uninformed voters to make a campaign
worthwhile. In that he was right, because Scotty Philip
wasn't the kind of a man anyone could ignore.

Scotty wasn't particularly surprised to find, when
the election results were in, that he had won handily.[2]
He would go to the temporary capitol in January to
stand up for the interests of his district, which was
primarily cattle country.

1899 was a very busy year for Scotty. Early in the
year, he took his seat in the senate at Pierre. There he
pushed for legislation that he felt was necessary to
preserve a healthy cattle industry in the state.

Young George Philip, Scotty's nephew, accepted
Scotty's invitation to come to South Dakota. Scotty was
living in Fort Pierre now with his family where it was
only a short trip on the ferry across the river to the

Mitchell Collection

James "Scotty" Philip as a senator.

temporary capitol. He put young George to work on his ranch a few miles north of Fort Pierre. George gave immediate indications that he was going to make a good cowhand.

One of the hot issues debated in the senate was the location of the permanent capitol of South Dakota.

George Philip, Scotty's nephew, shortly after he came to live in South Dakota.

Mitchell and Sioux Falls were vying with Pierre for the seat of government. In Scotty's mind, the only sensible place for a state capitol was within reach of all the state's inhabitants. Pierre was much more centrally located than either Mitchell or Sioux Falls.

Scotty pointed out that people from the Black Hills would have to cross the entire length of the state to get to their capitol if it was in either Mitchell or Sioux Falls. There were a lot of people in the Black Hills. To vote the capitol into any other city than Pierre would be a slap at the good citizens of the richest corner of the state. Scotty's oratory at times reached eloquent heights, but the issue was not settled. Pierre did gain some momentum, while Mitchell and Sioux Falls lost a little.

Scotty was busier than ever in the cattle business. In addition to his other partnerships, he had an interest in the Native Cattle Company, which normally ran about three thousand head.[3] Most of the stockholders were men from Omaha; Scotty was the only Dakotan.

Most of the cattle were shipped up from Texas and fattened on the grass in Dakota. It proved to be a profitable venture for Scotty, and it encouraged him to bring in more Texas cattle for himself.

The Native Cattle Company ran cattle from the White to the Cheyenne River. This vast area included some Bad River range. Many of the company's cattle were sold to the government for delivery to Indian reservations in Dakota and Montana.

Scotty had been partners with Joe Binder in their O and OO brands for years. This spring of 1899, Scotty and Joe decided to bring in a big herd from Texas and reap some of the large profits that were being made on the cheap southern cattle.

They formed a partnership with Carl Blasingame, and after the legislature adjourned, made a buying trip into the south. There they stumbled onto a cattle outfit that was going out of business, and they bought the entire herd. The stock was low grade, a mixture of cows, calves, steers and bulls. The partners had no intention of keeping any of this stock for breeding, but it was too good a buy to pass up. They shipped the cattle north on the railroad that ran into the Black Hills.[4]

At Brennan in the Hills, they unloaded the cattle. Here misfortune struck them. A terrific rain storm swept over the area, sending water down gullies and turning peaceful little streams into raging torrents. The water roared through the shipping pens at Brennan, washing some of them away.

Scotty and his partners and their crew struggled to save the cattle, but there wasn't much anyone could do. When the flash flood had subsided, they began the slow muddy work of rounding up the cattle that were left.

Some of the weaker cattle had drowned. A few of the better ones had become entangled with debris and had been dragged down, while still others had been trampled into the mud and water by their pen mates. But most of the cattle had survived although they looked even worse than before. They were caked with mud and gaunt from their long ride north on the train.

The men started moving the herd slowly east toward Joe Binder's ranch northwest of Hayes, which was almost due west of Fort Pierre. They crossed the Cheyenne River three days after leaving Brennan, letting the cattle fill up on grass as they went.

Scotty and Binder rode with the herd, talking to anybody they met, selling any of the cattle that caught a rancher's fancy. Each sale usually necessitated a stop while the cattle to be sold were cut out and often branded with their new brand right on the spot.

Before they got to Binder's ranch, a good portion of the herd had been sold. Scotty and his partners were assured of a profit from their trip to Texas because they had already taken in more money than the cattle had cost them, and they still had a fair sized herd to fatten up for sale this fall.

Carl Blasingame, who had been Scotty's and Binder's partner in this venture, stayed with Joe Binder on his ranch. That fall he was cut severely with a knife across one cheek and down his neck, narrowly missing his jugular vein. His assailant was identified only as "a crazy Russian."[5]

In the big roundup to bring back the cattle that had drifted off their home range, Scotty assigned his trusted cowhand, Si Hiett, to handle the throwback wagon for the 73. Si was also ordered to pick up any 7-L and S-7 cattle, Scotty's own brands.

The throwback wagon referred not only to the chuck wagon, but also the crew that headquartered at the wagon.[6] The wagon was set up in an area where a herd of cattle could be held, and as cattle from the brands the crew was to collect were cut out of the main

South Dakota State Historical Society

Roundup scene.

herd, they were brought to this area. Some of the cowboys then headed them back to their home range while the rest continued with the big roundup.

Most small outfits had only reps to pick out the cattle wearing their brands, but bigger outfits like the 73 needed a throwback wagon and crew.

Scotty put George to work on the roundup, letting him learn the rules of the range. He took to the work quickly and soon became a good hand. Scotty was proud of him. George liked it in South Dakota, and Scotty practically adopted him. Sally especially liked George and treated him as a son. George wrote in later years that Sally was like a mother to him. George was only a year older than Scotty's oldest living daughter, Emma.

In the fall, Scotty directed the annual roundup for the 73, from which the saleable cattle were to be cut out and trailed to market. It was a gigantic undertaking.

The cattle destined for market were pushed down to the river at Fort Pierre and loaded on the ferry, "Jim

Leighton." On the east bank of the Missouri, they were crowded into the shipping pens ready to load on the train. Both Charles Stuebe and the banker, Mr. Mullen, were on hand to watch the cattle being shipped to market.

Mr. Mullen made the mistake of trying to tell Scotty how the 73 should be run. Scotty considered the banker just that — a banker. He was out of his field trying to tell a cattleman how to handle cattle. Scotty's temper flared, and he cut the banker down to size without mincing any words.[7]

Mr. Mullen, used to respect, retorted in kind. The argument soon got out of hand. Scotty let the world around him know that he didn't have to associate with a man who was, in his opinion, too bigoted to have a right to mingle with decent people.

South Dakota State Historical Society

Stockyards scene at Pierre in 1896.

Leaving his cowboys to load the cattle into the waiting cars, Scotty went in search of his friend, Colonel R. W. "Bob" Stewart. Stewart was a practicing lawyer in the firm of Horner and Stewart. He was destined to become the head of Standard Oil Company of Indiana, and in that capacity, would stand up to anybody who crossed him.

Scotty offered Stewart a thousand dollars to find a buyer for his share in the 73. Scotty set sixty-five thousand dollars as the price for his third interest. Stewart told him he would look for a buyer, and Scotty went back to the loading pens.

Within a short time, Stewart looked up Scotty and told him he had found a buyer. Scotty was amazed when he learned that Stewart himself and Scotty's partner in the OO brand, Joe Binder, were the buyers. But Scotty had no objections. All he wanted was his sixty-five thousand dollars.

Although Scotty was no longer a partner in the huge 73 brand, he felt that the year had been a very profitable one for him. He had made out very well with the cattle he had helped bring up from Texas, and he had realized a very good profit from his years as partner in the Minnesota and Dakota Cattle Company. Now he was determined to use that money to build up his own brands. He didn't need partners with big capital to make himself a big rancher now, as he had when he'd joined up with Stuebe and Mullen.

Scotty interested Gaylord Sumner, cashier of the Stockgrowers Bank in Fort Pierre, in going to Texas with him the next spring to buy cattle. Scotty was a shareholder in the bank but Sumner was one of its biggest stockholders. Sumner was also one of the incorporators of the Empire State Cattle Company. This company ran cattle on one hundred sixty-five thousand acres of land along the Cheyenne River.[8]

In Texas, the two men bought over nine thousand

South Dakota State Historical Society

Main street of Evarts, South Dakota.

head of cattle and arranged to have them shipped to Pierre. Both Scotty and Sumner had their eyes on the new town called Evarts erupting on the east bank of the Missouri River opposite the Cheyenne River Reservation.[9] The railroad construction crew had started the town, and soon it would be the end of the rails. Evarts would be a better place than Pierre to unload cattle whose destination was the Cheyenne River, but the town was not ready to receive cattle yet.

Bringing nine thousand head of cattle into Pierre at one time presented a problem. There was a law that cattle coming from the south had to be dipped before they could be released onto the open range in Dakota. Indian Department officials were always present to make sure no undipped cattle set foot on Indian reservation land.

Even Scotty was staggered a bit at the thought of having to dip nine thousand cattle.

XXI

THE TWO DIPPING vats were huge, one nearly a hundred and fifty feet long while the other was about seventy-five feet long. The shorter vat was for the weaker cattle, those that could not stand the longer swim in the hot treated water.

Lime and sulphur were put in the water to kill the lice and ticks that the southern cattle carried on them. Thermometers were used to keep the water hot enough as the cattle were shoved through. The sulphur fumes were sickening, and everyone in town complained when cattle were being dipped down by the loading pens.[1]

With the vats ready, the cattle were forced up a long chute that ended in a steel slide into the vat. The vat was too narrow for an animal to turn around in. The only way he could go was ahead. Cowboys stood on either side holding long poles with curved hooks on the ends.

The animal usually slid out of sight on the first plunge into the vat, but before he had swum the hundred and fifty feet to the end where he could climb out, the cowboys usually ducked his head a couple of times to make sure every tick on his body got a good soaking in the lime and sulphur. The hook on the end of the stick was used to lift an animal's head up out of the water, if he didn't manage to do it himself.

For a few days after coming out of that vat, the cattle

would have a sickly yellow-blue color. There could be no question whether or not a critter had been dipped.

The long task began as the first of the nine thousand head were shoved into the vat. Some of the weaker cattle got down in the vat, and the others, in their frenzy to get out of the stinking water, trampled them under. Twice during the day, the dipping had to be stopped while the dead animals were dragged out of the vat. It didn't take many downed animals to make a floor high enough that the cattle coming into the vat could keep their heads above the water no matter how hard the cowboys tried to push them under.

Once out of the vat, the cattle were driven down to the ferry to be taken across the Missouri River. The river was too high this time of year for the cattle, weakened from their long ride and the dip in the hot sulphur and lime water, to swim across.

Scotty added his share of the new cattle to his 7-L herd, putting some on the range close to his ranch on the river and herding the rest to the range along Bad River. This fall he would bring many of these same cattle back across the river to ship them to market.

With his growing herds spread over two ranches, Scotty hired more men until he had dozens of riders on his payroll. He did very little riding himself any more. He weighed two hundred and forty pounds now, and riding was not only hard on him but on his horse as well. He usually used a light buggy or buckboard on his trips around the ranches to check his herds and the progress of the work.

Scotty had dreamed of returning home to Scotland someday, but he had never found the time or the spare money to make the trip. But now he had the money, and he had good men to leave in charge of his ranches. He decided to visit his old home.

He didn't want to make the trip alone, and none of his brothers would go with him. But the son of his brother George, at Victoria, Kansas, was eager to go back and see the land where his father had grown up. This nephew's name was George, too. To anyone outside the Philip family, so many Georges could be confusing. This George would be twenty-four years old in October, and Scotty decided he would make an excellent traveling companion.

It was a great trip for Scotty.[2] Memories of the first sixteen years of his life flooded over him as he walked again along the paths he had skipped over as a youngster, going to school or down to the Lossie to fish. It seemed only yesterday that he had lived those carefree days and dreamed of America. As he walked the old paths and remembered, he realized that America had not been all that he had expected it to be, but it had brought him the fortune he had dreamed of acquiring. He hadn't found it as quickly or as easily as he had

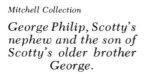

Mitchell Collection

George Philip, Scotty's nephew and the son of Scotty's older brother George.

Doug Philip Collection

Scotty with his sister Tina.

anticipated, and he certainly hadn't expected to have to work for it the way he had. But as he strolled along the paths of his old Highlands home, he felt no regrets that he had left this land to make his way in the new world.

From Scotland, Scotty and George went to Paris where they spent a few days at the Paris Exposition which was making headlines all over the world this year.

Then came the slow trip back across the Atlantic. In anticipation of the visit to his old home, Scotty hadn't noticed the time it had taken to sail from America to Scotland. He had many mixed emotions there, the thrill of walking the old paths along the Lossie and the sadness of visiting the graveyard where his parents were buried. But now that those emotions had all taken their place in his memory, he was chafing to get home.

As Scotty paced the deck, worrying away the hours until they reached New York, he began to think of all the things that could go wrong at home while he was away. Those possible misfortunes grew with continued worry until they were almost like accepted facts. It was actually a let-down when he reached home and found his worries groundless and everything under complete control. Scotty was almost irritated to think that things could run so smoothly without his guiding hand.

South Dakota State Historical Society

Ed Lemmon

The Stockmen's Convention was held in Texas that fall, and Scotty attended it with his good friend, Ed Lemmon, of the Lake, Lemmon and Tomb Cattle Company. Lemmon had also been connected in one way or another with the Sheidley Cattle Company since 1877. The Sheidleys branded a Flying V.[3]

As the year drew to a close, it seemed inevitable to Scotty that the country would soon yield to the plow, but he was convinced that this development would be a disaster to the Dakota plains.

Scotty heard that Pete Dupree up on the Cheyenne River Reservation had died. He had known Pete well and also his father, Frederick, before him. He had seen Pete's little herd of buffalo running loose with his cattle.[4]

The buffalo calves he had roped on the Grand River nearly twenty years ago had stayed with the cattle as they grew up, adopting the ways of their hosts. Most people had expected them to wander off, but they hadn't. It wasn't many years until Pete Dupree had several buffalo. He also had several animals he called cattalo, a cross between a buffalo and a domestic cow.

Scotty thought a lot about that little buffalo herd. There were very few buffalo left anywhere now, and little, if any, effort was being made to preserve them from extinction. That seemed like a crime of the greatest magnitude to Scotty.

Scotty made a trip up the Missouri to the Cheyenne Reservation. He learned that Dug Carlin, Pete's brother-in-law, was administrator of the estate. Scotty knew Dug Carlin well. He remembered the stories he had heard about the wedding of Dug and Pete Dupree's sister. It had been one of the big social events of the decade back in the '80s.

Scotty and Dug talked a long while about the buffalo herd. Dug estimated that there were seventy-five or eighty buffalo on the range along the Cheyenne River.

Scotty offered to buy every buffalo on the Dupree range.[5] Dug Carlin agreed, providing Scotty took the cattalo crossbreeds, too. Scotty really didn't want them. They were too much buffalo to be any good as cattle, and too much cattle to pass as buffalo.[6] They were good for nothing but butchering. Scotty agreed to take them, however, in order to get the buffalo.

Scotty went back to his ranch close to Fort Pierre and began making plans for a fence that would hold the big animals. He couldn't turn them loose to range with his cattle as Pete Dupree had done. They'd go right back to the Cheyenne River, which they would consider their home range.

Scotty faced a real problem because a fence that would hold a cow would scarcely slow up a buffalo if he wanted to go through. It would take a fence like no one on this range had ever seen to hold Scotty's new herd. But Scotty believed so firmly in the need to preserve the huge bison, a symbol of the past on these plains, that he didn't hesitate at the expense of building a fence strong enough to hold the big shaggy animals.

He bought rolls of heavy woven wire and loads of big heavy posts. He instructed his men to set the posts deep in the ground only five feet apart. Then they were to stretch the woven wire tight, nailing it to these posts. The wire was three feet high, and he had one panel of it put on top of the other so that the woven wire fence was six feet high. Two strands of barbed wire were stretched above the woven wire. This high tight fence was designed to discourage any buffalo from trying to jump over it. If a big buffalo could get his weight up on the fence, he would mash it down. But not even the wildest animal would have courage enough to try to go over that fence.[7]

The fence was built in the hills that rose above the bottom lands bordering the Missouri River just to the west of Scotty's ranch house. Even after spring work

Some of Scotty's buffalo near Fort Pierre.

began, Scotty kept some men working on the fence.

He hadn't realized much profit from the cattle he had brought up from Texas the summer before, but still he went south and bought another large herd and shipped it north.

This time, he shipped the cattle to the new town of Evarts north of Pierre. Evarts had a good ferry to take the cattle across the river. Like the ferries between Pierre and Fort Pierre, this ferry was owned by Captain Ed Senechal. Evarts also had brand new dipping vats. But more important, the railroad had negotiated with the Indians and the government for a strip of land six miles wide, running straight west from the river, over which cattle could pass freely through the reservation to and from the shipping pens at Evarts. They had built dams at intervals along the strip to hold water for the thirsty herds moving to and from Evarts.[8]

Scotty had a crew of men at Evarts when his cattle came in. After unloading the cattle and running them through the dipping vats, however, he discovered that the ferry was broken down. Scotty talked the situation over with his foreman, Si Hiett. They could hold the cattle in the shipping pens at Evarts until the ferry was repaired, or they could swim the cattle across the river.

The river wasn't especially high, and these cattle were in better shape than the ones Scotty had brought north last spring. Besides, there was grass waiting for them across the river. They had no feed here in Evarts except what they bought, and it would take a lot of feed for this many cattle. There was no guarantee when the ferry would be repaired, either. So they decided to swim the cattle across.[9]

Scotty got a horse for himself because all hands would be needed to get the cattle to the west side of the river. Although the river was far below flood stage, the crossing would be dangerous to both cattle and cowboys if the cattle should get excited and start milling in the river.

Before starting the herd across, Scotty rode down to the man who was working on the ferry. He asked him to keep an eye on the cowboys during the crossing and come out in his little rowboat to help anyone who got in trouble. The ferryman agreed to help if there was anything he could do.

The cattle started across, plunging reluctantly into the cold water as they were crowded in by those behind them. The cowboys, whooping and swinging their ropes, didn't give the cattle a chance to change their minds or their direction. Scotty helped push the stragglers into the water then plunged in after them.

The herd strung out, swimming well. It appeared to be an uneventful crossing. Scotty would be sore for the next day or two because he hadn't been in the saddle much lately and this was a strenuous job.

Then when he was about half way across the river, Scotty's horse got his feet tangled in some submerged debris and began to flounder. Scotty's two hundred and forty pounds handicapped the horse as he tried to free himself.

Scotty shot a glance at the banks of the river as it became obvious that his horse was not going to free himself without help. It was going to be a long swim to either shore. Scotty was sure that he couldn't make it.

XXII

THE HORSE CONTINUED to struggle and Scotty slid out of the saddle, hanging onto the stirrup, freeing the horse of the extra weight. But it didn't seem to help.

Then Scotty saw a boat coming toward him from the east bank. He had forgotten about asking the ferryman to help any cowboy who got in trouble. He certainly hadn't expected to be the one himself.

Scotty hung on to the stirrup until the boatman arrived. His horse got free about then but Scotty clambered aboard the boat, letting the weary horse follow the herd on to the west bank. The boat headed back for the east shore.

On land again, Scotty thanked his rescuer as he watched his cowboys corral the herd in the holding pens on the west bank of the river. Scotty introduced himself. He was amazed to hear that his rescuer was Boston Smith, the boy he had started to the Black Hills with back in October of 1875. After becoming separated while trying to get their horses back from a band of Indians that had stolen them, they hadn't seen each other since.[1]

Scotty asked his old partner why he hadn't met him on the Running Water the next day after their trouble with the Indians. Boston Smith explained that when the soldiers and Indians in the camp had seen him just as he caught his horse, he had fired that shot to stampede the Indians' horses so they couldn't follow him.

He'd been as afraid of being caught by the soldiers as by the Indians because he was an army deserter.

Boston Smith had no way of knowing that Scotty had already caught his horse when he fired that shot, and he supposed that the Indians had captured Scotty so he kept riding as fast as his horse could take him. The two men enjoyed their reunion there on the banks of the Missouri.[2]

After driving his cattle to the Bad River range, Scotty discovered that the Philip post office had been moved again, this time still farther west to Dr. Weikoff's ranch. Dr. Weikoff was the new postmaster.

Scotty rode to the Missouri to check on the progress of the buffalo pasture fence. He was impatient to get the buffalo inside the fence before someone decided to have a private buffalo hunt. Everyone knew that Dug Carlin didn't want to keep the buffalo, and some people might not recognize a new owner until he had established control of the animals.

In the late summer, the buffalo pasture was ready and Scotty sent six men to round up the buffalo on the Cheyenne River and drive them down to the pasture northwest of Fort Pierre. His nephew, George, was one of the six. All of the cowboys anticipated a lot of fun because this would be different from rounding up cattle.[3]

They hadn't realized just how different until they began to push the big shaggy animals south. Buffalo didn't drive like cattle. They were too big to rope and drag back into the herd when they decided to go off at an angle from the planned course, which was often. The men were worn out when they finally got the buffalo down to the west gate of the pasture.

There were fifty-seven buffalo and quite a number of cross breeds in the herd. They pushed them into the pasture then nailed the gate shut behind them. Scotty came out the next day with more men and cut the

Attempting to drive buffalo in the pasture.

cattalo out and herded them into separate corrals where they were to be held until slaughtered, the meat to be cured and salted down for winter use. Scotty was determined that there would be no more of the cross breeds on his ranch.

During the regular fall roundup, Scotty sent some men up to the Cheyenne River to claim any buffalo that got caught in the big sweeps of the plains. They brought back more of the stubborn animals and shoved them into the pasture. There were also several cattalo, but Scotty managed to sell them for beef, although he didn't get a good price for them.

Tales about the renegade buffalo bulls that had escaped the roundup on the Cheyenne River were brought to Scotty.[4] According to his purchase agreement with Dug Carlin, Scotty owned those bulls, and people along the Cheyenne were not slow in reminding him of the fact.

One rancher told Scotty of a particularly aggravating bull that had the habit of taking up a position by a gate through a partition fence. The gate was on the main road to and from the ranch. Whenever the bull was at the gate, nobody dared venture close enough to go through the gate. The old buffalo bull had pawed the ground so much that a hollow was being formed that the wind would soon turn into a blow-out.

The only way the rancher could get through the partition fence when the big bull was at the gate was to drive a quarter of a mile one way or the other and take down the fence to let himself through. Either Scotty had to come and get that bull, or the rancher was going to shoot him. Scotty agreed to come after that bull and some of the other renegades he had been hearing about.

Scotty's foreman, Si Hiett, warned him that they could never drive those big bulls down from the Cheyenne. Those animals had defied every attempt to move them and had broken out of the roundups in which they had been encircled. They were pure trouble.

Scotty sent an invitation to Governor Herreid to go with him after the renegade bulls.[5] They'd make a big outing of it. Scotty had discovered that a huge bull head would bring from five hundred to a thousand dollars on the market in New York. That was far more than a bull on the hoof would bring.

Scotty planned the buffalo hunt for winter when the cold weather would slow down the bulls' activities. It proved to be a wise decision. The bulls were not hard to find because they had come in close to the ranches where feed was more plentiful. Scotty's hunting party was welcomed by the ranchers who had been having endless trouble with the renegade bulls.

Scotty brought home several fine buffalo heads. Most of the meat from the animals was given to the ranchers on whose ranches the buffalo were killed. The weather turned very cold, so the heads were frozen until the hunting party got them to a taxidermist in Pierre.

Hunters of renegade buffalo bulls. Scotty Philip is seated second from left and Governor Herreid is seated fourth from left.

Most of the big heads were shipped east where sportsmen were waiting to pay good prices for them. Scotty shipped some of the big heads to his brothers in Victoria, Kansas. One of those mounted heads is still glaring down from the north end of the huge living room in the big stone ranch house on Alex Philip's original ranch. It is owned now by Alex's grandson, Douglas Philip.

Wolves were still bad on the range. Scotty had fought them ever since he had come to the Bad River. There had been a bounty on them for years, and some men, especially cowboys who found work rather slack

Scotty and Governor Herreid with a renegade bull they killed.

during the winter, spent weeks hunting and trapping the wolves. But wolves were not easy to catch. Scotty was convinced that, in most cases, they were smarter than their human hunters.[6]

Each winter the wolves accounted for many kills among the weaker cattle. In the spring they took a heavy toll of newborn calves and colts. Scotty was always willing to let some of his men take time off in the winter to hunt the wolves. If they got any, the bounty belonged to the man who made the kill.

It was a bad winter for snow, and cattle drifted south in some of the storms. The cold weather froze the rivers. Even the Cheyenne and the White were frozen over with a solid sheet of ice that the cattle could walk

A group of riders on Scotty Philip's ranch.

across and barely be aware that they were not on solid
ground.

When spring came, many cattle that were supposed
to be up on the Cheyenne River Reservation were
down on the Pine Ridge and Rosebud Reservations. So
were most of the cattle that ranged on the great pastures between the reservations.[7]

President Roosevelt was demanding that fences on
public lands be torn down and this was causing great
consternation among the cattlemen who had fenced
the land to discourage the homesteaders. The ranchers
reasoned that they had to protect the grass their cattle
ate and the water that they drank. Scotty shared this
belief, but he was convinced that, under the decree of
the government, the fences would come down. The
great profit making days of the rancher were over.

The ranchers gathered early that spring to plan
their roundup. Most of it would be concentrated on the
Rosebud and Pine Ridge Reservations. It would include outfits from the Cheyenne River, and even

beyond, and would be the biggest roundup these Dakota plains had ever seen.

Scotty sent a big crew. There were sixteen or eighteen throwback wagons, some with as many as sixty men. Scotty had only about half that many, but they could handle their share of the work. Besides all the wagons, many small outfits had reps riding with the roundup.[8]

Scotty instructed his men to watch for the brands of all his close neighbors along Bad River. They were to bring the neighbors' cattle in with the 7-L cattle, and they'd be cut out and sent to the right range when they reached Bad River.

The 7-L kept its throwback wagon to the north of the main roundup area as did most of the big outfits. Scotty had placed Si Hiett in charge of the crew.

They actually had two wagons, one to haul the bedrolls and the personal gear of the men; the other to

Ralph Jones Collection

A typical chuck wagon.

take care of the cook's needs. With so many men to cook
for over a longer period than usual for a roundup, the
cook insisted on taking a stove along. So a special cart
was pulled along behind the wagon. It had two wheels
and a short tongue that was fastened to the reach just in
front of the rear axle of the chuck wagon.

At each new camp, the stove was the first thing
unloaded and the cart pushed aside. A tent was set up
with one end fastened solidly to the corner of the grub
box on the rear of the chuck wagon. The tent covered
the stove and the grub box so that the cook could do his
job, regardless of the weather. The rear endgate of the
wagon flopped down to expose the grub box and to
form a solid table for the cook to work on. His first task
after getting the fire started was to grind some coffee
beans and get the coffee pot boiling. The cowboys
would wait for their grub, but they insisted on coffee as
soon as they had taken care of their horses. It was
seldom that they even had to wait for their grub. If they
came in too early for a meal, the cook informed them in
no uncertain terms that they had come out here to
work, not to loaf around the chuck wagon.[9]

There were the usual spring rains while the roundup was in progress, but with so many men on the job,
they handled the cattle with little trouble. There was
one serious accident when a cowboy named Walker
was struck by lightning while riding guard around the
herd. He and his horse were killed. Some cows close
by were stunned and burned, but none were killed.[10]

Scotty drove his buckboard down to the roundup
and stayed a while, watching the big operation. He had
never seen anything quite the equal of this. Si Hiett[11]
told him he had seen over a hundred different brands
that belonged along Bad River. With the brands that
belonged to the north along the Cheyenne and the
Moreau Rivers as well as those headquartered along
the White River nearby, it was estimated that well over

two hundred different brands could be found in that herd.

Scotty's crew cut out over forty-eight hundred head with Scotty's 7-L and S-7 brands on the left side.[12] Scotty got some real satisfaction from the fact that there were as many cattle here wearing his own brands as there were with the 73, the brand of the Minnesota and Dakota Cattle Company. Some people had hinted that they thought Scotty had come to the end of his rise as a big cattleman when he severed connections with Stuebe and Mullen and the 73. Now they'd have to admit that it was just the beginning for him.

In its meeting that year, the Western South Dakota Stock Growers Association issued a plea for unity between themselves and the Missouri River Stockmen's Association.[13] Scotty was a member of both. He had helped organize the Missouri River group and later had been at the organizational meeting of the larger Western South Dakota group. A year after that he had

South Dakota State Historical Society

Roundup scene.

Rheborg Collection

Rod and Annie Philip, Scotty's two youngest children, taken about 1900.

joined it. Dues were collected by both organizations by means of an assessment of one to four cents per head on the number of cattle each rancher owned. The larger organization felt that too much of the money it should be getting was going to the smaller organizations around the area and that the cattlemen would be stronger if all their memberships were placed under one head.

Scotty was in favor of consolidating the smaller groups, but he wouldn't abandon the group he had helped organize until the members were ready to throw their energy into the large association. The plea of the Western South Dakota Association at their meeting in Rapid City apparently had its effect, for the Missouri River Stockmen's Association gradually melted into the bigger group.

In spite of the good year financially for Scotty, his days were suddenly clouded with grief. His youngest child, Annie, who was now five years old, suffered severe injuries in a fall and died. It was the fourth child Scotty had lost. The other three had all died within a year of their birth and each loss had been hard for Scotty to take. But the loss of Annie hit him hardest. In five years, he had grown very fond of her. Also, being the baby of the family, she had taken over a special corner in the hearts of all the family.

XXIII

THE FALL ROUNDUP gathered a big herd of fat steers wearing Scotty's brands. Scotty decided to ship this year from Evarts. The shipping pens were three quarters of a mile south of the town itself. The town had a few permanent buildings, but it was mostly a tent city. It was on Gene Overholser's ranch and was named for his wife, whose maiden name had been Olive Evarts.

Evarts had two advantages over other shipping points along the river. It had holding pens on both sides of the river and a pontoon bridge which had been constructed this past summer. The bridge was safer than swimming the cattle across the river and faster than ferrying them across. Some of the cattle spooked when they first stepped on the pontoon bridge, but after a few of the gentlest cattle were started across, the others followed.[1]

During the roundup, Scotty had heard that more buffalo had been found along the Cheyenne River. On the way home from Evarts, Scotty and his men rode down the Cheyenne to pick up the buffalo.

They found several being held in a big corral on one ranch, and they started them southeast toward the buffalo pasture. There were a couple of big bulls in the little herd, and somebody made a bantering wager that no two cowboys could rope and hold one of them. Scotty's nephew, George, and a Negro cowboy, Bunk

South Dakota State Historical Society

Cattle being driven over the pontoon bridge at Evarts.

White, one of the best ropers in Scotty's crew, agreed to try it.[2]

It was a contest Scotty wouldn't have missed for the price of the bull. The two boys got their ropes on the big bull at almost exactly the same time. It was a hard fought battle that covered several acres of ground but the boys stayed with their victim, their ponies straining to hold the powerful animal. Eventually the big bull gave up, and the boys triumphantly flipped their ropes free. Neither cowboy volunteered to try it again, however.

More buffalo were brought in from other roundups and put in the buffalo pasture until Scotty eventually had eighty-three animals as a result of his purchase of the Dupree herd from Dug Carlin.[3]

In the fall, Scotty's final payment to Dug Carlin for the buffalo and the cross breeds was due. Scotty sent word to the bank in Pierre to send the money over at the first opportunity.

Buffalo in Scotty Philip's buffalo pasture.

Scotty was in Fort Pierre when young Ernest
Senechal, son of the river boat captain, Ed Senechal,
delivered a package to him from the bank. Scotty could
see that the boy had no idea what the package contained. He got a good laugh at the expression on
Ernest's face when he told him the package contained
ten thousand dollars.[4]

Some things were not amusing to Scotty, however.
After President Theodore Roosevelt's decree that all
fences had to come down on public lands, the interest
of the homesteaders had perked up.[5] Scotty expected
the next spring to bring a flood of settlers onto the open
prairies. They would take big bites into the open range
Scotty had been using.

A new ferry boat had taken the place of the old "Jim Leighton." It was named the "Scotty Philip." Scotty was flattered and proud of the gleaming white boat. It was busier than the old "Jim Leighton" had been because the settlements on both sides of the river were growing rapidly.

As Scotty had expected, homesteaders swarmed onto the prairies west of the river in the spring of 1903. The outlook for the big ranchers like Scotty would have been even darker if it hadn't been for the groundwork that Scotty's friend, Ed Lemmon, had done the year before in Washington when he talked to his friend and one time ranching neighbor, Teddy Roosevelt.

Lemmon had gone to Washington to protest the decree that all fences come down on government land. He didn't get a change in that decree, but he did get the president to sanction the opening of the South Dakota reservations to lease by the ranchers. The Interior Department had approved cattle leases on reservation land in some parts of the country as far back as 1891.

Ziemann Collection

"Scotty Philip" at Fort Pierre dock with the city of Pierre in the background.

But South Dakota had remained closed. It had been too soon after the Messiah Craze and the battle of Wounded Knee.

Ed Lemmon secured one of the first leases on the Standing Rock Reservation. That opened the door for other leases and Scotty was not blind to the possibilities of this. Scotty put in a bid on the Lower Brule Reservation. It was closer to his ranch at Fort Pierre than any other reservation, and he expected big outfits from Montana to Texas to bid on the larger tracts of land such as the Cheyenne River and the Pine Ridge Reservations.

Henry Hudson, foreman of the 73 since Scotty had stepped down as manager, told Scotty that the Minnesota and Dakota Cattle Company was bidding on a section of the Cheyenne Reservation. About three and a half cents an acre seemed to be the price most ranchers expected to pay for their leases. That was cheap grass, considering the price of beef. With the homesteaders flocking into the country and plowing up the prairie, a few cents an acre lease on grassland was a good deal for the cattlemen.[6]

With Si Hiett as his foreman, Scotty still ran cattle on open range near both his ranches. But every week, it seemed, a new tract of land he had been pasturing, especially along Bad River, was claimed by a homesteader and either fenced off or plowed up.

Scotty's buffalo were becoming quite an attraction for the nearby town of Pierre. There were more people in Pierre who had never seen a buffalo than there were who had. With the buffalo ranging down on the side hills close to the river in their fenced-in pasture, people on the river could usually see some of them.

It was as natural as sunshine after rain that someone would think of the idea of running excursion boats up the river, carrying people who wanted to see buffalo. It became a great tourist attraction that made good profit for the boat owners.

Scotty received notice that his bid for a lease on a section of the Lower Brule Reservation had been accepted. This reservation was downstream from Fort Pierre about forty miles. Scotty lost no time in moving some of his cattle down to this grass.

Most of the Indians on this reservation stayed in a small area close to the agency as they did on most reservations. Their main interest was in their allotments which came each month. What happened to their grassland was of little importance to them.

In spite of the dwindling of the open range, Scotty decided on one more trip into Texas and Old Mexico to buy cattle. He was sure he could find enough grass to fatten them up in the summer, then sell that fall at a good profit.

He boarded the train in Pierre and rode down the river to Omaha then on to Kansas City. There he made a side trip to St. Louis where the Louisiana Purchase Exposition was being prepared for the next year. He discussed with officials the possibility of bringing fifty head of buffalo to the big fair the next year and received enthusiastic support.[7]

Back in Kansas City, he was interviewed by a reporter before he went on south to buy his cattle. In writing up the story, the reporter called Scotty "the genuine buffalo man of the United States."

The interviewer asked Scotty why he admired the buffalo enough that he would go to such lengths to preserve the species. He quoted Scotty's reply.

"I have watched buffalo under all the conditions of their life. I have discovered many interesting things about the animal. I used to wonder how the comparatively delicate calves could withstand the terrible blizzards which occasionally sweep over our country, but now I know how it is done. When a storm comes, the

Doug Philip Collection

Buffalo on Scotty's ranch, showing some of the fence in the foreground.

buffalo form themselves into a triangle with the bulls along the sides — the boss bull standing at the apex facing the storm. Then the cows range themselves inside the lines of bulls and in the well protected center the calves and yearlings find their place. The mass is crowded well together into a warm and living whole, and even in the case of the outline of bulls only one side of any animal is presented to the blizzard.

"The herd will maintain this triangle so long as the storm lasts, and they are able safely to weather a storm that would kill our native cattle. There is something heroic in the stoicism with which the bulls will keep their places no matter how the storm may rage, and anyone who has seen the boss bull doggedly holding his head against a Dakota blizzard as he stands at the apex of the triangle will carry away a lot of admiration for the instinct and sacrifice. If a man wants to get a fine lesson in the advantage of 'standing together' he need only watch a buffalo herd in stormy weather."[8]

The article reported that there were fewer than a

thousand buffalo left alive on the North American continent, and by far the largest single herd belonged to Scotty Philip.

Scotty had about thirty thousand head of cattle on his South Dakota range now, and he bought another ten thousand head in the south. But he knew that this was going to be the last year he could run such numbers of cattle.

When he got back to South Dakota, more land had been fenced off by homesteaders, and he wondered if he'd find enough grass for his forty thousand head of cattle this summer. His Lower Brule Reservation lease was off limits to homesteaders, but it would handle only so many cattle. The size of the herd he had grazing on the open prairies would have to be cut down considerably next summer to fit the size of the available range.

Among the more than sixty hired hands that Scotty had on his payroll now was his stepson, Posey Moran. Posey, whose real name was Louis,[9] lived on the Cheyenne River Reservation with his wife, a full blooded Indian. He was a good rider and made a good hand in Scotty's crew.

When the Native Cattle Company, in which Scotty was a shareholder, found itself in need of a man to look after the three thousand head of cattle it ran on the range north of Scotty's old Bad River ranch, Scotty put in a good word for his friend, Tom Jones. Jones had been in some of Scotty's roundup crews and had worked as a regular hand on several ranches, often as foreman. Tom also had his own herd in addition to being in charge of Dick Mathieson's herd. Tom Jones accepted the job with the Native Cattle Company, whose brand was ZT, since it fit in with the work he was already doing.

Although Scotty trusted his foreman, Si Hiett, he was never surprised at any of the things that happened

Posey Moran, Scotty's stepson, on the right, Babe La Plante on the left.

to him. It seemed to Scotty that Si got into twice as much trouble as an ordinary cowboy, much of it of his own making.[10]

There was the time that summer when Si went to Fort Pierre for a load of supplies, including some sacks of lime. His team ran away as he left town, and he was thrown over the seat of the wagon and landed on the sacks. The sacks broke, and Si was liberally covered with the lime. He quickly forgot his anger at the horses and threw himself out of the wagon, running to a water trough to wash off the lime. He escaped without any serious burns from the lime, but he became the butt of many jokes when he told the story at the ranch.

Ralph Jones Collection

Tom Jones with chuck wagon.

Scotty was quite familiar with Si's love for the bottle, but this time he didn't blame whiskey for Si's trouble. If Si had been drunk, he might not have reacted as quickly as he had in getting the lime washed off.

Scotty did blame the bottle for the total failure of Si's trip to Sioux City. Si had gone down on the train with a car load of horses to sell. He had four hundred dollars in his pocket, just in case it took him a while to make a deal for the horses. He didn't want to be caught without a little cash. There were always games of chance and other attractions in a town the size of Sioux City. A man without any cash was a sad specimen in a place like that.

Si came home a few days later without either the horses or the four hundred dollars. He might have escaped a great deal of bantering if he had simply come home empty handed. But he had a nanny goat in the baggage car, the end result of some whiskey-fogged

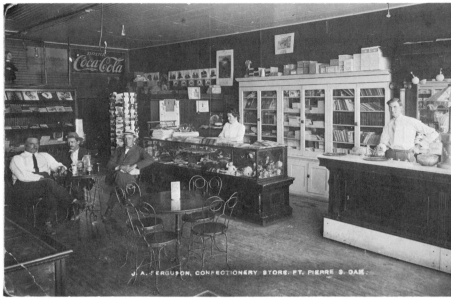

A confectionery store in Fort Pierre. Scotty Philip is seated at left.

trading. Si himself had no idea how he had ended up with a nanny goat. He never lived down the story about how he had gone to the big town and showed the city slickers that nobody could get his goat.

Scotty shrugged off Si's escapades because he was a good man when he was sober and on the back of a horse. Even Andrew Feeney, sheriff of Stanley County now,[11] accepted Si Hiett for just what he was: a carefree, hard working cowhand with plenty of good qualities. He lost those qualities only when he got hold of a bottle, which everyone, even Scotty, agreed was entirely too often.

Scotty bought some property in Fort Pierre, using some of the money that he would rather have put back into more cattle. But the cattle business was going to be squeezed into smaller operations, and he knew it. So he turned to other investments. As a director of the Stock Growers National Bank in Fort Pierre, he kept a finger on the financial pulse of the area, and he could plainly see the end of the big cattle operations on the open range. This foresight made him pull in his horns before they got nipped, and thus he survived the transition of the country from cattle to agriculture better than those who couldn't or wouldn't admit it was coming.

XXIV

DURING THE SUMMER, Scotty's friends often asked for a closer look at the buffalo herd. When they came to his ranch where his family lived during the summer, Scotty took them out to the pasture in a buckboard. While most visitors were content to stand on the outside of the six foot high woven wire fence and stare at the shaggy animals inside, occasionally there was one who was more venturesome. If the buffalo were some distance from the fence, he wanted a closer look. More often than not, Scotty was willing to oblige.

He would open the gate and drive his buckboard or cart inside. The buffalo usually just turned away from the vehicle as it approached and lumbered over the hill. But occasionally a big bull would take offense at the intrusion and shake his head as a warning.[1]

Scotty learned to recognize the signs and to beat an undignified retreat. But often there was no more than an instant between a warning and decisive action on the part of the bull. A big buffalo bull could make kindling out of a buckboard or cart in just a short time. Scotty had been put afoot more than once in the pasture when a bull decided to show him who was boss of that domain.

Usually the bull was satisfied to butt and trample the vehicle into fine pieces while the occupants of the wagon and the horses made a hasty retreat to the gate. Still Scotty considered some of his escapes close ones.

Rheborg Collection

Left to right: Clara Philip, Grace Goodsee, Olive Philip, and Scotty behind them.

He lost several carts and buckboards in that pasture. He marked those bulls that destroyed the vehicles for quick extermination. He had to thin out the bull population, anyway.

The buffalo were getting too crowded in the little pasture Scotty had built. He began talking to influential people about getting the government to lease a big section of land to him for a buffalo pasture to preserve the species. Scotty was convinced that if he didn't save the buffalo on his ranch, they could easily become extinct. Nowhere else in the world was there an animal exactly like the American bison, and there weren't many of them left now.

With the summer about over, Scotty helped his nephew, George, get off to the University of Michigan where he enrolled in law school.[2] Scotty found it hard to picture George as a lawyer. In Scotty's eyes, he was an excellent cowhand. On the other hand, a good

Scotty Philip's buffalo.

lawyer in the family could be most convenient once in a while. George liked law but had reached the decision to become a lawyer only after being caught by tricky phrases in some contracts. He vowed to become an expert in legal documents.

After the great influx of settlers in 1903 onto the Dakota plains, many ranchers had to cut down in size or move out. Some settled for a small spread on land they legally owned, obtained through homesteading and purchases. Feeling the pinch down on White River, Mike Dunn, Scotty's brother-in-law, moved to a homestead on the Cheyenne River, then later moved again to a site overlooking the Missouri River, just a short distance from Scotty's ranch north of Fort Pierre.[3]

George Philip, Scotty's nephew, during his college days at the University of Michigan.

George came home for his summer vacation from the University of Michigan, and Scotty let him work part of the time on the Lower Brule Reservation, where Si Hiett was foreman of Scotty's operations.

The fight for a permanent state capitol site was at its hottest this summer of 1904. Scotty was in the thick of it whenever the opportunity afforded itself. He approved of the plan to run excursion boats up the river loaded with important people to see the buffalo herd in Scotty's pasture. These trips were given free in an effort to influence certain people to support the drive to make Pierre the permanent capitol of South Dakota. Elaborate shows were put on for the guests on board these excursion boats each evening.[4]

The ranchers decided on one more big roundup along Bad River which would reach down to the White. Scotty, along with Jim Cox, Dick Mathieson, March Brothers, and W. I. Walker ramrodded the roundup. Walker was a stockholder in the Native Cattle Company, the ZT brand, in which Scotty also had an interest.

They picked Tom Jones for foreman of the roundup.[5] He was the ranch foreman for the Big Pool Wagon, Dick Mathieson's brand. Scotty had very few cattle left along Bad River, but this extensive roundup picked up a few. Jesse Knight ran Scotty's wagon on the roundup.

One of the crews working the roundup had a Mexican cook named Edward Sanchez. He was shot at the Peno stage barn, but no one could prove who did it. Having a good crew member killed left a blight over all the others until the killing was solved.

It was some time later that a man named Bob Adams got too much to drink while at a dance at Morrison's close to Fort Pierre and told how he had killed the cook. With no one else available to do something about it, Scotty had Adams arrested and charged.[6] Later at his trial, he was sentenced to two to fourteen years in the penitentiary.[7]

In the fall, after George had gone back to law school at the University of Michigan, the battle for the permanent site of the South Dakota capitol was finally settled with Pierre the winner.

Scotty sold more cattle than usual that fall because he had to cut down his herd so it fit his range. The only grazing land he could depend on controlling was the land he owned or leased.

The spring of 1905 was warm and wet. Grass started early, and all the ranchers, including Scotty, began spring branding ahead of the usual time. Then on May 5, the weather suddenly changed. The morning was warm and cloudy, but by noon, a cold rain began to fall. Early in the afternoon, a chilling wind sprang up, and the rain turned to big wet snowflakes. These became thicker, and alarm spread through the oldtimers on these plains as they read the signs. This storm could be a tailtwister.[8]

The oldtimers weren't mistaken. For two days the blizzard raged. The snow was so blinding that a man couldn't see an object ten yards away. The cold wind drove the cattle and horses before it. Cowboys couldn't hold the stock and finally gave up, seeking shelter for themselves. The cowboys felt they were lucky to survive, and if one of them had two blankets, he wrapped one around his horse and used the other himself.

The third morning found the storm gone, but so was the chance for a profitable year for most ranchers. Draws and fence corners were piled high with dead sheep and cattle. Some ranchers also lost as many as a hundred horses.

Thousands of sheep and cattle and over a hundred horses were piled up at the foot of the "death wall" in the edge of the badlands. This wall was a cliff that broke off sharply from the plateau, and the animals, drifting with the storm, reached the top of this and stopped, only to be pushed over by those crowding in behind them seeking shelter.[9]

The losses of the ranchers from the Cheyenne River to the Pine Ridge Reservation ran into the millions of dollars. There hadn't been anything like this since the Big Die-Up back in the winter of '87. For some ranchers, the loss in young stock was almost total. Even when the cows survived, the calves didn't. Scotty's cattle had some protection in the hills and breaks along the river, but still his losses were huge.

Ground was broken that spring for the new capitol building in Pierre. The capitol would stand on the hill

*Part of the old Capitol, with the new Capitol under construction
in the background.*

to the northeast of the main part of town and overlook
the city and the river.

Scab showed up in the cattle that summer and dipping vats were constructed all over the range.[10] It was
the worst outbreak of scab in years, and most ranchers
made sure that all their cattle were run through a vat.[11]

June was a wet month. Roundup crews working late
after the spring blizzard were mired down in mud so
deep they couldn't move their wagons. The gumbo
mud balled up between the wheels and the wagon box
until it locked the wheels. Horses sank to their knees in
the mud, even in the grassed-over lowlands. The in-
teriors of rope corrals were churned into knee deep
mire holes.

Dipping was still in progress in some places when
the flood hit in early July. The big rain started on the
second day of the month. Millions of barrels of water
that couldn't be absorbed by the water-soaked plains

South Dakota State Historical Society

Bad River Bridge in Fort Pierre. It was taken out by flood in 1905.

poured down the tributaries into Bad River. The river went on a rampage that was unparalleled by anything ever seen by those who had spent much of their lives on its banks.

Again there were huge livestock losses. Even men drowned. Four men were caught in a flash flood in a draw close to Bad River where they were dipping cattle. They drowned before anyone could reach them.[12]

In Fort Pierre, the water rose quickly and roared through the streets, swamping shacks and rising to the second stories of some of the bigger houses on the low land. Boats that were normally used on the Missouri River were pressed into service, rescuing people from second story windows.[13]

Some of Scotty's property suffered mud and water damage in town, but Scotty had his family out at the ranch north of Fort Pierre where they lived during the summer.

Ziemann Collection

Ann Senechal, wife of Ed Senechal who owned the Missouri River ferries. The town of Philip is in the background.

Shortly after the flood, Ed Senechal, the river boat captain, came to Scotty with an offer to buy twenty head of buffalo. He had made over an old ferry boat into a big barge enclosed with a strong fence. He planned to stage a wild west show on the barge, moving from town to town on the river.[14]

Scotty agreed to let Senechal have a few buffalo since he was getting crowded for space in his buffalo pasture, anyway. He still hadn't heard any favorable word on leasing more land from the government for preserving the buffalo.

They picked out twelve animals and moved them down to Fort Pierre where the show boat was tied up. Senechal had hired fifteen Indians from the Pine Ridge Reservation. His plans were to give exhibitions at river towns all the way down to New Orleans then up both the Red River and the Ohio River.

Scotty decided he wanted to see that show when it was ready. The show boat was named the "City of Fort

South Dakota State Historical Society

"City of Fort Pierre."

Pierre." Scotty's oldest daughter, Emma, and her husband, Peter Joslin, were going along on the voyage down the river with Captain Ed Senechal and his family. The cook, Billy Henrickson, and the watchman, Ray Munson, completed the crew. The show was presented at Fort Pierre the last of August then the boat moved down the river toward Sioux City and Omaha.

The grass had grown tall that summer and when the normal dry weather of fall came, it was prime fuel for prairie fires. Big fires broke out at various spots over the prairie. Some of the fires were started by lightning from the almost rainless electrical storms that swept over the prairies. Occasionally a fire was blamed on a careless homesteader burning trash around his soddy or dugout.

It was the unwritten law of the plains that every ablebodied man must turn out to fight a prairie fire. Some of the fires came in on a high wind from far to the west, and these fires had a wide front by the time the fighters from along the river could get to them.

Fire drags were kept at ranches and camps all over the prairie. These drags were made of asbestos squares held together top and bottom with welded chains. Men on horseback dragged these over the edge of fires, squelching the blaze and leaving only smoldering ashes.[15]

Backfires were started far ahead of the main fire because nobody dared get close to that roaring fury. Strips of sod were plowed across the path of the fire and a backfire set a hundred yards from the plowed ground. This fire burned the grass to the turned-over sod, where it went out because it wasn't big enough to jump the plowed strip. When the main fire swept up to the burned over area, it was supposed to die for lack of fuel. Sometimes the wind was strong enough to carry blazing embers over the burned area and start a new blaze. Fires with this kind of momentum burned until the wind died down or they reached a river too wide to leap across. The fire fighters could only beat out the sides of such a fire and try to keep it from spreading.

Men fighting the fires faced the constant threat of being trapped by a sudden shift in the wind, and Scotty always warned his men about this. Every big fire claimed its victims, human as well as animals.

In late October the show boat came back from down river. Scotty was disappointed when his daughter and son-in-law told him that the boat had gone only as far as Omaha. Their show had done well in Sioux City but nowhere else. In Omaha, Ed Senechal had given up, sold the buffalo, paid off his Indians, and come home, showing a loss for the venture.

That winter, Scotty made a trade with some men in

Ziemann Collection

Elk in Scotty's buffalo pasture.

Elgin, Illinois, sending two buffalo cows and a bull in exchange for three elk. Scotty thought that elk roaming the pasture with the buffalo would be an added attraction.[16]

They had to drive several buffalo to town to get the three they wanted. The pens in town had been reinforced to hold the buffalo. The two cows and the bull were forced into a twelve foot wide heavy crate, and the crate was consigned to the Narrigan Transfer and Dray for transport to the rails at Pierre.

Scotty heard that they had trouble with the buffalo at Elgin, but he had too much trouble with his elk to worry about the buffalo. His six foot high buffalo fence with the two strands of barbed wire on top wasn't enough to discourage the elk from trying to jump over. One did manage to jump part way over and got tangled in the fence and a big drift of snow. Scotty's men had to untangle it and put it back in the pasture.

Scotty placed a high value on his buffalo. When making one shipment of animals to some men in Omaha, he insured them for a hundred and fifty thousand dollars.[17]

XXV

THERE WERE MANY train loads of cattle shipped out from Pierre and Evarts that fall. Ranchers were cutting down on the number of cattle they were holding over as the homesteaders gobbled up more and more of the open range. The railroads, trying to be fair to all shippers, allowed each rancher to send out only one train load of cattle a day. That was approximately four hundred head.[1] Scotty had several train loads to sell so he sent them in small bunches to the shipping pens, never more than eight hundred at a time.

In the spring of 1906, George graduated from law school at the University of Michigan. He immediately set up a law office in partnership with Alvin Waggoner in Fort Pierre. Later Waggoner would move his share of the practice to Philip, but the two would remain partners and work together.

Scotty attended the meeting of the Western South Dakota Stock Growers Association along with many former officers of the Missouri River Stockmen's Association. There had not been a formal merger of the two associations, but very little was ever heard of the Missouri River organization after this. Many credited Scotty with bringing over the members to strengthen the larger organization.[2]

A couple of things happened that summer that Scotty considered important. The railroad bridge that had been started the year before was completed across

*George Philip, Scotty's
nephew, after his gradua-
tion from the University
of Michigan law school.*

the Missouri River.[3] There was no longer any need for
the ferry. With the trains able to cross the river to Fort
Pierre, the ranchers could now load their cattle on the
train on the west side of the river.

Scotty profited in another way. The railroad was
planning to build west to Rapid City as fast as possible.
The crews needed gravel to use in the roadbed for the
rails, and Scotty had that gravel in abundance in the
hills at the south end of his buffalo pasture. He signed a
contract with the railroad company to sell gravel and
the company built a spur line from Fort Pierre out to
the pits to haul the gravel.[4]

Also that summer Scotty secured more land for his
buffalo pasture. Congress passed a special act, with-
drawing thirty-five hundred acres of land from public
entry. This land joined Scotty's buffalo pasture and ran
along the bluffs above the west bank of the Missouri
and out on the prairie behind the bluffs. It was leased
to Scotty for the express purpose of pasturing the native
buffalo. The cost of the lease was fifty dollars a year.[5]

Scotty set about immediately to fence the entire

thirty-five hundred acres buffalo tight. That took a lot of money and labor, but it guaranteed that Scotty's buffalo herd would have room to increase.

Si Hiett, still ramrodding Scotty's cattle interest down on the Lower Brule lease, often came to Fort Pierre to check with Scotty on important matters. On one occasion, Si came to Fort Pierre looking for Scotty and found a place at a local bar instead. Later when he did run into Scotty at the corner of the Stock Growers National Bank where Scotty was a director, he was too drunk to state the purpose of his trip clearly.

Scotty fired him on the spot as he had often done before when he found his foreman drunk. But he always relented when Si sobered up. Si took offense this time and pulled a knife, making a stab at Scotty. The knife blade cut through Scotty's coat and Scotty retaliated instantly with a blow that sent his foreman reeling. Si crashed to the sidewalk, hitting the back of his head a sharp blow, knocking him unconscious.

Scotty immediately picked up his foreman and carried him up the flight of stairs to Dr. Walsh's office and had the doctor look after him. Then he paid the bill.

The next day back on the home ranch, Si recovered from his drunk and wondered why he had such a terrible sore head along with his hangover. He had no recollection of pulling a knife on Scotty or of getting hit in return. Scotty was full of remorse because that was the first time he could remember having hit a man in anger. That anger was gone now, and he sent Si back to his job on the Lower Brule, never letting him know that he had been fired yesterday.[6]

Two local men asked Scotty for permission to try to break some buffalo calves to ride and possibly to work in harness. Bob Yokum[7] and Red Fuller were good men with plenty of patience. Scotty was convinced that it would take unlimited patience to train a buffalo to do anything he didn't want to do. He gave his permission,

Red Fuller with two buffalo calves that he broke to harness.

and the two men started working with some calves that they caught out of the pasture.

The calves were barely past weaning age, and the two men had quite a battle training the calves just to stand still when anchored with a rope. Later they taught them to lead, and Scotty began to have some hope that the men might succeed in their endeavor.

An early fall that year promised a bad winter, and the promise was fulfilled. The first blizzard swept down from the northwest early in November.[8] Shortly after this storm died, another one roared in. It reminded Scotty of the bad winter of '86 and '87.

Scotty's cattle were in good shape because he had plenty of hay stacked for them. The buffalo had no shelter in their pasture, but that didn't worry Scotty. He had seen them weather the worst storms this country could muster.

The big buffalo bulls formed a triangle, heads to the

wind, shielding the cows and calves from the storm.[9]
The cattle, on the other hand, if they weren't protected
by sheds or bluffs, turned their tails to the wind and
drifted, pushing each other over canyon walls or piling
up in fence corners when the leaders couldn't go any
farther.

Scotty thought it was too bad that when the buffalo
and cow crossed, the calf couldn't inherit the natural
sense of the buffalo and the better disposition and meat
qualities of the cow. But it seemed to be the other way
around.

Temperatures dropped near zero in November,
which was too early for cold of that intensity. December brought even colder weather and more storms.
Cattle started drifting with the storms as all grass and
forage disappeared beneath the growing drifts of snow.
Cattle from the Cheyenne River Reservation and even
from up in North Dakota, wandering aimlessly south
and east with the wind, arrived at Scotty's buffalo pasture fence. Not many things would turn cattle drifting
with a storm, but that woven wire fence did. The cattle
slid around the fence, trying always to keep their tails
to the wind.

Most of them stopped at the river. But some ven-
tured out on the ice and went over to the east side.
There they found the hay that the small ranchers and
farmers had stacked for their stock for winter feed. The
starving animals made that hay disappear like snow-
balls in a hot oven. The farmers tried to run them off but
nothing would stop those starving cattle from eating
the hay except a bullet between the eyes.

Scotty couldn't protect his stacks, except the few
that were behind a fence equal to that of the buffalo
pasture. He saw his cattle's winter feed disappear in a
matter of a couple of days, then his cattle joined the
others in drifting south seeking shelter from the
weather and something to eat. Neither was to be found
anywhere on the plains.

Scotty sent a few men to follow the cattle and keep track of as many of them as possible. They were to find feed for them if they could, wherever they were. The cattle couldn't be brought back home as long as the cold north winds were blowing. There was nothing to feed them, anyway, if they were home.

It was a terrible winter for all ranchers on the northern plains. Scotty's losses might have broken a weaker man. But he had fought many rounds with these great plains that promised so much but sometimes dealt from a stacked deck. He had lost many battles, but he was winning the war. He had settled on these plains to make his fortune, and he was succeeding. He wasn't finished yet. He had plans for greater things, and he didn't have the slightest doubt that he would accomplish them.

On one occasion, during some nice weather between storms, some Mexican officials were among the spectators who came out to see Scotty's buffalo in their pasture. They made some condescending remarks about the laziness and slowness of the big animals. A fighting bull of Mexico, they said, would make a fool of a buffalo bull.

Having had the buffalo herd for over five years, Scotty had become intensely proud of the big animals. By nature, he couldn't allow a challenge like this to go unanswered, anyway. He made a stinging reply, and one Mexican retorted angrily that a Mexican fighting bull could whip one of Scotty's shaggy animals with one foot tied.[10] Scotty's answer was equally hot and exaggerated, declaring that the Mexican bull wouldn't last long enough against a buffalo to give the buffalo any exercise.

Bob Yokum, who was working with Red Fuller in trying to train those buffalo calves to work in harness, was formerly from Texas. Yokum operated saloons in both Pierre and Fort Pierre. His nephew, Billy Harral,

South Dakota State Historical Society

Bob Yokum with his trained buffalo.

who worked for him, was also from Texas. They heard of the challenge and took up the argument. They had watched the Mexican fighting bulls in the ring at Juarez on many a Sunday afternoon. After observing Scotty's buffalo for the last few years, they were convinced that they could whip anything on four legs.

Both men knew Tom Powers, one of the proprietors of the famous Coney Island Saloon in El Paso. They talked to Scotty about the idea they had. The result was that, through their connections, a letter was written to Felix Robert, the manager of the bull ring in Juarez, offering to send down a couple of buffalo bulls to challenge the Mexican fighting bulls. The challenge was quickly accepted.

Excitement ran high around Fort Pierre as the news spread about the coming fight. Scotty made preparations to go with the bulls to Mexico. He was confident

that his big buffalo bulls would trample the smaller
Mexican bulls like they would a crippled wolf. He
intended to be on hand to see it happen.

The first job was to reinforce a box car to hold the
two bulls. No ordinary box car would hold the animals
if they got excited. And they would be excited long
before they got inside the car.

The box car was prepared at Pierre.[11] Bob Yokum
was one of the men chosen to go with the bulls because
he knew Felix Robert and because he was as interested
in this fight as any man involved in it.

A heavy crate was built, similar to the one constructed for the three buffalo that had been shipped to
Illinois in exchange for the three elk. Scotty and several other interested men, including Bob Yokum and
his nephew, spent a lot of time choosing the two bulls
they would take to Mexico. They finally settled on a big
eight year old bull and a smaller four year old. They
gave them the names of Pierre and Pierre, Jr.[12]

After much effort, they got the bulls loaded into the
crate. They put the crate on a heavy sled and pulled it
over the snow to the river. The river was covered with a
thick layer of ice so they pulled the sled across to the
special box car waiting at the loading pens in Pierre.
The weather had been very cold since early in
November. Now, the first part of January, the cold had
reached an intensity that matched the severity of the
blizzards that swept down over the land with irritating
frequency.

Scotty planned to take Eb Jones and Bob Yokum
with him on the trip, but a severe blizzard blew out of
the northwest only hours before the scheduled departure of the train. Scotty, thinking of the cattle still at his
ranch and the care they would need in this kind of
weather, decided that he didn't dare leave right now.[13]

Hurrying up to the new law office of his nephew,
George, he asked him if he would go to Mexico in his

Eb Jones

place. It took very little persuasion because George had wanted to go with the bulls ever since he had heard about the proposed fight. He had only a small business as yet because he had opened his office just a few months ago.

This brick building on the corner of Dead-wood Street in Fort Pierre is where George Philip, Scotty's neph-ew, had his law office.

So George Philip, Bob Yokum and Eb Jones left Pierre in a blizzard with the two buffalo bulls. All the pride of Pierre and Fort Pierre went with them. The importance of the battle had grown until it encompassed the entire community. If the buffalo bulls lost their fights in Juarez, it would be a sad homecoming for the adventurers. But only supreme confidence rode with the men on the train as it raced southeast on the blizzard winds.

At Omaha, the buffalo car was switched off on a sidetrack to be picked up by a train on the Rock Island line. The three men got a room at a hotel since the train wasn't scheduled to leave until six thirty the next morning. However, when they went down to the yards in the dark the next morning to take care of the buffalo before the train headed on toward Kansas City, they couldn't find the special car anywhere.

The three men began a frantic search. Half the day was gone before the buffalo car was located on a siding about ten miles from the switching yards where some other train had discovered its mistake in picking up the car and had switched it off on a siding.[14]

They hooked the car onto another train and left Omaha. Toward evening a conductor pointed out the wreck of a caboose that had been the victim of a rear end collision earlier in the day. The conductor explained to them that that caboose was the one they would have been riding if they had not been delayed in finding the buffalo car.

As they left the bad weather belt, people crowded the stations where the train paused. Word of the coming bull fight had spread up and down the line, and people were on hand to cheer or jeer, depending on their personal sentiments. The upcoming fight was going to be followed with keen interest by more people north of the border than any fight ever held in the bull rings of Mexico.

XXVI

THE BULL RING in Juarez was crowded well before time for the bulls to meet in the arena. People from miles around on both sides of the border were crowded into the seats to see what would happen when a gallant Mexican fighting bull challenged the ponderous buffalo bull. It was a prospect that enticed every sporting mind.

The rules governing the fight were reviewed and the bulls put in their pens. Pierre, the eight year old buffalo, was chosen for the first fight. The quickest and fiercest of the Mexican bulls was chosen to oppose him. As honored guests for the occasion, George, Bob Yokum and Eb Jones were put in the presidential box where they could see every move made in the arena.

The day's activities began with the ceremonial parade, led by the matadors. Behind them were the banderilleros and the picadors. All were decked out in their brightest finery, the tinsel and sequins dazzling the eyes of the Americans.[1]

Four regular bull fights were first on the afternoon's program. Yokum had seen these fights often in the past, but it was something new to George Philip and Eb Jones. They understood why the bull was furious enough to kill when they saw the darts jabbed into his withers the moment he appeared at the gate entering the ring.

They didn't like the second act in which the picador

irritated the bull with his spear because three of the picadors' horses were gored to death that afternoon. That didn't set well with any cowboy who loved horses.

After the picadors had their turns, the banderilleros got in their licks before the matadors took over. The Americans were impressed with the quickness and determination of the fighting bulls. But when their Mexican hosts suggested that they might do well to concede defeat for their buffalo bulls before the contest, they laughed off the possibility that any animal Mexico could produce could conquer the mighty king of the prairies.

A murmur of sound from the crowd rose to a roar as the time came for the buffalo and bull fight. The big buffalo, Pierre, was turned into the ring. He had come from the land of blizzards, and the warm sun felt so good to him that he simply walked a short distance into the arena and laid down, contentedly absorbing the warm sunshine. Even the taunting yells of the crowd failed to disturb him.[2]

Then a cheer ripped the afternoon as the other gate was opened and a fighting bull appeared. Two darts were jabbed into his withers to make sure he didn't forget his role once he got into the arena.

He charged into the open and stopped as he spied the buffalo across the arena from him. For a minute he simply stared at the animal, apparently trying to decide just what it was. Then he started toward him.

The buffalo, seeing the Mexican bull coming at him, got up and pawed the ground, warning the other bull to keep his distance. There was no animosity in the buffalo's actions. He would have given the same warning to another buffalo that happened to come too close to him.

But the Mexican bull was not in the mood to take any friendly warnings. He came closer, gaining speed

"The Bull Fight of the Century" – the bull ring in Juarez, Mexico, in January, 1907.

as he advanced. He evidently expected the big buffalo either to retreat or come charging to meet him. Pierre did neither. He simply stood his ground and when the Mexican bull reached him, met him head to head.

The Mexican bull got his first lesson in facts about the buffalo. There are few things attached to living animals harder than a buffalo head. The Mexican bull staggered backward, shook his head, and glared at his adversary. Pierre shook his shaggy head, too, eyeing this intruder on his peaceful afternoon as if he were surprised that such a runt would think he could push him around.

The Mexican bull showed his intelligence by not attacking head on again. He circled warily, evidently expecting the buffalo to keep facing him, at least. But the buffalo practically ignored the other bull. This seemed to infuriate the Mexican bull. He suddenly charged again, this time aiming at the flank of the big buffalo. Those sharp horns would have ripped Pierre's flank and crippled him if they had found their target.

But just before the Mexican bull reached his foe, the buffalo made a move that no Mexican bull had ever seen before. Every bull they had fought in their pasture duels pivoted on their back legs as all respectable bulls did. Not so the buffalo. The bulk of his weight was in his shoulders, so he pivoted on his front legs.[3] His back legs were not weak, though, because he could kick with twice the force of an army mule.

Just as the Mexican bull was about to deliver the fatal blow to the buffalo's flank, Pierre pivoted and let the Mexican bull crash into his head again. The blow sent the Mexican bull reeling to his knees.

Still the buffalo didn't follow up his advantage. He seemed content just to let the other bull know that this was his territory, and he only wanted to be let alone.

The Mexican bull backed off, obviously considering the situation carefully. Then once more he tried a flank attack. He was rapidly gaining respect for that hard head. But as before, the buffalo spun around at the last second and met the other bull head on. This time the Mexican bull went all the way down.

A horrified gasp went up from the spectators. In all their years of watching bull fights they had never seen one of their favorites humiliated. Not even death from a matador's sword carried any disgrace. But to be flattened in the arena by a foe that even disdained to follow up his advantage was more than they could accept.

The Mexican bull refused to accept it, too, and tried once more, circling even farther behind the buffalo before charging. But once again a swift swivel of the huge buffalo's shoulders brought about a head-on crash. Once more the Mexican bull was knocked flat, then ignored by the buffalo.

When the Mexican bull got up this time, he'd had enough, and he began circling the arena, looking for a gate to let him out.[4] The crowd roared its disappointment and anger and in a couple of minutes, the manager, Felix Robert, came to the presidential box and asked George if they could put in another bull. His handlers had just told him the bull in the ring was not feeling well this day; another bull would put up a much better fight.

Feeling the heady confidence of victory, George told him to bring on all the bulls in Mexico if he felt like it.

So the defeated bull was let out of the arena and another bull turned in. This bull was jabbed with the darts and he came into the ring full of fire and fury. He didn't find a buffalo lying down enjoying the sun, but neither did he find an angry foe. To Pierre, this was just another annoyance to be met and disposed of if it got out of hand.

This fight was almost a duplicate of the first one. A third bull was turned in with Pierre with the same result. The arena manager asked to be allowed to try one more bull, apparently feeling that the big buffalo must surely be worn down by now. Permission was granted, and the fourth bull was let in.

By now, the buffalo was becoming annoyed. When the Mexican bull pawed the ground in a defiant challenge, the big buffalo pawed the arena dust in reply.

The Mexican bull came charging straight at the buffalo, and for the first time, the buffalo moved to meet the enemy. The crash when they met made even the Americans in the presidential box wince. But it did more than that to the Mexican bull. He shot backward as if he'd been hit by a freight locomotive. He landed in a heap, and when he got up, he didn't need a second encounter with the buffalo to know that this was just not his day for triumph.

He turned and began circling the arena, his head in the air as he looked for a place in the wall low enough that he could leap over. The spectators watched in horrified silence. They were simply stunned. The only happy customers that day were the Americans who had expected victory for the buffalo but not by such a convincing margin.

As the last bull was let out of the ring, the crowd suddenly voiced its displeasure at the outcome of the widely advertised fight. It appeared to the Americans that things could easily get out of hand. But there was still one event on the program, and anticipation of this slowly calmed the fury of the crowd.

A small fighting bull was turned into the ring. A brass knob was clamped over the end of each horn so he couldn't gore anybody. A small sack was tied with a string to the base of his right horn. The Americans were informed that this sack was filled with money.

A swarm of boys of all ages and sizes rushed into the arena and converged on the bull. The point of the game was to get the sack of money off the bull's horn. The boy who succeeded got to keep the money.

It was a grand melee for a while. The bull snorted and charged the boys, tossing several of them over his back. But they rolled to their feet and returned to the fray, intent on getting that money. One boy got his pants caught on the bull's horns and he took a merciless beating as the bull tried to throw him. But by the time the bull had dislodged him, the boy had the money.[5]

He held the sack high in triumph as he raced for the stands where his parents apparently were watching. All the other boys headed for the gates, too, leaving a perplexed bull in the middle of the arena, snorting and glaring around for another enemy to fight.

Ziemann Collection

The bull ring at Juarez – Eb Jones, third from left, Bob Yokum, third from right, and George Philip, far right.

Although the actual battle between the Mexican bulls and the buffalo had turned out to be a fiasco to the faithful patrons of the bull ring, the financial reward to the owners was just the opposite. George Philip accepted his share of the money, and it more than paid for all the expenses of bringing the two bulls down here from South Dakota.

At the same time, plans were made for a matador to fight the younger buffalo bull at next Sunday's fights. The Americans were confident that the younger bull would do as well against the matador as the older bull had against the fighting bulls. None of the Americans who had seen the buffalo bulls fight in their pasture at home thought that any man would dare face an angry four year old buffalo bull with nothing more lethal than a sword.

A capacity crowd filled the bull ring again on the following Sunday. After the usual parade and ceremonies, the first scheduled fights were between matadors and Mexican bulls. The big fight everyone was waiting for, between their best matador and the buffalo, was the last event.

The very first fight, however, took an unexpected turn. The bull chosen for this fight was one of the four that had been bested the week before by the buffalo. As the bull was ushered into the ring, he was jabbed with the darts but they didn't have the usual effect. The bull came in, looking around the arena for his opponent, and it was obvious to all that he expected the buffalo bull to be there.[6]

After one quick look over the arena, he turned to the wall and began trotting around, his eyes on the top of the wall, looking for a place to escape. No amount of hazing or efforts by the picador could bring him into the middle of the arena to fight. In disgust, the bull was turned out and another brought in. But this, too, was one of the vanquished bulls from the week before. His performance was a duplicate of that of the bull that had gone before him.

With little to cheer about in the early fights, the crowd was ready with all its energy to yell for their favorite matador in his fight with the buffalo bull.

Pierre, Jr., the younger of the two buffalo bulls, was brought into the ring and given the same treatment the Mexican bulls got to make him ready to fight. But the buffalo bull had been cooped up down here in the warm sunshine for a week now, and he was ready for action. After the picador and the banderilleros had pestered the buffalo for a while, Pierre, Jr. was furious.

The matador came on with his red cape, swishing it past the buffalo a time or two.[7] Lacking the quickness of the Mexican bulls, the buffalo wasn't liable to get to the matador, but neither was the matador going to do any damage to the buffalo. If it came to a matter of endurance, the odds were on the side of the buffalo.

The buffalo, matador, and the crowd were just warming up for a long battle when the governor of the province called off the fight.[8] Rage swept through the spectators, but they couldn't overrule their governor. The crowd calmed down when it was announced that all gate receipts would be refunded since there hadn't been one good fight today.

George Philip was convinced that the governor and his advisors had decided, after last week's fiasco, that they didn't want to risk having their best matador humiliated by a buffalo. They were using this excuse, flimsy as it was, to avoid that possibility. George was sure that Pierre, Jr. would have worn down the matador and either killed him or made him admit defeat.

When George tried to take the buffalo bulls back across the border at El Paso, he ran into trouble with the Mexican authorities. Pat Garrett, the man who had put an end to Billy the Kid's murderous career, was then collector at the port at El Paso by appointment of President Theodore Roosevelt.[9] But George's trouble was on the Mexican side of the border, and Garrett couldn't help him.

When it appeared that clearance for the buffalo bulls wasn't going to be granted, George made a deal with an El Paso butcher to buy the animals for two hundred dollars each.[10] The butcher could kill them and bring the carcasses across the border to his shop where he would charge plenty for buffalo steaks. Some of his customers who had been so furious at the buffalo for defeating their prize fighting bulls could now get some measure of revenge by eating the victor.

XXVII

WHEN GEORGE PHILIP and his two companions, Bob Yokum and Eb Jones, returned to Dakota from their Mexican adventure, they stepped right back into the depths of winter. George made a complete report on everything that had happened, making Scotty wish more than ever that he could have gone on that trip. How he would have enjoyed seeing his buffalo bulls run the famous Mexican fighting bulls out of the ring! He would also have appreciated exchanging this timeless world of cold wind and snow for the warm sunshine George described.

But the snow stayed. More blizzards piled the drifts deeper until the cattle could no longer plow through them. It seemed that spring would never come. But the days grew longer, and the snow drifts began to settle.

As the drifts disappeared, they revealed the staggering cost of the past winter. Dead cattle were in every draw and fence corner and even among the trees where ranchers had thought they would be sheltered from the storms. Shelter alone hadn't been enough. The grass was buried, and every edible twig had been chewed up long before the snows melted enough to expose the grass that could have sustained life.

The railroad grade moved west from the place where the snows of early November had stopped it. The rails had started from the river last summer, and now in April of 1907, they were in Midland.[1] As the

South Dakota State Historical Society

Philip, South Dakota.

trains roared west from Fort Pierre, they carried loads of settlers, intent on making their fortunes from the soil.

By June, the rails had reached a spot close to Scotty's old Bad River ranch.[2] A new town sprang up there and was named Philip, in honor of the most famous rancher along Bad River. The post office of Philip was moved from Dr. Weikoff's ranch into the new town.[3]

Rheborg Collection

Main Street, Philip, South Dakota.

In spite of the winter's loss, Scotty felt optimistic about the future of the cattle business. Fat steers were bringing around forty-five dollars a head, which was ten dollars more than the price a year ago.[4] In spite of his losses, Scotty's herd was worth more money now than it had been last year.

Scotty was doing well in the real estate business since so many people were pouring into the country. He and his partners, Young and McPherson, had the oldest real estate business in Stanley County. He was still a director of the Stock Growers National Bank. These jobs, in addition to overseeing his big ranch, allowed Scotty few idle moments.

During that summer, part of the Lower Brule Reservation was opened to homesteading, and settlers swarmed in. The land Scotty leased, however, was not included in the portion opened to settlement.

Bob Yokum and Red Fuller continued to work with their buffalo calves. Since the calves had been around people all their lives, they lacked the fear and animosity that characterized some of the older buffalo.

Scotty was amazed at the progress the two men were making. They had first broken the calves to ride, but they admitted that buffalo weren't about to replace saddle horses. The calves were rough riding and stubborn in their choices of speeds and directions.

Harness was made to fit them, using collars like horses rather then yokes. There were some gay runaways as the men tried to teach the buffalo to answer the tug of the reins and listen to commands of the drivers. Eventually the calves learned to respond. Hooked to a cart in the summer or a sled in the winter, they made passably good work animals. They were seldom used for anything but exhibitions, giving people pleasure rides.

Frequent excursion trains ran up to the edge of the buffalo pasture where passengers could see the buf-

Ziemann Collection

The Scotty Philip cigar, sold all over the United States.

falo. These trains ran on the track used by the railroad
to haul gravel from Scotty's pits. Scotty liked to be at
the pasture when the trains came. Most of the visitors
were getting their first look at a buffalo, and Scotty
found that, after seeing the shaggy animals, they were
interested in hearing everything about them.

Scotty looked forward to the fall roundup to find out
how well he had done for the summer. But when time
came for the roundup down on the Brule Reservation,

Scotty's nephew, George Philip, on the right. At left is Gaylord Hudson.

he discovered that his foreman, Si Hiett, was in Sioux City on one of his big benders. It could be days before he sobered up and returned.

Scotty was not one to put off doing anything if there was a way to get it done immediately. He went into Fort Pierre, an idea in his head, but he knew he'd have to handle things carefully if he was to be successful.

He dropped into the law office of his nephew, George, as if on a casual visit. George was idling away his time, waiting for a client. Scotty made the remark that George looked peaked; he should get out into the sunlight for a day or two. He asked George if he had his saddle, and George admitted that it was handy.

At Scotty's suggestion, George threw his saddle into the back of Scotty's buggy, and they headed out of town, following the river to the southeast. Not until they reached the Lower Brule Reservation did Scotty tell George what he had in mind.

With Si Hiett out of action, Scotty informed George that he was to ramrod the roundup until Si returned. After some hesitation, George agreed. His law practice in Fort Pierre had not built up to the point yet where his partner couldn't handle it for a few days. Besides, he liked the work of a roundup.

As foreman, George set up a camp and got the men busy bringing in the cattle. Just before dark, Scotty drove his buggy into camp after completing an inspection tour. He got the surprise of his life when George ordered him out on first guard duty around the newly gathered herd. His first reaction was to remind George who owned these cattle and hired these men. But then he remembered the code of the roundup. The foreman is top boss, even over the owner.

So Scotty got a horse and rode guard around the herd. He didn't ride much any more, and this was both exhilarating and tiring. Soft muscles complained. But it

Ralph Jones Collection

Catching horses for the day's work on roundup.

brought back memories of the years when he had spent
up to twenty hours a day in the saddle. Two hours
weren't going to kill him now.

It was a dark night, threatening storm, and before
Scotty's two hours were up, lightning began zigzag-
ging across the sky and thunder rolled heavily. Just as
the rain began to fall, Scotty saw George leading the
rest of the crew out from camp. The cattle, unused to
their bedding grounds, were up and moving around
restlessly. A terrific clap of thunder just as George
arrived sent the herd rumbling away.

George shouted the order to let the herd run. Scotty
objected, yelling that they could stop the stampede.
But George ignored him. Once more, Scotty bowed to
the code of the roundup. He had put George in charge;
he had to abide by his orders now.

The men followed the stampeding herd and after a
short run, the cattle stopped and broke into bunches to
look for grass. The men gathered on the crest of a hill to
discuss the task of rounding up the cattle again.

Sore from the unaccustomed hours in the saddle,
Scotty declared he was going back to camp. As he
started his horse down the slope, his nephew called to
him that he was going the wrong way. Scotty, who
prided himself in knowing his directions, argued that
he was right.

During the argument, the clouds began to break
and the Big Dipper appeared, proving that George was
correct. Scotty was in no mood to admit defeat.

"To hell with the Big Dipper," he grumbled. "I still
think I'm right."[5]

Scotty went back to Fort Pierre in his buggy the
next morning before George could put him to work
again. But in late September, he returned to see how
the roundup was coming. He took the buckboard this
time with Bull Marshall, a half blood Indian, driving
for him. Scotty admired Marshall's skill with a team
and often had him drive his buckboard or buggy.

After spending the night on the reservation, they began checking the cattle that had been rounded up. At a corral near the mouth of Medicine Creek, Scotty got out of the buckboard to look over some cattle being held there. When he was almost to the corral, a rattlesnake struck him. If the snake had rattled a warning, Scotty hadn't heard it.

The snake sank its fangs into the calf of Scotty's leg. Scotty leaped back, but he knew he'd been hit hard. Bull Marshall helped Scotty back to the buckboard where he tied a cloth around Scotty's leg above the puncture wounds, then took a stick and twisted it into the cloth, pulling it tight, trying to keep the poison from circulating through Scotty's body.

The first remedy for snake bite that most men of the plains thought of was whiskey. No one could say exactly how it helped a person bitten by a rattler, but at that time all agreed it was the best thing to do until a doctor could be reached.

Scotty was on an Indian reservation, however, where whiskey was banned. That fact didn't dismay the half breed, Bull Marshall. Leaving Scotty in the buckboard, he ran to an Indian shack close by. In record time, he was back with a bottle half full of whiskey.

Scotty was not a drinker, but like all plainsmen, he knew the accepted cure for snake bite, so he took a drink of the whiskey. Bull Marshall whirled the team around and started his run for the nearest doctor, which was in Fort Pierre.

Word traveled fast on the reservation. Before they got off the Indian land, they were stopped a couple of times and offered fresh bottles of whiskey. It seemed that whiskey grew magically in the grass of the Lower Brule.

Bull Marshall got the maximum effort out of the buckboard team. Scotty, fortified by the whiskey, found it hard even to remember he'd been bitten, much less worry about it. Marshall showed his skill with horses by covering the forty miles to Fort Pierre in record time without ruining the horses.

Just as the weary team pulled up in front of the house, Scotty's nephew, George, rode up. George had just come home from the roundup a few days ago, after turning the foreman job over to Si Hiett when he staggered in from Sioux City. At this moment, George was on his way home after being out rather late. When he saw the buckboard, he dashed after it in alarm, demanding to know what was wrong.

"I'm snake bit and drunk," Scotty informed him in slurred words.

George helped Bull Marshall get the big man out of the buckboard and up the hill to his house. There Sally helped get him in bed while George sent one of the boys for Dr. Walsh.

"I believe I'll get over the snake bite all right," Scotty said, once he was in bed, "but oh, Lord, when I start to get sober!"[6]

Dr. Walsh arrived and lanced the wound. Scotty's prediction was close to the truth. His hang-over was more painful than the effects of the snake bite. He was a healthy man, and he threw off the poison with little trouble.[7]

Scotty was up and around in time to see his potato crop harvested from the rich bottom land on his ranch.[8] He gathered approximately twenty-five hundred bushels; enough, according to one observer, to feed the town of Fort Pierre through the winter.

In late October, Scotty and a man named Barker formed a company to dig a well for an indoor swimming pool.[9] This 'plunge' was to be on the lots adjoining Scotty's home in Fort Pierre.

Scotty was a shareholder in the new Northwestern Hospital that was opened in Fort Pierre the first of January in 1908.[10] This was a great achievement for the

*Deadwood Street in Fort Pierre at approximately the time
of Scotty's death.*

town, and Scotty was proud of it. In April, the name was
changed to the Fort Pierre Hospital.[11]

That spring Scotty sold his interest in the Native
Cattle Company when it marketed most of its cattle and
moved the rest from its range north of Bad River to the
Cheyenne River Reservation. Tom Jones, who had
been range foreman for the company, stepped out.[12]

Scotty had other plans for his friend, Tom Jones.
Although some of the Lower Brule Reservation had
been opened to homesteading, most of it was still
available for lease. Tom Jones was looking for land,

*Tom Jones and his wife
Clara.*

Rheborg Collection

Emma Philip with Ann Garrow in the aspen grove.

Rheborg Collection

Ann Garrow, left, with Clara Philip. Taken in Scotland during Clara's visit there.

and he and Scotty went into partnership, leasing every acre of the Lower Brule Reservation that was available.

Si Hiett, Scotty's foreman on the Lower Brule for the last few years, decided to return to the Cheyenne River where he had an offer from the Turkey Track Cattle Company.[13] So Scotty's operations on the Lower Brule underwent a big change in 1908. But with Tom Jones, an expert cattleman, as a partner, he saw nothing but profitable days ahead for him in the cattle business.

Scotty was a member of the Masonic Lodge in Fort Pierre. Though a bit unusual in Masonry, he belonged to both the Scottish Rite Bodies at Yankton and the Chapter and Commandery at Pierre. He was also a member of the Shrine at Sioux City.

Four other men had received their Scottish Rite degrees from Yankton Masons at Pierre at the same time Scotty did. One was Governor Andrew Lee; another was Alex C. Johnson, who later made a big name for himself with the Chicago and Northwestern Railroad. The other two were also very prominent men in Fort Pierre, Dr. C. J. Lavery and George D. Mathieson.[14]

Although 1908 was a good year for Scotty, it ended on a tragic note. His oldest living daughter, Emma, who was married to Peter Joslin, suffered a heart attack following surgery at the new Fort Pierre Hospital. She died on the second day of December when she was only twenty-seven years old. On Monday, the 7th of December, her funeral was held in the Episcopal Chapel and the burial was in the aspen grove north of town.

This was another heart-breaking experience for Scotty. Emma was the fifth of his ten children that he had seen laid away. He had three girls and two boys left, ranging from Olive, who was twenty-five, to Roderick, who was only fourteen.

After the funeral, Scotty found it hard to return to

Rheborg Collection

Olive Philip, left, and her sister Hazel with an unidentified man.

normal living. Half his family was gone, and Scotty himself was only fifty years old. He wanted to do something to commemorate these children he had lost.

An idea struck him one day when he was visiting the graves of his daughters who were buried here on the Missouri River. He would choose a peaceful site overlooking the river and lay out a cemetery plot. The plot would be enclosed with a cement curb and a strong fence. Then he would gather the caskets of all his children and bring them to this plot, erecting a headstone for each. He would make it a fitting memorial. When he and Sally and the other children died, they would be buried here, too. They would all be together in death, even if they had never been together in life. Three of his children had died before the younger ones were born.

As the year ended, Scotty found some consolation in his plans.

XXVIII

SCOTTY BEGAN WORK on his cemetery immediately. He had big plans, and he knew it would take time to complete them, but eventually he would have things the way he wanted them.

He made arrangements for help in bringing his children from the places where they had been buried to his new cemetery north of Fort Pierre. But he couldn't find the grave of his oldest daughter, Mary. Mary had died on the trail before they reached Bad River, and neither Scotty nor Sally could recall exactly where the grave had been dug. The fact that he couldn't find Mary's grave was a bitter disappointment to Scotty.

With the four graves together in his new cemetery plot, Scotty began work on the curbing and iron fence around the plot. He ordered a big stone marker. Set on a cement base in the center of the plot, the monument appeared to be in three sections. The lower part and the top section, which protruded out over the center, were both white. The center was of darker stone. The word 'PHILIP' stood out in big raised letters on the white lower section.[1]

Scotty had plans for some trees at the corners of the plot, and there was some landscaping to be done. But he resolved to get it just the way he wanted it before he invited anyone to come and see it.

As he looked at the four graves, Scotty often re-

flected about how much sadness had been mingled
with his joy of success.

There were spots on the Lower Brule Reservation
that were so far from a creek or river that Scotty and his
partner, Tom Jones, contracted to have some wells
drilled and windmills put up, reasoning that if the
cattle didn't have to walk so far for water, they'd put on
more weight.

Scotty never lived down the story they told about
his reaction when one of the men working on the drill-
ing crew raced into Fort Pierre to report to Scotty that
the driller had hit oil instead of water.

Scotty had an immediate reply. "Tell him to dig
deeper. The cattle can't drink that 'dommed' stuff." An
oil well on his own land might have been welcomed by
Scotty, but down on the leased land of the reservation,
all he wanted was water for his cattle.[2]

Rheborg Collection

*Stanley Philip at left
and Rod Philip, right.*

Scotty's niece, Ann Garrow, came from Scotland for a visit that fall. She had never seen a roundup, so Scotty invited her to the Lower Brule to watch some of the fall roundup there.

He took a good tent, so his niece could keep warm and dry in case the weather turned bad. Scotty himself had no aversions to the comforts of a snug tent during a rain storm, either.

Shortly after they arrived at the roundup site, a storm did strike. Scotty and his niece got inside the tent only moments before the rain began. The storm had all the elements of the typical prairie shower: thunder, lightning, wind and dashing rain.

The crew had a big herd of steers rounded up ready to trail to the railroad for shipment to market. Scotty paced the ground inside the tent, worrying that the herd might stampede and run off many valuable pounds. A bad stampede could cost a man a big share of his summer's profits.

"Don't worry, uncle," his niece said. "Place your trust in the Lord. He'll take care of everything."

"All right," Scotty agreed reluctantly. "I'll trust Him a little bit, but most of it I'm placing in Tom Jones."[3]

When the roundup was complete, Scotty and his partner found that their year on the Lower Brule had been a profitable one. They made even bigger plans for the next year.

All of Scotty's cattle operations went well. It was hard for him to recall those hard days when his liabilities had far exceeded his assets. He had a partner in Tom Jones who was wise in the ways of cattle and a man Scotty completely trusted. Their partnership was a profitable one.

The buffalo herd continued to grow and, until the railroad abandoned upkeep of the gravel pit spur, excursion trains came out almost daily to let visitors see

Race between two of Scotty's buffalo trained by Bob Yokum.

the shaggy animals. The trained buffalo calves were big enough now that they were in demand for every parade in the area. Red Fuller and Bob Yokum drove their buffalo teams and carts in the parades and took the venturesome for rides. Two of the buffalo calves which had been broke to ride were raced against each other and created far more excitement than any horse race.

Scotty became intrigued with the automobiles showing up on the streets of Pierre. He traveled in a buggy or a buckboard with high stepping horses, but compared to an automobile, they were slow. A car, he reasoned, would save a lot of time. So, having decided that, he bought one of the first cars to be used much outside town.

His big problem now was learning how to operate the vehicle. He was first taught how to start and stop the car, and he didn't bother to learn much more. He seldom stopped the car without yelling "Whoa!," sometimes at the top of his voice if he forgot to apply the brake and the car didn't stop as ordered.[4]

He found ways of avoiding any unnecessary stops. He usually had someone riding with him, and when he arrived at a pasture gate, instead of stopping, he would wheel the car into a big circle while the man with him had to hop out on the go and open the gate. Scotty would then bring the car around, shoot it through the gate, then go into another big circle while his man shut the gate and caught onto the car as it went past.

In town Scotty often had trouble getting the car stopped where and when he wanted to. He just "couldn't do a 'dommed' thing with it." Yet he used the car a great deal because it saved him so much time. And Scotty had many things to do.[5]

The state capitol building was completed in 1910, and Scotty was as proud of it as if he owned it himself. It cost eight hundred thousand dollars, and that was a lot of money, even in Scotty's estimation. That same year, the St. Charles hotel was built only a few blocks down the hill from the capitol. It was the fanciest building in town, with the exception of the capitol itself.

The spring of 1911 was dry. On the thirtieth of May, Scotty's nephew, George, was married to Isle Waldron, daughter of George Waldron, one of Scotty's old neighbors out on Bad River. George seemed almost like a son to Scotty, an older brother to Stanley and Roderick.

The drought that hit the land revived Scotty's dream of irrigating the meadows on the river bottom. Selecting a site close to his ranch north of Fort Pierre, Scotty made plans to pump water out of the Missouri and ditch it out over his meadows. There were billions of gallons of water racing past, doing nobody any good. Scotty couldn't bear to see it wasted. Searching through catalogs, he decided what engine and equipment he would need and sent off his order for them.[6]

In the meantime, he got another project under way.

Isle Waldron, the bride of George Philip, Scotty's nephew.

For some time he and Sally had been talking about a new house. They had a nice place in town to live in the winter, but the house on the ranch north of town was getting old. Scotty liked the old house with its porches that ran along three sides, but a new house would be more in step with his current needs. Scotty felt that he had finally attained the fortune he had dreamed of getting when he sailed from Scotland. It was time now to use some of it for his own comfort.

The site Scotty and Sally chose for their new home was just below the cemetery where four of their children lay. It was at the edge of the buffalo pasture on a high rise of ground with a commanding view of the valley for miles up and down the Missouri. Three miles to the southeast was Fort Pierre, and across the river, the capitol building in Pierre was clearly visible from

The interior of Scotty's town home.

the new home site. Scotty was convinced there wasn't a prettier building site anywhere along the river.

He completed the plans for the house, then went into town and carefully selected the lumber, making sure it was free of knots. Then he followed the first load of lumber out to the site where the house was to be built.

The irrigation machinery came in, and he hired men to freight it up the river to the place where water would be pumped out onto the meadows. It was a happy summer for him. He was getting a great deal of satisfaction out of being able to buy what he needed to put the frosting on his dream.

Now Scotty turned again to the task of completing the cemetery plot. He had the stone in place, and the iron railing was set in the cement curbing. When he

Doug Philip Collection

Scotty Philip cemetery about 1920.

had cleaned and leveled the ground inside the curbing, gently mounding the four graves, and set out some
trees, he finally had the cemetery plot finished to his
satisfaction.

On Saturday evening, the 22nd of July, Scotty drove
his car into Fort Pierre to announce proudly that his
cemetery plot was finished.[7] He had been talking
about the work he was doing for over a year, but he
hadn't invited anyone out to see it. He wanted it completed before they got a look. It was done now, and he
made the rounds of the places where he knew he could
find his friends in town that Saturday night and invited
them all out to see his handiwork.

After getting assurances from his friends that they
would be out soon, perhaps tomorrow, to see his
cemetery, Scotty headed his car north toward his old
ranch house where the family was staying during the
summer. He had to cross Indian Creek to get to his
house. There was no bridge, just the ford that he had

Scotty Philip in the aspen grove southwest of the cemetery.

driven teams across hundreds of times. But a wagon
ford didn't always make a good crossing for a car, although he had put his car across it several times.

Tonight, however, the car stalled in the edge of the
creek, its wheels spinning in the mud. Scotty had to
work several minutes to get the car's wheels up where
they could get traction. It was only by hard work and
the sheer strength of his big frame that he got the car
moving again and drove it on home.

But the damage had been done. Whether it was
damage caused by the exertion of getting the car out of
the creek or from some other cause, no one could tell.
The cause was not important; the effect was. He was
struck down about seven o'clock Sunday morning, July
23rd, by a cerebral hemorrhage.

Dr. Walsh was called. It was the doctor's duty a
little later to announce to a stunned community that
Scotty Philip was dead at the age of 53.[8]

It was a funeral that Fort Pierre would never forget. The services were held at the ranch home on Wednesday afternoon, July 26. From there the procession made its way slowly to the cemetery which Scotty had just completed to his satisfaction a few days before.

Friends who had promised to come and see his cemetery were there. But these were not the circumstances under which they had hoped to view Scotty's handiwork. Even these special friends found it hard 'not to get lost in the huge throng that had gathered.

In preparation for the funeral, Scotty's good friend, Alex Johnson, one of the men who had received the Scottish Rite with him in Pierre and now a high official in the railroad company, had examined the tracks of the spur line railroad had laid out to the gravel pit on Scotty's land. The railroad was no longer using the gravel, so the track had been allowed to deteriorate. Alex Johnson quickly put men to work repairing the grade, replacing ties and fastening down rails.

On the day of the funeral, the line was solid again, and a special train was run out on this line, which came very close to Scotty's cemetery. On this train were more dignitaries than were usually found in a president's entourage.[9]

Besides railroad officials, there were governors, senators, and other high government officials, and as room would allow, bankers, commissionmen, and merchants. All were given free passage to the funeral as the railroad's gift to Scotty's memory.

There were cattlemen present from near and far. The Bad River ranchers were there in nearer perfect attendance than any important meeting had ever been able to draw them. Ranchers from the Cheyenne River to the north and the White River to the south stood there in the hot sun, their heads bared, tears trickling unashamedly down their cheeks.

Indians, who had always found Scotty to be a good

Mitchell Collection

George and Isle Philip in Scotty's car. Scotty got this car stuck the night before he died.

friend, were there from the Pine Ridge, Rosebud, Lower Brule and Cheyenne River Reservation. Cowboys, many of whom had worked for Scotty and many who only knew him from what they had heard, stood there that day, hats in hands. There were enough of them present to have handled the roundup of a hundred thousand head of cattle.

The pall bearers who carried the casket up from the hearse to the grave were all long time friends of Scotty's. Louis LaPlant, who had the ranch downstream on the Bad River from Scotty's ranch where Scotty had spent many a day watching races and even racing his own horses; George D. Mathieson, another ranching neighbor, and Dr. Charles J. Lavery, both of whom were with Scotty and Alex Johnson when they received the Scottish Rite in Pierre; Tex Hemphill; W. H. Frost; Fred S. Rowe.[10]

But perhaps the most significant onlookers who came to pay their last respects to this great man were the buffalo that Scotty had saved from extinction. Hundreds of them, attracted perhaps by the huge crowd gathered at the cemetery just outside their high fence, came slowly and quietly down from the hills to the north and west and bunched up on the hillside directly above the cemetery.

There they stood motionless during the graveside services. When the ceremonies were over, and the coffin slowly lowered into the grave, the buffalo turned almost as one and moved slowly and again without any sound back over the hill and out of sight.[11] Spoken words could not have expressed it more eloquently — the greatest man in their lives was dead.

The multitudes who knew Scotty found the words and they said the same thing. A great man had died.[12]

EPILOG

PRACTICALLY EVERY NEWSPAPER in South Dakota and many outside the state carried an obituary of Scotty Philip. Until then, even Scotty's closest friends hadn't realized how well known and respected he had been.

The famous buffalo herd, which numbered nearly a thousand head at Scotty's death, gradually disappeared. Most of the herds found in parks and reserves today over a great part of the west are descendents of Scotty Philip's herd.

The management of the herd fell to Scotty's son-in-law, Andy Leonard, Hazel's husband. He kept the herd until 1925 when he staged a big buffalo hunt and brought in important men from almost every state of the union. The festivities were filmed because many motion picture dignitaries from Hollywood were invited. Two hundred of the buffalo were marked for killing during the hunt while the rest were distributed to parks and reserves over the west. Thus ended the great Scotty Philip buffalo herd.

Scotty's widow, Sarah (Sally as Scotty always called her), lived until 1938. She was well up in her eighties when she died. She is buried beside Scotty in the little cemetery. The cemetery has been enlarged to become a Masonic cemetery. It is still called the Scotty Philip Cemetery with the name in big letters on the gate. The original plot that Scotty constructed so carefully is still

Scotty's wife Sarah at about the age of 80.

preserved just as it was. The only difference in it now is that there are more graves. Nine of Scotty's ten children are buried there with him.

Scotty Philip was elected to the National Cowboy Hall of Fame in Oklahoma City on January 5, 1958. He and Ed Lemmon were the first two South Dakota men so honored. Although he was in turn prospector, freighter, cowboy, army scout and rancher, he is best remembered and so honored as the preserver of the buffalo.

Truly, he left the world a richer place for having lived here.

FOOTNOTES

CHAPTER I

1. *The Cheyennes and Black Hills Stage and Express Routes*, by Agnes Wright Spring, p. 25. The Fort Laramie Treaty, signed in 1868, forbade white men to enter the territory north of the Platte River between the Big Horn mountains and the Black Hills.

2. *South Dakota Historical Review*, Vol. 1, No. 1. *James (Scotty) Philip* by George Philip. George Philip was a nephew of Scotty's and wrote more about his famous uncle than any other man. Orphaned young, he migrated to the United States at 16 and spent many years on Scotty's ranch. He graduated from law school at the University of Michigan and was Assistant United States District Attorney for South Dakota from 1914 to 1922. In 1933 he became United States District Attorney.

3. *South Dakota Historical Review*, Vol. 1, No. 1, p. 7.

CHAPTER II

1. *Outline Descriptions of the Posts in the Military Division of the Missouri. Commanded by Lieutenant General P. H. Sheridan*, p. 123.

2. *Wild, Wooly & Wicked* by Harry Sinclair Drago. Chapter 25, Dodge, Last of the Cow Towns, pp. 279-280.

3. In this, Jimmie was mistaken. The cattle herds began stopping in Dodge City in 1875 to be shipped out and Dodge wasn't ready for them. But almost overnight, the town got ready with new shipping pens and saloons. By 1876, it was the biggest shipping center for the Texas cattle coming up the trail.

4. *The Cheyenne and Black Hills Stage and Express Routes* by Agnes Wright Spring, p. 49.

5. *The Cheyenne and Black Hills Stage and Express Routes* by Agnes Wright Spring, p. 54. The *Cheyenne Leader* headlined the story: Glorious News from Washington; The Black Hills and Northern Wyoming to be Opened; Nine Cheers for Everybody in Washington! Let Old Glory Wave!

CHAPTER III

1. *The Cheyenne and Black Hills Stage and Express Routes* by Agnes Wright Spring, pp. 105-107. Hi Kelly became a good friend of Scotty's. One of Kelly's neighbors was John (Portugee) Phillips, who made the famous ride through a blizzard from Ft. Phil Kearny to Ft. Laramie in December of 1866 to report the

Fetterman massacre and request help for Col. Carrington and his depleted garrison at Ft. Phil Kearny.

2. *South Dakota Historical Review*, Vol. 1, No. 1, p. 11.

3. *The Cheyenne and Black Hills Stage and Express Routes* by Agnes Wright Spring, p. 42. Approval for the construction of this bridge came in 1872 but the bridge wasn't completed until late in 1875 and officially accepted in February, 1876. Mrs. Spring says that bridge was tested by Captain Stanton by running thirteen army wagons loaded with stone across the bridge in close formation.

4. *Outline Description of the Posts in the Military Division of the Missouri. Commanded by Lieutenant General P. H. Sheridan*, pp. 93-97.

5. *South Dakota Historical Review*, Vol. 1, No. 1, p. 13.

CHAPTER IV

1. Runningwater was a translation of the Indian name for the little river in northern Nebraska. It is called the Niobrara River on the maps of today.

2. *Scotty Philip, Living Legend*, by Joe Koller, Golden West Magazine, November 1968, p. 12.

3. *South Dakota Historical Review*, Vol. 1, No. 1, pp. 34-35. Scotty had reason to recall this episode more than once in later years, especially when he was saved from drowning in the Missouri at Evarts in 1901. It is recorded in various places, including this story by his nephew, George.

CHAPTER V

1. *South Dakota Historical Review*, Vol. 1, No. 1, p. 15. In his letter to his father in Scotland, Scotty mentioned the lot he had drawn. His grand-niece, Mrs. Jean Mitchell of Sturgis, South Dakota, and his granddaughter, Mrs. Billie Ann Rheborg of Pierre, South Dakota, have dug into records and tried to locate this lot and discover how Scotty disposed of it but they could find no trace of it.

2. *South Dakota Historical Review*, Vol. 1, No. 1, p. 14-15.

3. *South Dakota Historical Review*, Vol. 1, No. 1, p. 15.

4. The reputation that Wild Bill Hickok had made in Hays, Kansas, was very current when Scotty arrived at Victoria, Kansas, only eleven miles from Hays. Discovering that Hickok was in Deadwood was like finding that someone from home was there. Hickok was killed by Jack McCall on August 2, 1876, in Deadwood.

CHAPTER VI

1. *Fort Robinson, Outpost of the Plains*, by Roger T. Grange, Jr., pp. 210-211.

2. *South Dakota Historical Review*, Vol. 1, No. 1, p. 18.

3. *South Dakota Historical Review*, Vol. 1, No. 1, pp. 22-23. In some accounts Larabee's name is spelled Larvie. Mari Sandoz uses this spelling in writing about him. Joseph Larabee was a French Voyageur who married a Sioux Indian woman in the territory south and west of Ft. Robinson and years later moved to the Ft. Robinson vicinity with his family.

4. *Fort Robinson, Outpost of the Plains*, by Roger T. Grange, Jr., p. 214. Frank Grouard was the interpreter. Grouard had lived in the Indian camps of Sitting Bull and Crazy Horse and was considered their friend. However, he later led the army in campaigns against the Indians and some suggested that he was afraid of Crazy Horse and his 'mistake' in interpretation was intentional.

5. *Fort Robinson, Outpost of the Plains,* by Roger T. Grange, Jr., p. 216. There is much controversy over Little Big Man's part in the death of Crazy Horse. He had been a friend of Crazy Horse. Some historians say that, instead of trying to save Crazy Horse's life by restraining him, he was actually holding him so he could be bayoneted.

6. *South Dakota Historical Review,* Vol. 1, No. 1, p. 18. In a letter to his brother, dated Nov. 4, 1877, Scotty told of the Indians burning his hay that was stacked some distance from the house.

7. *Fort Robinson, Outpost of the Plains,* by Roger T. Grange, Jr., p. 217. The northern Indians broke away from Spotted Tail's band before they had gone far from their former Nebraska camp. They joined Red Cloud's band briefly on their march north and east but soon broke away from this column, too. They fled north, carrying Crazy Horse's bones. Although the army first reported 1700 Indians missing, a recheck later proved that only about 800 made the break north, apparently to join Sitting Bull in Canada.

CHAPTER VII

1. *South Dakota Historical Review,* Vol. 1, No. 1, pp. 18-19.

2. *South Dakota Historical Review,* Vol. 1, No. 1, pp. 19-20.

3. *Fort Robinson, Outpost of the Plains,* by Roger T. Grange, Jr., p. 217.

4. *Fort Robinson, Outpost of the Plains,* by Roger T. Grange, Jr., p. 217.

5. *Reminiscences of a Ranchman,* by Edgar Beecher Bronson, p. 130. Bronson was the first rancher to go into business on the land recently vacated by the Indians close to Ft. Robinson.

6. *South Dakota Historical Review,* Vol. 1, No. 1, p. 20.

7. *South Dakota Historical Review,* Vol. 1, No. 1, pp. 20-21.

8. *Fort Robinson, Outpost of the Plains,* by Roger T. Grange, Jr., p. 217.

9. *South Dakota Historical Review,* Vol. 1, No. 1, p. 21.

CHAPTER VIII

1. *South Dakota Historical Review,* Vol. 1, No. 1, pp. 21-22.

2. *The Cheyenne and Black Hills Stage and Express Routes,* by Agnes Wright Spring, pp. 122, 169, 208-209, 221-222, 228. Hat Creek Ranch, a station on the Cheyenne-Deadwood Stage Line, was established in the fall of 1876. It was near bluffs and broken country which harbored outlaws and Indians. It was the most dangerous stretch of road between Cheyenne and Deadwood and was the scene of many holdups, raids and murders. There is little doubt that this dangerous stretch of road was the main reason why this road was not more popular than it was.

3. *The Sidney-Black Hills Trail,* by Norbert R. Mahnken, Nebraska History, September, 1949, p. 211.

4. *The Sidney-Black Hills Trail,* by Norbert R. Mahnken, Nebraska History, September, 1949, p. 211.

5. *The Sidney-Black Hills Trail,* by Norbert R. Mahnken, Nebraska History, September, 1949, p. 216. Prices in the Black Hills were so high that freighters who arrived safely with their goods could make fortunes in a hurry. Even whiskey, which was plentiful at every stop, was 25¢ a drink.

6. *The Sidney-Black Hills Trail,* by Norbert R. Mahnken, Nebraska History, September, 1949, p. 218.

7. *The Sidney-Black Hills Trail,* by Norbert R. Mahnken, Nebraska History, September, 1949, p. 222.

8. *The Sidney-Black Hills Trail,* by Norbert R. Mahnken, Nebraska History, September, 1949, pp. 216-217.

9. *The Sidney-Black Hills Trail,* by Norbert R. Mahnken, Nebraska History, September, 1949, p. 213. With a toll of $2 a wagon and driver plus 50¢ for each additional man or beast, the big freighters paid dearly to cross the bridge but it was safer and cheaper in the long run than trying to ford the river, especially in high water.

CHAPTER IX

1. *Fort Robinson, Outpost on the Plains,* by Roger T. Grange, Jr., p. 223.

2. *Fort Robinson, Outpost on the Plains,* by Roger T. Grange, Jr., p. 223. General Crook had been put in charge of recapturing Dull Knife and his band. He gave orders to General Bradley at Ft. Robinson to set up the third line of defense. After a skirmish close to Dodge City between Dull Knife and two companies of the Fourth Cavalry and several cowboys from Dodge City, the next line of defense was set up on the Kansas Pacific Railroad from Ft. Wallace eastward. The second line of defense was along the U.P. line in Nebraska and General Bradley was to establish a third line close to Ft. Robinson. Also General Wesley Merritt was to prepare his Fifty Cavalry to intercept the Indians in the vicinity of Ft. McKensie, Wyoming, in case Dull Knife slipped through and tried to establish himself on his old hunting grounds.

3. *Reminiscences of a Ranchman,* by Edgar Beecher Bronson, p. 149. Bronson was fearful for his ranch close to Ft. Robinson and kept daily watch over the reports of progress of the Indians and gives an accurate report in his book.

4. *Reminiscences of a Ranchman,* by Edgar Beecher Bronson, p. 150.

5. *Mayor Jim,* by Fred Carey, pp. 31-32. Jim Dahlman was a life-long friend of Scotty's. His account of the fear of the white men of the sandhill region was shared by other writers. Even the soldiers dreaded being ordered into the region for fear they'd never get out.

6. *Reports of Persons and Articles Hired,* Dec. 1878 (payment for work in October, 1878) from National Archives. This page, signed by C. A. Johnson, 1st Lieut. 4th Inf. A. A. Quartermaster, shows that the contract with James Phillips (name misspelled) was "employed in Carrying Dispatches" at $50 a month.

7. *Reminiscences of a Ranchman,* by Edgar Beecher Bronson, p. 156.

8. *Reminiscences of a Ranchman,* by Edgar Beecher Bronson, p. 162.

9. *Reminiscences of a Ranchman,* by Edgar Beecher Bronson, p. 163.

CHAPTER X

1. *Reminiscences of a Ranchman,* by Edgar Beecher Bronson, p. 166.

2. *Reminiscences of a Ranchman,* by Edgar Beecher Bronson, p. 167.

3. *Fort Robinson, Outpost on the Plains,* by Roger T. Grange, Jr., p. 223.

4. *Reminiscences of a Ranchman,* by Edgar Beecher Bronson, pp. 171-173.

5. *Fort Robinson, Outpost on the Plains,* by Roger T. Grange, Jr., p. 223.

6. *Reminiscences of a Ranchman,* by Edgar Beecher Bronson, p. 174. The Indians suspected treachery and wouldn't allow their head chief, Dull Knife, to go to the conference called by Captain Wessells. When Wild Hog and Old Crow refused to yield to the demands, they were ordered put in irons. Wild Hog stabbed and seriously wounded Pvt. Ferguson of Troop A.

7. *Fort Robinson, Outpost on the Plains,* by Roger T. Grange, Jr., p. 224. Surgeon Mosely in his report says, "The great proportion of fatal wounds is remarkable and their concentration on the trunk of the body show a deliberation and skill in handling the improved breech-loaded arms with which they were liberally supplied, a fact which explains why this particular tribe enjoys the reputation of being the best warriors on the Plains."

8. *Reminiscences of a Ranchman,* by Edgar Beecher Bronson, pp. 185-186.

9. *Reminiscences of a Ranchman,* by Edgar Beecher Bronson, pp. 187-197.

10. *Fort Robinson, Outpost on the Plains,* by Roger T. Grange, Jr., p. 224.

CHAPTER XI

1. *Mayor Jim,* by Fred Carey, pp. 32-33.

2. *South Dakota Historical Review,* Vol. 1, No. 1, p. 17.

3. *South Dakota Historical Review,* Vol. 1, No. 1, p. 22.

4. *South Dakota Historical Review,* Vol. 1, No. 1, p. 23.

5. The marriage certificate has Scotty's name wrong, too, calling him John instead of James. It is also dated January 1, 1882, the day it was made out, not the day of the marriage. The certificate was recorded at the Pine Ridge Agency. All accounts of the wedding clearly indicate that the wedding took place at Ft. Robinson in the early summer of 1879.

6. *South Dakota Historical Review,* Vol. 1, No. 1, p. 23.

CHAPTER XII

1. *Roundup Years, Old Muddy to Black Hills,* by Bert Hall, p. 96. Charley Zabel, an overland freighter on the Ft. Pierre-Deadwood Trail, gives a detailed description of the old bull trains.

2. *Roundup Years, Old Muddy to Black Hills,* by Bert Hall, p. 97.

3. *Last Grass Frontier,* by Bob Lee & Dick Williams, pp. 128-129. The Northwestern Railroad agreed to purchase right-of-way across the reservation from the Indians for $100 a mile and land for stations at $5 an acre. The agreement included a section of land at Fort Pierre for a freight depot for $3,200.

4. *South Dakota Historical Review,* Vol. 1, No. 1, pp. 25-26. Scotty's brother, George, back in Victoria, Kansas, had tried repeatedly to get an answer to his letters to Scotty and, when he failed, decided in 1881 to find out whether or not Scotty was still alive. His trip to visit Scotty brought a promise from Scotty to keep in closer touch with his family, a promise he kept the rest of his life.

CHAPTER XIII

1. *Roundup Years, Old Muddy to Black Hills,* by Bert L. Hall. Ralph Jones of Midland, South Dakota, whose wife is the daughter of the former Cowboy Governor of South Dakota, Tom Berry, says that his father, Tom Jones, well known early day rancher and a partner of Scotty Philip's from 1903 till Scotty's death, said that trees were plentiful along the rivers when he came to South Dakota in 1890. Men who had come earlier such as Scotty and the LaPlant brothers said these trees were native, not planted. But they were confined to the river bottoms and stream banks. Flora Ziemann verifies this.

2. *Last Grass Frontier,* by Bob Lee & Dick Williams, pp. 131-132.

3. *Last Grass Frontier,* by Bob Lee & Dick Williams, p. 131, 139-140. Richard

F. Pettigrew was a Sioux Falls surveyor and attorney. He was a delegate in Congress from the Dakota Territory in 1882. After the territory became two states in 1889, he was one of the first U.S. Senators from South Dakota.

4. *Last Grass Frontier,* by Bob Lee & Dick Williams, p. 148.

5. *Last Grass Frontier,* by Bob Lee & Dick Williams, p. 144.

6. *Roundup Years, Old Muddy to Black Hills,* by Bert L. Hall, p. 58. Scotty and Dan Powell became good friends when Dan worked for Scotty putting up hay near Ft. Robinson. Powell was credited with killing the last wild buffalo close to Ft. Robinson.

7. *Roundup Years, Old Muddy to Black Hills,* by Bert L. Hall, p. 58-60.

CHAPTER XIV

1. *Last Grass Frontier,* by Bob Lee & Dick Williams, p. 143. Senator Henry L. Dawes was chairman of the Committee on Indian Affairs and a powerful member of the senate.

2. *Last Grass Frontier,* by Bob Lee & Dick Williams, p. 145.

3. *Roundup Years, Old Muddy to Black Hills,* by Bert L. Hall, p. 87.

4. *Last Grass Frontier,* by Bob Lee & Dick Williams, pp. 149-150. Failing to get clearance for a railroad through the reservation from Fort Pierre, the Northwestern Railroad built north from Chadron in Nebraska and brought its first train into Rapid City on July 3, 1886. It was greeted with wild cheering but the real celebration was held until the next day, July 4th. That was a celebration Rapid City would long remember.

5. *Roundup Years, Old Muddy to Black Hills,* by Bert L. Hall, p. 531.

6. *The Cattlemen,* by Mari Sandoz, pp. 409-413.

7. *Roundup Years, Old Muddy to Black Hills,* by Bert L. Hall, pp. 531-532.

CHAPTER XV

1. *Roundup Years, Old Muddy to Black Hills,* by Bert L. Hall, pp. 87-88.

2. *Last Grass Frontier,* by Bob Lee & Dick Williams, p. 155.

3. *The Cattlemen,* by Mari Sandoz, p. 259.

4. *Last Grass Frontier,* by Bob Lee & Dick Williams, pp. 154-156. In the Big Die-Up, many ranchers had a loss of 85 to 90 percent of their stock. Many big outfits were wiped out and numberless small ones went bankrupt. Theodore Roosevelt, whose ranch was in northern Dakota Territory, lost an estimated $75,000. He went out of the cattle business "without any effort on his part," as Ed Lemmon described it.

5. *Last Grass Frontier,* by Bob Lee & Dick Williams, p. 159.

6. *The Cattlemen,* by Mari Sandoz, pp. 405-406.

7. *Last Grass Frontier,* by Bob Lee & Dick Williams, p. 158.

8. *Last Grass Frontier,* by Bob Lee & Dick Williams, pp. 158-159.

CHAPTER XVI

1. *Last Grass Frontier,* by Bob Lee & Dick Williams, p. 165. This bill was introduced by Delegate Oscar Gifford of Dakota.

2. *Last Grass Frontier,* by Bob Lee & Dick Williams, p. 165. Sitting Bull's refusal to sign the agreement and its eventual success in spite of his veto broke the

old chief's power over the tribe. This cession opened up nine million acres to white settlement. Each Indian family was allotted 320 acres of land, two milk cows and a pair of work oxen.

3. Billie Ann Rheborg, Scotty's granddaughter, says that Scotty had over 1000 head of cattle when the reservation land was opened up to settlement in 1889.

4. Flora Ziemann, perhaps the best 'Scotty Philip historian' alive, visited almost daily with Sally Philip during the last several years of her life and learned hundreds of details about Scotty's life on the Dakota prairies.

5. *Tragedy Strikes at Wounded Knee*, by Will H. Spindler, pp. 4-5.

6. *Last Grass Frontier*, by Bob Lee and Dick Williams, p. 166.

7. *Prairie Progress in West Central South Dakota*, Historical Society of Old Stanley County, p. 743. Stanley County was organized April 25, 1890.

8. *South Dakota Historical Review*, Vol. 1, No. 1, p. 28.

9. *Prairie Progress in West Central South Dakota*, p. 743.

10. *South Dakota Historical Review*, Vol. 1, No. 1, p. 28.

11. *Last Grass Frontier*, by Bob Lee & Dick Williams, p. 126.

12. *Roundup Years, Old Muddy to Black Hills*, by Bert L. Hall, p. 59. Midland was established in 1890, just fifty miles up Bad River from Fort Pierre.

CHAPTER XVII

1. *Tragedy Strikes at Wounded Knee*, by Will H. Spindler, p. 5.

2. *South Dakota Historical Review*, Vol. 1, No. 1, p. 31.

3. *South Dakota Historical Review*, Vol. 1, No. 1, p. 39.

4. Some of the buildings that used lumber from the old Stanley Hotel in Stanley are still standing (1971) in Fort Pierre.

5. *South Dakota Historical Review*, Vol. 1, No. 1, pp. 26-27.

6. *South Dakota Historical Review*, Vol. 1, No. 1, pp. 26-27.

7. *Tragedy Strikes at Wounded Knee*, by Will H. Spindler, p. 7.

8. *Tragedy Strikes at Wounded Knee*, by Will H. Spindler, p. 11.

9. *Tragedy Strikes at Wounded Knee*, by Will H. Spindler, p. 11. Chief Big Foot was a Minneconjou Sioux.

10. *Tragedy Strikes at Wounded Knee*, by Will H. Spindler, pp. 12-15.

CHAPTER XVIII

1. *Tragedy Strikes at Wounded Knee*, by Will H. Spindler, pp. 14-15.

2. *Last Grass Frontier*, by Bob Lee & Dick Williams, p. 186.

3. *Roundup Years, Old Muddy to Black Hills*, by Bert L. Hall, p. 447.

4. *Last Grass Frontier*, by Bob Lee & Dick Williams, p. 186.

5. *Queen City Mail*, Spearfish, South Dakota. Although the number of cattle had more than doubled in 1891, the assessed value had risen only from $4,600,000 in 1890 to $5,700,000 in 1891.

6. *Last Grass Frontier*, by Bob Lee & Dick Williams, p. 185.

7. *Prairie Progress in West Central South Dakota*, p. 743.

8. *Last Grass Frontier*, by Bob Lee & Dick Williams, p. 187.

9. *Last Grass Frontier*, by Bob Lee & Dick Williams, p. 189.

10. *Roundup Years, Old Muddy to Black Hills*, by Bert L. Hall, p. 509.

11. Emma Philip is referred to more often as Amy than Emma and sometimes causes confusion among those looking at Scotty's family tree.

CHAPTER XIX

1. From the old record books in the County Clerk's office in the court house in Fort Pierre, county seat of Stanley County, South Dakota.

2. *Roundup Years, Old Muddy to Black Hills,* by Bert L. Hall, p. 200. The letterhead of the Minnesota & Dakota Cattle Company shows the three brands owned by the Scotty Philip and Charles Stuebe partnership as well as other brands that Scotty owned personally or in partnership.

3. *South Dakota State Brand Book.* This brand book giving complete descriptions of all South Dakota brands was published in 1898-1899 in Fort Pierre by John Hayes of the Sioux Stock Journal Press. My thanks to Flora Ziemann for locating this for me.

4. *Last Grass Frontier,* by Bob Lee & Dick Williams, p. 197.

5. *Last Grass Frontier,* by Bob Lee & Dick Williams, p. 197.

6. *Last Grass Frontier,* by Bob Lee & Dick Williams, p. 198.

7. *Roundup Years, Old Muddy to Black Hills,* by Bert L. Hall, p. 296.

8. *Roundup Years, Old Muddy to Black Hills,* by Bert Hall, p. 320. All who worked with Scotty testified to his remarkable memory.

9. *Last Grass Frontier,* by Bob Lee & Dick Williams, p. 209.

10. *Roundup Years, Old Muddy to Black Hills,* by Bert L. Hall, p. 200.

11. *Roundup Years, Old Muddy to Black Hills,* by Bert L. Hall, pp. 205-206.

12. *Prairie Progress in West Central South Dakota,* p. 743.

13. *Roundup Years, Old Muddy to Black Hills,* by Bert L. Hall, p. 218. In the main event of the day, George LaPlant bet $175 and 35 of his horses on the race. After his horse, Two Bits, lost the race, he tried to buy the winning horse but was turned down. He did manage to get his 35 horses back for $450.

14. *Roundup Years, Old Muddy to Black Hills,* by Bert L. Hall, pp. 270-271.

15. *Roundup Years, Old Muddy to Black Hills,* by Bert L. Hall, p. 296.

16. *South Dakota Historical Review,* Vol. 1, No. 1, p. 32.

17. *Roundup Years, Old Muddy to Black Hills,* by Bert L. Hall, p. 60.

18. Billie Ann Rheborg, Scotty's granddaughter, supplied the information about the movements of the Philip Post Office, the dates of moving and locations and postmasters until it moved to the new town of Philip in 1907.

CHAPTER XX

1. *Roundup Years, Old Muddy to Black Hills,* by Bert L. Hall, p. 465.

2. *South Dakota Historical Review,* Vol. 1, No. 1, p. 39.

3. *Roundup Years, Old Muddy to Black Hills,* by Bert L. Hall, p. 145.

4. *Roundup Years, Old Muddy to Black Hills,* by Bert L. Hall, pp. 417-418.

5. *Roundup Years, Old Muddy to Black Hills,* by Bert L. Hall, p. 417. Jim Brown and a companion were credited with saving Blasingame's life. The man who had knifed Blasingame was sent on to Yankton to stand trial.

6. *Roundup Years, Old Muddy to Black Hills,* by Bert L. Hall, p. 124.

7. *South Dakota Historical Review,* Vol. 1, No. 1, pp. 32-33.

8. *Roundup Years, Old Muddy to Black Hills,* by Bert L. Hall, p. 474.

9. *Roundup Years, Old Muddy to Black Hills,* by Bert L. Hall, p. 355. Evarts came into existence as a railroad town in 1900. It was named for the wife of Gene Overholser, whose maiden name was Olive Evarts. The town was a wild one but lasted only 7 years. The site of Evarts is now under the water of Oahe Reservoir formed by the Oahe Dam just north of Pierre

CHAPTER XXI

1. *Dakota Cowboy,* by Ike Blasingame, p. 36.

2. *South Dakota Historical Review,* Vol. 1, No. 1, p. 34.

3. *Boss Cowman, Recollections of Ed Lemmon,* edited by Nellie Snyder Yost, pp. 203-204. Both Ed Lemmon and Scotty Philip were delegates to the Stockmen's Convention in Fort Worth in 1900. Ed Lemmon's memory was faulty when he said that one of Scotty's sons was a member of the state legislature. It was Scotty himself. Scotty's oldest son, Stanley, was only 10 in 1900.

4. *South Dakota Historical Review,* Vol. 1, No. 1, pp. 35-37. Pete Dupree, son of Fred Dupree, had roped five buffalo calves in the last big buffalo hunt on the Grand River and took them home to the home ranch on the Cheyenne River.

5. *Roundup Years, Old Muddy to Black Hills,* by Bert L. Hall, p. 297. In later years, Cy Hiatt said that Scotty paid $150 a head for the buffalo he bought from Dug Carlin, Pete Dupree's brother-in-law.

6. *South Dakota Historical Review,* Vol. 1, No. 1, p. 35. Scotty had no use for the cattalo cross-breeds. He catalogued them as "not worth a damn."

7. *Stock Growers News,* February 22, 1905 issue. "Truths About the Buffalo," was written by Scotty. The bulls were so big that they required this special fencing. One large bull dressed out 1300 pounds of meat. They weighed between 2000 and 2600 pounds on the hoof.

8. *Dakota Cowboy,* by Ike Blasingame, Preface. The Milwaukee Railroad had a lease on the whole north end of the Cheyenne River Reservation and they fenced a lane six miles wide and eighty miles long over which cattle could be driven to and from Evarts. This was used extensively and helped make Evarts a very busy railroad shipping point.

9. *South Dakota Historical Review,* Vol. 1, No. 1, pp. 34-35.

CHAPTER XXII

1. *Scotty Philip – Living Legend,* by Joe Koller, Golden West Magazine, Nov. 1968.

2. *South Dakota Historical Review,* Vol. 1, No. 1, p. 35.

3. *South Dakota Historical Review,* Vol. 1, No. 1, p. 37. 'Buffalo George' was one of the six men who drove the buffalo into the new pasture. In later years, he became a rather notorious outlaw.

4. *Roundup Years, Old Muddy to Black Hills,* by Bert L. Hall, pp. 399-400. Ike Blasingame tells of the renegade buffalo bulls that gave them trouble on the Cheyenne River Reservation. Ernest Eidson drove one away with a .38 revolver. The bull was blocking a gate they wanted to drive a herd of cattle through. Eidson fired at the buffalo from some distance while the bull was pawing and goring the ground. "Doubtless the monarch of the plains sustained a rude shock in spite of his thick hide," Blasingame says, "for it brought his horn out of the ground pronto. The next blast got him off his knees; the third, he curled his short tail up over his back and plunged away in a fast lumbering gallop."

5. *South Dakota Historical Review*, Vol. 1, No. 1, p. 38. Tom Phillips (no relation by Scotty; even his name was spelled differently) was also on this hunt with Scotty and Gov. Herreid.

6. *Dakota Cowboy*, by Ike Blasingame, pp. 156-159. Trapping wolves required a skill not every man had. Blasingame tells the story of Baldy Sours and how he had to dangle a live rabbit from a tree limb above his traps to entice one wily wolf into his traps. Other schemes, equally as clever, were used by other trappers and hunters to get the wolves which were a serious menace during bad winters on the Dakota plains.

7. *Last Grass Frontier*, by Bob Lee & Dick Williams, p. 224. Heavy snow on the northern ranges forced the cattle to drift in search of food. North winds pushed them south until spring found most of them on the Pine Ridge and Rosebud Reservations close to the Nebraska line.

8. *Last Grass Frontier*, by Bob Lee & Dick Williams, pp. 224-225. Henry Hudson was the general foreman of the roundup. He became range foreman for the 73 brand (Minnesota & Dakota Cattle Co.) after Scotty had sold his interest in the company. He had worked as a cowboy for Scotty. Scotty's own L Bar 7 and S Bar 7 brands constituted one of the largest outfits in the roundup.

9. *Dakota Cowboy*, by Ike Blasingame, pp. 18-19. This was the common procedure for the range cook. Not many cooks were able to convince their bosses they should have a stove brought along in a 'stove cart' for the cooking but some did. Around the cook wagon, the cook was absolute boss.

10. *Roundup Years, Old Muddy to Black Hills*, by Bert L. Hall, p. 558.

11. Si Hiett was foreman for Scotty on this roundup. Hiett was Scotty's regular foreman on his Missouri River ranch.

12. *Roundup Years, Old Muddy to Black Hills*, by Bert L. Hall, p. 290.

13. *Last Grass Frontier*, by Bob Lee & Dick Williams, p. 219.

CHAPTER XXIII

1. *Roundup Years, Old Muddy to Black Hills*, by Bert L. Hall, p. 355.

2. *Roundup Years, Old Muddy to Black Hills*, by Bert L. Hall, p. 558.

3. *South Dakota Historical Review*, Vol. 1, No. 1, p. 37.

4. *Roundup Years, Old Muddy to Black Hills*, by Bert L. Hall, p. 482. This ten thousand dollars was part payment to Dug Carlin for the buffalo that Scotty had bought.

5. *The Cattlemen*, by Mari Sandoz, p. 442.

6. *Last Grass Frontier*, by Bob Lee & Dick Williams, p. 229.

7. *Wild Animals in Kansas*, Clippings, Vol. 1, pp. 54-56.

8. *Wild Animals in Kansas*, Clippings, Vol. 1, pp. 54-56.

9. *Roundup Years, Old Muddy to Black Hills*, by Bert L. Hall, p. 54. Many of the hired hands who worked with Posey Moran didn't know that his real name was Louis although most knew he was the son of Sally Philip by a former marriage.

10. *Roundup Years, Old Muddy to Black Hills*, by Bert L. Hall, p. 558.

11. *Prairie Progress in West Central South Dakota*, p. 743.

CHAPTER XXIV

1. Douglas Philip, grandson of Alex Philip, Scotty's brother, says he heard his

father tell many times of hearing Scotty's first hand accounts of narrow escapes in his buffalo pasture.

2. *Roundup Years, Old Muddy to Black Hills*, by Bert L. Hall, p. 535. George Philip was an ambitious man who usually achieved any goal he set for himself. He entered the University of Michigan law school in the fall of 1903 and graduated in the spring of 1906 after only three years of study. Scotty was proud of this nephew and predicted great things for him, a prediction that was borne out after Scotty's death. Among his many achievements, George was U.S. Attorney for South Dakota from July, 1934 to April, 1947. He suffered a cerebral hemorrhage on September 29, 1947, that led to his death shortly thereafter.

3. Flora Ziemann pointed out Mike Dunn's homesite not far from Scotty's home north of Fort Pierre.

4. *Roundup Years, Old Muddy to Black Hills*, by Bert L. Hall, p. 482.

5. *Prairie Progress in West Central South Dakota*, pp. 204-205. Tom Jones kept a day book with tallies for each rancher.

6. *Roundup Years, Old Muddy to Black Hills*, by Bert L. Hall, p. 549.

7. *Roundup Years, Old Muddy to Black Hills*, by Bert L. Hall, p. 452.

8. *Dakota Cowboy*, by Ike Blasingame, pp. 95-96.

9. *Roundup Years, Old Muddy to Black Hills*, by Bert L. Hall, p. 337. This "death wall" is between the present towns of Kodoka and Wall. An estimated 10,000 head of stock plunged over this wall during this blizzard, according to Mrs. Martin Johnson of Murdo, South Dakota.

10. *Prairie Progress in West Central South Dakota*, p. 200.

11. *Last Grass Frontier*, by Bob Lee & Dick Williams, pp. 231-232. For the prevention of scabies, a mixture of lime, sulphur and Black Leaf 40 was heated and poured into the vats then the cattle were pushed in.

11. *Prairie Progress in West Central South Dakota*, p. 200. The four men, Arthur Austin, Fred Trumbo, Ed Cook, and Perry Riffenberg were working at the mouth of Jack Daly Draw just west of the town of Midland when the flash flood hit.

13. *Roundup Years, Old Muddy to Black Hills*, by Bert L. Hall, p. 482. Ed Senechal, who operated the ferry boats between Pierre and Fort Pierre, rescued 25 families from upstairs windows during this flood that roared down Bad River into the Missouri.

14. *Roundup Years, Old Muddy to Black Hills*, by Bert L. Hall, p. 481.

15. *Dakota Cowboy*, by Ike Blasingame, pp. 135-136.

16. *Roundup Years, Old Muddy to Black Hills*, by Bert L. Hall, p. 297.

17. *Roundup Years, Old Muddy to Black Hills*, by Bert L. Hall, p. 297.

CHAPTER XXV

1. *Dakota Cowboy*, by Ike Blasingame, p. 137. Limiting shipment to one train load per rancher per day curtailed only the biggest ranchers. Scotty was one of those.

2. *Last Grass Frontier*, by Bob Lee & Dick Williams, p. 234.

3. *Last Grass Frontier*, by Bob Lee & Dick Williams, p. 129.

4. Flora Ziemann pointed out the route of this track and the hills from which the gravel was taken.

5. *South Dakota Historical Review*, Vol. 1, No. 1, p. 38.

6. *South Dakota Historical Review*, Vol. 1, No. 1, p. 44.

7. *South Dakota Historical Review*, Vol. 2, No. 2, p. 51. Bob Yokum, who trained buffalo calves for Scotty, was a former Texan. He operated saloons in Pierre and Fort Pierre.

8. *Dakota Cowboy*, by Ike Blasingame, pp. 226-231. Blizzard after blizzard swept over South Dakota until four wire fences were hidden and all feed was buried.

9. *Wild Animals in Kansas*, Clippings, Vol. 1, pp. 54-56.

10. *Rapid City Daily Journal*, May 13, 1965. Article by Mrs. Arnold Raben, Journal Correspondent.

11. *South Dakota Historical Review*, Vol. 2, No. 2, p. 52.

12. *Rapid City Daily Journal*, May 13, 1965.

13. *South Dakota Historical Review*, Vol. 2, No. 2, p. 53.

14. *South Dakota Historical Review*, Vol. 2, No. 2, pp. 54-55.

CHAPTER XXVI

1. *South Dakota Historical Review*, Vol. 2, No. 2, pp. 60-62. George Philip, Scotty's nephew, describes his reaction to the Mexican bull fights: "It is no place for a timid, a cross-eyed, or a clubfooted man."

2. *Rapid City Daily Journal*, May 13, 1965.

3. *South Dakota Historical Review*, Vol. 2, No. 2, p. 63.

4. *South Dakota Historical Review*, Vol. 2, No. 2, p. 64.

5. *South Dakota Historical Review*, Vol. 2, No. 2, p. 65.

6. *South Dakota Historical Review*, Vol. 2, No. 2, p. 68.

7. *South Dakota Historical Review*, Vol. 2, No. 2, p. 67. El Cuco was the matador chosen to fight the buffalo bull. He was considered the best of the Mexican bull fighters.

8. *South Dakota Historical Review*, Vol. 2, No. 2, p. 69. Both Felix Robert, the ring manager, and Cuco, the bull fighter, pleaded with the president to let the fight go on. But the president warned them he would fine them both and suspend Cuco if they didn't get out of the ring immediately. Thus ended the buffalo bull fights in Mexico.

9. *South Dakota Historical Review*, Vol. 2, No. 2, p. 66.

10. *South Dakota Historical Review*, Vol. 2, No. 2, pp. 70-71. Felix Robert insisted that he was going to keep the two buffalo to pay for the $1500 expenses of the last Sunday's fights. He said he'd sue the Americans for the money and keep them locked up until he filed the suit. The Americans were glad to sell the buffalo and leave the country.

CHAPTER XXVII

1. *Prairie Progress in West Central South Dakota*, p. 266.

2. *Prairie Progress in West Central South Dakota*, p. 275.

3. *Roundup Years, Old Muddy to Black Hills*, by Bert L. Hall, p. 447. The post office, started by Scotty Philip back in July, 1891 and moved two or three times, finally moved into the new town of Philip on July 31, 1907.

4. *Last Grass Frontier*, by Bob Lee & Dick Williams, p. 241.

5. *Roundup Years, Old Muddy to Black Hills*, by Bert L. Hall, p. 558. Scotty's nephew, George, enjoyed telling the story of the time Scotty thought he'd gotten the best of his nephew only to have the tables turned when he put George in charge of the roundup.

6. *South Dakota Historical Review,* Vol. 1, No. 1, pp. 41-42.

7. *Wokama Leader* — September 27, 1907. "Scotty Philip stepped on rattlesnake at his camp on Lower Brule Reservation. Getting along OK."

8. *Wokama Leader* — October 25, 1907.

9. *Wokama Leader* — November 1, 1907 — "Barker and Philip incorporated Monday, October 28, to dig well for Plunge in Block 19 and will furnish gas — also will build rental houses."

10. *Wokama Leader* — January 3, 1908.

11. *Wokama Leader* — April 17, 1908.

12. *Roundup Years, Old Muddy to Black Hills,* by Bert L. Hall, p. 145.

13. *Roundup Years, Old Muddy to Black Hills,* by Bert L. Hall, p. 539.

14. *South Dakota Historical Review,* Vol. 1, No. 1, p. 40. Scotty's nephew, George, explains that "Scotty was not a 'joiner' and restricted his fraternal affiliations to those mentioned."

CHAPTER XXVIII

1. This stone still stands in the center of the Scotty Philip plot in the cemetery northwest of Fort Pierre that is now called the "Scotty Philip Cemetery."

2. Douglas Philip of Hays, Kansas, grand-nephew of Scotty's, related many stories about Scotty that had been handed down to him by his father. Included was this one.

3. *Roundup Years, Old Muddy to Black Hills,* by Bert L. Hall, p. 558. This is one of the many stories that George Philip, Scotty's nephew, put into print for the benefit of his children. Some have been reprinted for all to read.

4. *South Dakota Historical Review,* Vol. 1, No. 1, p. 43.

5. From the files of Douglas Philip's stories on Scotty.

6. *South Dakota Historical Review,* Vol. 1, No. 1, p. 43. Flora Ziemann said that this irrigation machinery lay out there by the Missouri River after Scotty's death until it rusted and had to be hauled away when the engineers began surveying for the Oahe Dam.

7. *South Dakota Historical Review,* Vol. 1, No. 1, p. 45.

8. *South Dakota Historical Review,* Vol. 1, No. 1, p. 45.

9. *South Dakota Historical Review,* Vol. 1, No. 1, p. 45.

10. *South Dakota Historical Review,* Vol. 1, No. 1, p. 47.

11. *South Dakota Historical Review,* Vol. 1, No. 1, p. 47. Many of the obituaries of Scotty mentioned the buffalo herd that came down quietly to watch the funeral ceremony then, just as quietly, went back over the hill. The actions of the buffalo made more impression on most of those attending the funeral that hot afternoon than the fact that most of the dignitaries of the state were present.

12. *South Dakota Historical Review,* Vol. 1, No. 1, pp. 47-48. Following is one of the many obituaries printed immediately after Scotty's death. It is representative of the many.

"Scotty Philip, frontiersman, cattle king, promoter, financier, genial and whole-souled friend, and withal the most prominent pioneer in the trans-Missouri country, is no more. 'Scotty' has gone the way of all men, and the familiar haunts and hosts of friends who have known him will see his face no more. Only in memory will his life and genial personality be perpetuated.

"James Philip was ushered into the world in Bonnie Scotland, at Morayshire, in the year 1858, and departed this life at his ranch near Fort Pierre at seven o'clock on Sunday morning July 23, aged fifty-three. The summons was swift, and apoplexy the instrument. The call came to him in the prime of life, and in the fullness of life's interest and activities.

"Scotty Philip came to this country a lad of sixteen, and at once cast his lot in the far west, first locating in Victoria, Kansas, in 1874, and removing to the Hills section of this state a year later. In the early eighties he located on a ranch near the present site of Philip, and engaged in the stock business on a large scale and became famous as a cattle baron, but for a number of years has lived at or near, Fort Pierre, where he has been identified with a large number of public and private undertakings, his operations covering real estate, banking and mercantile lines. His most recent venture was a large irrigation project, which was only well started at the time of his death. In business he readily adapted himself to circumstances, was a square dealer, and was the type of man that misfortune could not down, having survived many reverses that would have crushed the ordinary man.

"He was a man of large stature, large plans and large heart, and will be mourned by a host of friends, not only locally, but all over the West and South, where he was perhaps the best known plainsman of Dakota, being widely known as the owner of the famous Dupree buffalo herd which roam the confines of a large pasture on the banks of the Big Muddy.

"He leaves a wife, three daughters, and two sons and his nephew, George Philip, who have the sympathy of the many who claimed James Philip as friend.

"The funeral was held Wednesday afternoon and was attended by a multitude of old timers and friends of the deceased, being the largest funeral and the most remarkable gathering that ever congregated in this section. The pioneer of Indian days and the homesteader mingled their tears with the citizenship of Fort Pierre and the Capitol City in a tribute of respect to the departed. Burial took place in a spot but recently selected by the deceased, in a grassy meadow at the foot of the rugged bluffs and overlooking the course of the mighty Missouri and the little city whose interests he had made his own. Here rest the ashes of 'Scotty' Philip, in surroundings typical of the environment in which he spent his life."

BIBLIOGRAPHY

BOOKS

Blasingame, Ike *Dakota Cowboy,* G. P. Putnam's Sons, New York, 1958.

Bronson, Edgar Beecher *Reminiscences of a Rancher,* University of Nebraska Press, Lincoln, Nebraska, 1962.

Carey, Fred *Mayor Jim,* Omaha Printing, Omaha, Nebraska, 1930.

Drago, Harry Sinclair *Wild, Woolly & Wicked,* Bramhall House, New York, 1960.

Grange, Robert T., Jr., *Fort Robinson, Outpost of the Plains,* Nebraska History, Vol. 39, No. 3, Nebraska State Historical Society, Lincoln, Nebraska, September, 1958.

Hall, Bert L. *Roundup Years, Old Muddy to Black Hills.* The Reminder, Inc., Pierre, South Dakota, 1954.

Historical Society of Old Stanley County, *Prairie Progress in West Central South Dakota.* Midwest Beach, Inc., Sioux Falls, S.D., 1968.

Lee, Bob & Dick Williams *Last Grass Frontier,* Black Hills Publishers, Inc., Sturgis, South Dakota, 1964.

Mahnken, Norbert R. *The Sidney-Black Hills Trail,* Nebraska History, Vol. 30, No. 3, Nebraska State Historical Society, Lincoln, Nebraska, September, 1949.

Sandoz, Mari, *The Cattlemen,* Hastings House, New York, 1958.

Sheridan, Lt. Gen. P. H. *Outline Descriptions of the Posts in the Military Division of the Missouri.* Originally published — Chicago, 1876; Facsimile Edition — The Old Army Press, Belevue, Nebraska, 1969.

South Dakota Historical Society, *South Dakota Historical Review,* Vol. 1, No. 1, Pierre, South Dakota, October, 1935.

South Dakota Historical Society, *South Dakota Historical Review,* Vol. 2, No. 2, Pierre, South Dakota, January, 1937.

South Dakota State Brand Book, 1898-1899, Sioux Stock Journal Press, Pierre, South Dakota.

Spindler, Will H. *Tragedy Strikes at Wounded Knee,* News/Star, Rushville, Nebraska, 1955.

Spring, Agnes Wright *The Cheyenne and Black Hills Stage and Express Routes,* University of Nebraska Press, Lincoln, Nebraska, 1948.

Wild Animals in Kansas Clippings, Vol. 1.

Yost, Nellie Snyder *Boss Cowman,* University of Nebraska Press, Lincoln, Nebraska, 1969.

MAGAZINES

Blasingame, C. M. *Scotty Philip, Man of the Plains,* Frontier Times, Austin, Texas, September, 1966.

Koller, Joe *Scotty Philip – Living Legend,* Golden West, Freeport, New York, November, 1968.

NEWSPAPERS QUOTED

Queen City Mail — Spearfish, South Dakota
Rapid City Daily Journal — Rapid City, South Dakota
Stock Growers News
Wakoma Leader

INDEX